LIKE THE WIND I GO
A MEMOIR OF IRAN, AMERICA, MY STRUGGLE TO FREEDOM

This book is a work of creative nonfiction. The author has re-created events, locales, and conversations from his memories of them and from personal journals, using some well-known historical and public figures. To maintain their anonymity, in some instances, the author has changed the names of individuals and places. He may have changed some identifying characteristics and details. In some instances, he may have used literary license to reconstruct the conversations from many decades ago to reflect the intrinsic nature, style, culture and emotions of the time and places and certain scenes have been dramatized.

Copyright 2020 © by Vahid Imani

All rights reserved. This book contains material protected under International and Federal Copyright Laws and Treaties. Any unauthorized reprint or use of this material is prohibited. For permission requests, please contact:

Stormtop Publishing

P.O. Box 132

Solvang, CA 93464 U.S.A stormtopublishing.com www.stromtopublishing@gmail.com

Editors:

Jeanette Morris, CA, freelance editor, www.jeanette-morris.com

Susan Leon, NY, an independent book editor

ISBN- 978-0-9911103-7-7 (Soft cover)

ISBN- 978-0-9911103-8-4 (Hard cover)

ISBN: 978-0-9911103-9-1 (eBook)

Library of Congress Control Number: 2020906549

Library Subject headings:

1-Memoir- Iran 2- Iranian American man- Biography

3-Iranian revolution 1978- history 4-Culture – Iran

5-Iran -nonfiction I. Title

www.LiketheWindIGo.com

To Carole Eckhardt
May she rest in peace

LIKE THE WIND I GO

A MEMOIR OF IRAN, AMERICA, MY STRUGGLE TO FREEDOM

VAHID IMANI

Stormtop Publishing

"I have sworn upon the altar of God eternal hostility against every form of tyranny over the mind of man."

--*Thomas Jefferson*

1

THE PURSUIT OF HAPPINESS

> *We hold these truths to be self-evident, that all men are created equal, that they are endowed by their Creator with certain unalienable Rights, that among these are Life, Liberty and the pursuit of Happiness.*
>
> — The Declaration of Independence of the thirteen United States of America (July 4, 1776)

The phone rang. I sprang up automatically, causing the kitchen chair to slide against the floor with a loud screech. In 1978 in Tehran, my family had just one landline in our house, and that big, black rotary phone was our major link to the outside world. Every time it rang, we all jumped for it.

My mother, who sat at the table with me, pushed her chair back and rushed toward the phone also. She told me to sit down and finish my lunch. A typical Middle Eastern mother, she was always worried about what I ate and how much I ate.

Her attempt to keep me in the kitchen was too late. I had beat her out of the starting gate and was already in the living room, where the phone sat proudly on a white, curved metal telephone console table with a dark brown cushioned seat. I didn't want her to answer the phone. She had a bad habit of cutting my friends short or asking them to call back later. This was getting old and unbearable for me, already a man of twenty-one and not needing her intervention. Nevertheless, in our house, she was the telephone tsar, among other things.

"Hello?" my mouthful of food garbled my words.

The voice on the other side of the phone belonged to my father. He asked me not to respond to his words. He didn't want my mother to know about what he was going to tell me. I cunningly acknowledged his wish and pretended it was a neighbor.

My mother didn't care about my intention of withholding the caller's identity. "Who is it, Vahid?" she pressed.

I didn't acknowledge her and continued to listen to my father. The receiver felt heavy after hearing what he had to say.

My hand slowly placed the receiver back onto its cradle. My eyes stayed fixed on the phone, while Mother stood next to me, wringing her slender hands and repeatedly asking me who it was and what had transpired.

There was no way I was going to tell her. I grabbed my house key from the hook near the door and left the room without looking at her.

She whined, her authoritarian tone switching to pleading as she followed me, asking me where I was going.

I mumbled something like, "I'll be back soon," and shut the heavy metal door behind me with a loud bang.

Iran had become a tumultuous and unstable place to live. The people's efforts to attain freedom from the shah, the king-dictator, had gained momentum. For thousands of years Iran had been led by tyrant kings. In 1906, a people's uprising moved the political system a small step toward democratization by changing it from an absolute dictatorship to a constitutional monarchy. However, the change remained mostly superficial and kings continued ruling as dictators. Attempts by many brave people to gain a democratic system of government failed. Nevertheless, the political wind changed significantly around 1977, and dissident movements had picked up steam.

Unrest and turmoil had prevailed. News of deaths and disappearances of friends and relatives were a regular, weekly event. The telephone ringing had become synonymous to unsettling news. Some people believed that we were on the verge of a revolution. But I didn't.

In the past, the shah's government had suppressed many uprisings and attempts at changing the government to a more democratic form. For me, there was not enough evidence of a revolution. My guess was that the shah's generals would soon tire of people's demonstrations and would heavy-handedly end the dissent.

A large crowd had gathered in front of my destination, the local lumberyard at the end of our short street. Two police cars were parked there. The front entrance was not guarded, but for some reason, most people gathered outside of the business. Not many had ventured inside.

I had walked past this lumberyard thousands of times before. But that day, for the first time, I set foot inside the large warehouse. The exceptionally high ceilings combined with the dim lighting, cool inside air, and sweet smell of fresh-cut wood gave the warehouse a dark and eerie atmosphere.

A few men from the neighborhood stood in the middle of the warehouse watching the police. Somebody pointed his finger to the far corner of the ceiling and whispered to the man next to him. My eyes followed to where he was pointing.

There, in the corner of the warehouse, up high near the ceiling, a body dangled, swinging gently.

A chill went up my spine and I stepped back a few meters. I had never seen a person dead by hanging or any other means. My head felt funny, like I was about to lose my balance. I leaned against the nearby wall and looked up again. An onlooker next to me whispered that the deceased, Akbar *agha*, was a nice, quiet man.

My eyes were fixed on the man's lifeless body. It rocked ever so slightly. Two policemen had climbed up into the rafters and were crawling on a narrow wooden beam toward the dead man. I shivered again.

Akbar *agha* was an acquaintance of my father's, and once he had mentioned that Akbar was a religious man. In Islam, suicide is forbidden—so could this really be a suicide? Or?

Suddenly, death felt closer to me than ever before. I kept my lips together, sealed against the possibility of secret police and informers, who were everywhere, reporting any suspicious activities or any negative comments about the regime. So even though my mind wanted to stick around and learn more, my roiling stomach forced me out of the warehouse and back to the relative security of my home.

On my walk back, I thought about Akbar *agha's* suspicious demise and how it added yet another mystery to the recent occurrences and inexplicable disappearances or deaths of people we knew. Yes, these times were turbulent, and a sense of change was everywhere. People were fed up, and more and more braved the streets in long and sometimes violent demonstrations. This was my world, but not my destiny.

I was convinced that karma had a different call on me.

Then I thought of my father. How well does he know Akbar *agha*? How about Akbar *agha's* wife, his children? And could my father be in danger too? Oh God! A tremble slithered up my spine and I ran the rest of the way home.

Up until three years ago, my father was a charcoal distributor with a large, dark warehouse. When I was twelve years old, he bought and added a six-room house next door to his warehouse. The empty rooms in the back of that house were used as a storage area. If anything happened to him in any of those rooms, it would go undiscovered for days! I remembered the large pile of charcoal in his warehouse. Just like a tall black mountain, it was the dream of any kid to climb up, and then slide down on the small pieces of dark charcoal. Once a week a large truck with a hydraulic lift came and dumped a mountain of new charcoal into his warehouse yard. I was lucky to sit behind the wheel of some of the trucks and pretend I was driving them. Sometimes the driver allowed me to honk the loud horn. And the donkey rides! Yes! Often vendors showed up with their donkeys to buy charcoal, and I got to ride those donkeys whenever I was there.

When I burst through the front door, panting, my mother asked many questions. I answered them to the best of my ability. She said she didn't know the man well. Nevertheless, he was a neighbor.

She went to the kitchen and reheated my unfinished lunch. The aroma of her Persian cooking filled the house. It enticed to my growling stomach, which had settled down some. I washed my hands and splashed cold water on my face, hoping to rinse away the images from the warehouse, and sat again at the table.

The moment she placed the food in front of me, the phone rang again. The same game started once more. My rush to the living room won me the phone receiver one more time.

This time the voice on the other end of the line belonged to Farhad, my best friend from high school. I hadn't heard from him in a long time. He had basically disappeared on me about a year prior. On the phone, he mentioned that he was in Tehran for two days with some free time. I seized the opportunity and asked if he could accompany me to my afternoon mission, a visit to the Higher Education Ministry for processing my request to study abroad.

He agreed, but with a touch of reluctance in his voice.

Mother had eavesdropped, as usual, and made a pejorative comment about my friend. She immediately followed up with an order to go back and finish my lunch, trailed with a comment about the importance of good hot meals for skinny boys like me.

Every time she called me a boy, my resentment toward her flared.

Would I ever become a man in her eyes?

On my return to the kitchen she drilled me about what Farhad was after. She wasn't fond of him, and thought that he wasted my time.

My nod, and the stuffing of my mouth with food, kept her quiet momentarily. Then I employed my usual solution to avoid her never-ending inquiries by hustling downstairs to my room in the basement. The make-shift bedroom occupied half of the small underground area. My living space was separated from the stored junk by a heavy curtain. The room was barely furnished on purpose, of course. It was to remind me of the hellhole I was in. There was nothing in that room that gave me a sense of belonging or enticed me to stay. In fact, I could say the same thing about the whole country.

On my way out of the house, my mother blocked me in the upstairs hallway. My attempt to evade her was unsuccessful. She shoved a big, rolled-up sandwich into my chest. "God protect you, my son. Stay out of trouble. The streets are dangerous these days!"

I nodded, grabbed the sandwich and proceeded to exit. She wasn't satisfied with her earlier comment, and she shouted on my way out the door to stay out of the soldiers' ways and to not engage them.

A few steps down the street from our house, a beggar was sitting on the ground hitting his metal plate with a spoon-his way of asking for help. I dropped the sandwich into his plate, and walked briskly toward Farhad's apartment.

In June, a month prior, my graduation from college had brought me closer to grasping my life's dream of leaving the country. During the past four years, I had planned, strategized, and carefully lined-up supporters to assist me in getting out of Iran. Ever since childhood, Western societies, their cultures, their ideas and way of life were relentlessly pumped into my mind. Every cartoon, the majority of TV programs, shows, movies, most music, and other forms of modern communication were promoting the glories of the Western world. It was during my high school years when I realized that my life as an independent individual would begin after high school graduation. The West was where I wanted to live my adult life. Perhaps, at first, it was all the razzle-dazzle that the Western world promoted. All the happy endings of the American stories, all the fantastic, brave endeavors that westerners would take, from *Flash Gordon* to *Lost in Space* and *Star Trek*. Not all the entertainment imports were necessarily from America. Iran imported plenty of European shows during the sixties and seventies as well.

My knowledge of the Western world during my adolescent years was augmented by reading translated literature such as *Twenty Thousand Leagues Under the Sea* and *Around the World in Eighty Days* by Jules Verne and *Les Misérables* by Victor Hugo, and *The Old Man and the Sea* by Ernest Hemingway. Reinforcement came through association with my cousins' friends from Europe who traveled to Iran during summers, and my American teachers at the Iran/America Society language school.

Yet it was during the college years that I realized my wings were clipped in Iran. My intellect, my sense of adventure, my self-expression, even my imagination were all impeded by a set of political, cultural, and religious chains. It had become suffocating. I felt as if fate had trapped me in a storm in the middle of an ocean.

During 1977 and 1978, the whole country went into turmoil. Strong new political winds created heavy social swells, and the unrest made my life even more unbearable. Being in the midst of it all was exuberating, yet unsettling. In those years, people in Iran tasted the sweetness of populous power and learned that once united, the power of the masses could actually supersede modern weaponry. The shah's powerful security forces were faced with strong challenges by a mass of unarmed civilians. The government had become reactionary to the persistent, continuous, and forward-moving mass demonstrations. People were demanding changes. Daring attempts were made by a captive nation to break the chains of oppression and dictatorship that had suffocated her for millennia.

But my shackles were multitude. Traditions, and unwritten rules of customs and rituals were holding me down, keeping me from the future I had imagined for myself. I knew refusing to submit to those rules while living in Iran would be the end of me— becoming socially banished at best or imprisonment with torture at worse. I had to get away, far away, before I drowned.

Farhad's place was about twenty minutes walking distance from my house. Our relationship had been strained in the past couple of years. My mind contemplated our upcoming encounter. I rehearsed my conversation with him over and over on my way to his place with the hope of getting to the bottom of his recent strange behavior.

He stayed at his mother's apartment on the fourth floor of a commercial building on a busy street. My climb of four flights of stairs ended with me panting at his doorstep. Soon after I knocked, he opened the door, slid himself out of the doorway, and immediately shut the door behind him, quite in contrast to the Persian practice of hospitality.

I extended my hand for a friendly handshake and was ready for the possibility of the customary two kisses, one for each cheek. He shook my hand with his usual strong grip and proceeded to descend from the stairs without delay.

Farhad had always kept his body in a good shape with a daily, regular workout regimen. I could see his muscle tone was still good, his biceps prominent. His height of a hundred-seventy-five centimeters was considered slightly taller than average. His dark hair had been recently cut. Pretty much the same Farhad. Yet …

"We're going to have to take a bus," I said as I rushed to keep up with him flying down the stairs. "My car is in the shop again."

He asked about the purpose of going to the Higher Education Ministry as we entered the busy street. Walking toward the bus stop I raised my voice to be heard over the loud traffic noise. "The Higher Education Ministry's clearance is required in order to attend graduate school abroad."

The look of surprise on his face was unmistakable. I reminded him that my plans had not changed for the past four years, as he should have remembered. The process was very involved and comprised of many steps.

"You shouldn't leave," he said, interrupting my explanation.

Surprised by his comment, I was about to ask him for clarification when our bus appeared out of the black smoke of exhaust fumes, and the rumbling engine of the previous bus.

We ran toward the bus and waved our hands, gesturing to the driver to wait for us. The bus stopped and a few people exited, but the driver immediately pulled the lever to shut the door.

A mild pain traveled through my elbow as I wedged my right arm into the bus' two folding doors to prevent its closing. Fortunately, the sensors triggered the doors to open.

"Hustle up," the agitated driver shouted.

We both hopped on, and immediately after, the driver pulled the lever again so he could shut the doors on the overcrowded bus. We slowly moved toward the center of the aisle and stood. My grip on the nearby rail handle secured my position.

It was as good a time as any to ask Farhad to explain why he didn't want me to leave Iran.

He repeated his previous comment. "Like I said, you shouldn't leave the country."

"Where are you going?" a stranger standing next to me asked.

Privacy was a rare commodity in my world. Living in a busy metropolitan city with a culture that encourages physical closeness, I had learned early on to tolerate such invasions, but never felt comfortable with it. I turned my face away from the stranger and paid no heed to him. My tactic didn't work, however. He asked again.

"He is probably going to America," said another man, who stood on the other side of Farhad, interjecting himself into the unsolicited conversation about me.

"America? I have a cousin in Los Angeles," the first man said.

"Gentlemen, mind your own business, please," clearly irritated, I interrupted the chatty passengers.

My comment didn't set well with them.

"He is a *West-toxicated*, stuck up, sissy. Leave him alone," a guy behind me said, jumping into the discussion, also uninvited.

I turned around to look at him. He stood so close to me that my nose almost hit his face.

"I'm standing right here. You are calling me a sissy?"

"Yes, I'm *telling* you. Not only you're a sissy, but you're a coward too. Now get the hell out of my face." He shoved me and I lost my balance, stumbling into the young man next to me. My grip on his denim jacket prevented my falling.

"Are you picking my pocket, you West-toxicated bastard?" the young man asked, punctuating his question with a punch to my stomach.

Farhad saw that, and returned the guy's punch to my gut with a punch to his face. The man behind me then hit Farhad in the face, and suddenly we were brawling.

A second or two later, someone shouted, "Knife. He's pulling a knife!"

The bus jerked to a stop in the middle of a busy street, blocking the traffic. The driver opened the side door in the middle of the bus near us, stood up, and shouted, "Get off the bus, you savages!"

Farhad and I jumped out and sprinted up the street. After several minutes, Farhad slowed down and looked back to see if anyone had chased us. He declared that we were clear, his words accompanied by heavy breathing. "But we didn't have to run," he complained. "I could've taken care of those idiots."

Also breathing heavily, I stopped and bent forward to ease inhalation. A few wet drops fell on my left hand.

It was blood.

"Where is it coming from?" I gasped. Panic was clearly detectable in my voice, and I felt the heat rising up my neck for showing my fear in front of Farhad.

He offered his help and turned my face toward him. A moment later he let out a loud chuckle. "Clean up your face man. It's covered in blood."

The cotton handkerchief I always carried in my pant's pocket came in handy, but a moment later it was drenched in blood. I winced. I never could stomach the sight of blood.

Farhad saw the fright on my face, chuckled again and said, "It's just your nose. It has already stopped."

That was good news. But I now had another dilemma. I couldn't go to the ministry with a bloody face.

The rushing water in the nearby *jube,* a narrow canal running down both sides of almost every street, seemed to be the only solution at hand. The *jube's* water, as usual, carried debris and trash from the north of the town toward the south. I found a clear spot and dipped my handkerchief in the water, just enough to dampen it, and then cleaned my face.

Farhad sneered, commenting that this was the first time he had seen me, Mister Clean, touch the dirty *jube* water. I ignored his comment and cleaned up my face.

We walked for a few minutes in silence. It was hard to ignore what he had said earlier. Why was he opposed to my leaving? Curiosity was killing me. I couldn't take it anymore. So I asked again.

"People like you shouldn't leave the country," he replied.

"People like me? What's wrong with me?" I asked.

He went to explain that the country needed people like me to stay and fight against the regime, as we were at a historical point. Big changes were happening; a revolution could soon emerge.

His comment sounded like a compliment to me at first. It felt good.

The country needs people like you. No one had ever said anything like that to me before. I felt flattered and accomplished. Then, the burden of responsibility he put on my shoulders hit me. He asked me to stay and fight!

Fight for what? I thought. Fight for whom? He was asking me to endanger or perhaps give up my most important possession, my dream, and even my life.

He also said *we*. What group was he connecting himself with? Who were these "we" he was talking about?

Farhad was a student at the military academy, and therefore he was considered a member of the military. The recent public face of the military was smeared with resentment for their daily harassment, shooting, and arresting of civilians on the streets. However, there was a growing number of armed forces' personnel who sympathized with the opposition groups. They, nevertheless, were considered heroes by many. Risking their lives by opposing the brutal regime and facing the possibility of a court-marshal for the good of the nation. Of course, the assumption was that a change of regime would be good for the nation.

Which side is he on? Is he turning? Is he in trouble? I was deep in thought when he blurted, "It's a cop-out!" shattering my thoughts.

I stopped and looked at his face, which wore a much-too-serious expression. "Cop-out? What the heck is that supposed to mean?"

He kept his head down and continued walking. He philosophized that it was convenient to take the easy way out and leave the country when there were troubles--when the future was unclear and the lines between friends and foes were ambiguous at best. When our enemies were dangerously illusive and ready to pounce, stealing our national treasures. Especially when our independence, and most importantly, our very freedom was at stake.

These words were a bit strange coming from my childhood friend. They seemed like memorized propaganda to me. A melancholy feeling came over me listening to his words. Was I a coward as he implied? I wasn't sure how to respond to him. Fortunately, we reached our destination.

"Here's the building."

2

SILENT TALK

 The wound is the place where the Light enters you.

— RUMI, PERSIAN POET (1207 – 1273)

A large, eight-story building with white marble stones stood before us. My smile turned into a frown when I saw the long line of people waiting to enter, curved around the building. Mostly college students. The few older people in line seemed to be parents standing next to their daughters in the heat of the summer afternoon. Everyone was behaving with civility and calm for the sake of efficiency. The line moved slowly but steadily.

Farhad shook his head and started complaining, questioning if anyone would remain in Iran. I sighed, and immediately warned him that I wasn't finished with him. He would soon find out why I wanted to leave the country. The bus incident taught me a good lesson—not to talk about those subjects in public, as people listen and want to participate.

We arrived at the front desk inside the building after twenty minutes of sluggish and agonizing progress. The cool air inside was a welcome relief. The first clerk I had to interact with was a woman in her mid-twenties, thin with short dark hair. She looked up, smiled, and greeted us.

Her smile piqued my curiosity. Iranian girls typically didn't smile at male strangers. She inspected my documents and flipped a few pages as she kept her smile. Then, with a soft voice asked if I was going to America.

Returning her smile, I confirmed I was.

With her eyes on the documents she said, "I just returned from America myself."

With those words, she suddenly seemed even prettier than before. I surmised that her smile was the residual side benefit of her stay in America, a nation of smiling people. Desperate for more information about America, I asked her where in the US she had studied.

She kept her smile as she flipped more pages of my documents. After a moment, with a softer voice she explained that after completing her graduate school in Raleigh, North Carolina, she had returned home a month ago.

"What did you study? Did you finish your degree?" I asked, eager for more details.

Farhad elbowed me. "Slow down. You're asking too many questions."

She looked up at Farhad and replied politely, "It's okay." Then she looked at me and continued, "Yes, I received my master's degree in management."

I moved my head closer to her and whispered, "But *why* did you come back?"

She raised her shoulders and angled her head, placed her eyes back on my papers and answered, "I love my country! I also felt homesick." After a short pause she continued, "Besides, I am looking forward to settling down and having a family here." She looked up at me, a flirtatious spark lighting up her eyes.

"But with all the troubles lately, this is not a good time to be back here," I whispered again.

Her smile disappeared, and her face took on a serious, professional expression. She slammed the stamp on my documents a couple of times and handed them back to me. In a formal tone she explained that I had six months to secure acceptance from a graduate school in order to continue my education. Otherwise, I would be drafted to the military services. My next step was to go to office number twenty four, on the second floor, for the final approval.

I knew at that point to hold my remaining questions, and let the long line behind me move forward. I found her motives odd. Why would someone come back from a free and prosperous world to a hot bed of troubles? Was she unaware of the dangerous path the country was taking? Perhaps she returned to partake in the change, like what Farhad was talking about. I wondered how many more students shared her views and had returned from abroad. Was I making a mistake?

The political turbulence of Iran at that time was uncharted water for everyone. No one knew where it was heading. However, one thing I knew for sure was that the turmoil we were experiencing in Iran was not going to end well, at least for a while. Chaos was not what I was looking for, quite the opposite. I was after a period of low-key and peaceful endeavors to learn more about myself.

A few hours later, my work was finished at the ministry. The air had cooled down a bit and it became tolerable to take the long walk home instead of risking another confrontational bus ride.

As we walked, I was overcome with the excitement of accomplishing an important step toward my final objective. I announced, "It's official now. I have six months to exit Iran. Otherwise, I will be drafted. And that, my friend, would be the end of my life."

"And why is that? What's wrong with being drafted?" Farhad asked.

Was he joking? I launched into a monologue on how dangerous it had become with daily protests everywhere. Soldiers in the streets were shooting ordinary citizens during peaceful demonstrations. How chaos was prevailing, and more importantly, the possibilities of the draft now looming over my head. My fear of ending up on the streets pointing a gun at my friends, family, and innocent people was a real and serious one. As a matter of principle, I refused to handle military weapons, and I explained to him that the military had a simple solution for my kind—it starts with a court marshal and ends with a firing squad.

He dismissed my worries and said that I was educated, and men with college degrees wouldn't become foot soldiers. They were more likely to become officers after boot camp.

"Great! As an officer I'd be in charge of a group of soldiers with multiple weapons. So then the disgruntled soldiers will shoot me!" I went over a few tales of distressed soldiers who, refusing to shoot innocent people, turned to their commanding officers and had shot them. "No thanks!" I paused a bit to rein in my emotions and redirect the topic. "Plus, I need to figure out some stuff for myself."

Farhad didn't say anything more. We continued our brisk walk in silence, but my mind continued to process our conversation. No one had ever asked me to stay in Iran for the sake of the country before. My friend's comments touched me. Someone thought I could make a difference. But then quickly my suspicions took over again. It seemed he had some other unspoken agenda.

After a few more minutes, I broke the silence by telling him about the dead body I saw that day.

"Was he shot?" Farhad asked.

"No, he was hanged." I paused for his reaction. But he didn't say anything. I gave up waiting and continued the story in more detail.

At the end he asked if it was a murder or a suicide.

Shrugging my shoulders, I related everyone's first impression of the incident as a suicide, but followed it quickly with my own hypothesis that perhaps it was SAVAK who killed the man and made it look like a suicide. The secret police were notorious for such things.

Farhad chuckled. "The secret police don't bother to make it look like anything anymore. They would kill him in their torture chambers and then dump the body into the dead salt lake in the desert, where the body sinks in the soft salt, and no one can find any trace."

Our path took us near our favorite music store, a small retail establishment packed with instruments. We went in to browse. Rows of acoustic guitars, violins, saxophones, trumpets, flutes, and other instruments were eye candy to me, in spite of the crowded aisles. The store had a unique odor—the scent of the wood mixed with the fragrance of the resins used to varnish it. And perhaps combined with the smell of the brass instruments' polish. Whatever it was, it invoked some nostalgia in me. I asked Farhad if he remembered the first time we stepped into this store. He shook his head, rifling through a stack of sheet music.

"It was four years ago in the fall. I exchanged my accordion for a classical guitar here," I explained.

"Oh yes, was that the first time?" he asked.

It had been difficult to part with my accordion that day. It was the instrument that started me on my journey into learning music. But I recall comparing it to the passing of a torch. The accordion gave up its position in my life to another instrument that would take me deeper into the wondrous world of music. Four years earlier, the afternoon walk from that music store back home, with my best friend Farhad and my brand new Yamaha classical guitar, had become unforgettable.

It changed my life.

Farhad asked why I would remember it. I looked at him in disbelief. For the first time in my life I owned a guitar. That was important.

"So what? Why was owning a guitar so important to you?" He pushed me to dig deeper.

I thought about it for a few minutes. The best I could come up with was that for me, every "first" became memorable.

Examining a guitar, Farhad asked if I would remember the date and the place I got my first accordion. To my own amazement, I couldn't remember.

"How come your first accordion wasn't that significant?" he philosophized.

My right hand fingers gently traveled along the curves of another classical guitar on display. My eyes examined the details of its curves and bindings closely. After a short pause, without taking my eyes off the guitar, I replied, "Well, guitar players have more sex appeal than accordion players."

That wasn't true. In reality, it was because of him. But admitting it to him wasn't necessary. During the last year of high school, Farhad often played his classical guitar for me. Life became unbearable without a guitar. I had to have one. Its soft tone, versatility, and the beautiful body contour were irresistible. But more importantly, it was an excuse for us to spend more time together.

Farhad exposed a half smile and admitted that he did remember that day. Especially, our conversation about my plans for my new best friend, the guitar that I just bought.

Yes, I acknowledged it. We chatted about how I would pamper the new friend, where I would place it in the house, and how I was going to play it.

"And the next day, I taught you the 'House of Rising Sun,'" he said.

Yes, and then I confessed that I would never forget that day. We both chuckled.

When we stepped out of the store, the sun had set and the sky was dark. The cool breeze of the summer evening was a welcoming break from a hot and difficult afternoon. A street vendor's kerosene lamps seduced pedestrians to his display of fresh, moist walnuts in front of the music store.

We continued our walk back home. Farhad remained quiet while I talked about my plans to travel abroad. He usually had many ideas, and before you knew it, our conversations would turn into farfetched plans and fantastic activities. But not that afternoon.

His silence bothered me, so I decided to join him in it. We walked shoulder to shoulder, jumped over the *jubes* and crossed streets together without a single word. Our muteness turned thick, like a blanket. No, it became more like a deep black cloud hovering over us as we walked home. Curious about this new game, I was determined not to be the first one to break the silence.

Farhad was my best friend from the fifth through twelfth grades. We were inseparable. However, since his first semester of college three years ago, his behavior had changed, and his sudden quietness disturbed me. This might be the last time we would see each other for a long time.

The cloud of silence threatened to overshadow potentially one of the greatest moments in the lives of two friends. Moments like these, if treated well, could engrave the happiness, the bonding, and the delight of a friendship for the rest of our lives. It was peculiar that my senses didn't detect any particular trouble. I began to wonder if his silent walk next to me was just some mischief he was trying out on me.

Right after his boot camp, two and a half years prior, Farhad was sent to study at the University of Shiraz, the most prestigious university in Iran located in the southern city famous for its tall, handsome spruce trees and temperate weather. The trouble started there, as he hung around with the wrong crowd.

My mind stayed busy as a way to avoid speaking before he did. I had talked enough. It was his turn to speak.

How could Farhad, a mediocre student at best, end up in a top university in Iran? Scholastically, one needed to be among the top one percent of students in the country to be accepted there.

I knew the answer: the military academy. He joined it right after high school. Every year, the military academy selected and planted cadets interested into engineering and medical studies directly in the classrooms of the top universities, bypassing the difficult national college entrance exam. That was one of the perks. The academy approved Farhad's decision to study electronic engineering, one of the most sought after and competitive fields of study in Iran. In retrospect, I didn't think they should have placed him there. Mentally and scholastically he wasn't prepared. Being among the cream of the crop was too stressful for him.

His decision to join the military academy was a surprise to me. He wasn't the military type. Was it the unexpected death of his father in his last year of high school that forced him to make that decision? Or did he know that through the academy he could be placed in a good school studying engineering with a stipend? I never received an answer to that question. He kept it to himself. In Shiraz, Farhad, not an introvert, thrived amongst his new, smart friends.

In my mind, I contemplated going easy on him. Away from home, with the newfound freedom of college life, perhaps he had fallen into a trap. For the first time in his life, he sat in co-ed classes and was introduced to liberal arts studies. Those were big changes for a boy who spent his twelve years of schooling in an all-boys school, influenced by conservative education.

Our quiet walk continued.

Farhad's new friends, in the new city, at a large university that was heavily influenced by Western standards, were a group of smart engineering students. These super-smart students turned into philosophers by devouring philosophy books and immersing themselves in the new-found world of liberal arts; a world not emphasized in Iranian high schools.

Finally he broke the silence. My wait was over. "We must be drifting apart as friends."

I challenged him on the origin of that insight.

"Close friends don't need verbal communication to connect. They can feel and read each other's minds."

These words must have been a product of his newly found self-confidence and demeanor that projected a search for a deeper sense of life. But somehow, it felt like a farce. Although truthfully, the sense of a fading friendship happened to be mutual.

Repeatedly throughout the past year, he had proudly displayed masochistic behaviors such as burning the backs of his hands with cigarettes. I suspected these mannerisms were attempts to fit in with his new group of friends. That worried me. How far would he go? Where would he draw the line? Did these new friends find him vulnerable? Were they playing games with him? Were they testing him?

He crossed the street and jumped over a wide *jube* onto the sidewalk. I followed.

"Look," I said, "all this mumbo jumbo about real friends' silent communication and philosophizing relationships has its time and place. It is certainly not now, and not here." I was sure that impatience could easily be detected in my tone. I didn't care. I further explained how thrilled I was about my journey to a new country, to experience an exciting way of life. I wanted to talk to him about it as my friend. Or, if that subject was boring to him, we could talk about music, art, or even politics. "I'm sorry if my telepathic powers are not strong enough to carry a non-verbal conversation about these subjects with you," I continued.

He must have thought that I had missed the point and continued philosophizing, explaining that close friends can feel each other's vibes and energy. Their togetherness can be satisfying even without verbal communication. They don't need to talk in order to enjoy each other's presence. He further emphasized that spending time in silence with a good friend could be very elevating. But, he warned that usually it happened when both were more or less at the same level of understanding the universe.

I was livid. He alluded that he had evolved beyond my level of intellect, and that's why we didn't connect silently. I confronted him with that thought.

He picked up his walking pace; I matched it. He explained, "Well, earlier you said we could talk about music. Music, for example, is about feeling. How you connect with the world impacts your sentiments and that, my friend, is reflected in your understanding of music. If you don't push your limits, how will you know where the real boundaries are?"

I wasn't clear on what he meant by pushing our limits. Impatiently, I asked him to explain.

"For example," he continued, "on the subject of pain: how do you know how much pain you can withstand if you don't try?"

"Trust me," I immediately replied, "I can withstand pain and a lot of it. Ask my dentist. He never used any anesthesia, even on root canals. Since I was six years old I have been tortured by the same dentist year after year. I have screamed as loud as humanly possible. But I'm afraid that's not what you are talking about."

He extended the back of his hands. "Here, can you do this? Can you bear the pain without a sound, without the twitch of an eye?" The backs of his hands showed what looked like burn marks.

He admitted that he had burned the back of his hands with cigarettes without uttering a sound and that he was extending the time.

Has he flipped? I thought. His behavior and new beliefs combined with his brief military training made him a prime target for the recruiters of the two guerrilla organizations that were actively fighting the government. A dangerous lifestyle. Members of those groups were routinely tortured once arrested; and often executed. On the other hand, SAVAK recruiters loved to hire cadets like him to spy on other students. I reminded myself to be careful, and not share my thoughts freely with him.

I wondered if his new group of friends had suspected him of being an agent of SAVAK because he was from a military academy and were playing him.

SAVAK had infiltrated every aspect of Iranian society. SAVAK's agents, trained by the world's most feared intelligence organizations such as the CIA, and Israel's Mossad, were the eyes and ears of the dictatorial regime inside and outside of the country. They had developed a large network of informers. Seen and unseen, informers reported on whomever they perceived as a threat to the regime, not excluding friends and family members. Everyone was a suspect.

Or perhaps my friend's extremist behavior stemmed purely from his youth, wanting to experiment with pushing limits? Or had he become a masochist?

Suddenly, Farhad stopped and asked an older man on the street, who was enjoying a few minutes of quiet time smoking, if he could borrow his cigarette.

The man took his cigarette out of his mouth with thick fingers hardened with callouses that resembling dried leather. "What? My cigarette? This one?"

"Yes, for just a moment, please," Farhad insisted.

The man chuckled, the wrinkles on his skinny face undulating with his laugh, and handed Farhad his cigarette. Farhad took the cigarette and gave it a good puff. The tip went bright orange. He exhaled the smoke and said, "Watch this."

He placed the tip of the burning cigarette on the back of his left hand and held it.

"What are you doing?" My shout and quick move to brush the cigarette off his hand alerted him. He turned his body to block my action, and held the cigarette on the back of his hand.

Cigarettes burn at 900 degrees Celsius, equivalent to 1652 degrees Fahrenheit during puffs, and 400 C/752 F between puffs. A glancing touch would not burn the skin, as the coal at the end of the cigarette is surrounded by a thin layer of ash. But his skin turned black as he held and pressed the cigarette for nearly three seconds. I turned my face away, unable to watch.

"There, I held it a second longer than ever before," he told me and returned the cigarette to its owner. The stranger took his cigarette, looked at me, and asked if Farhad was a psycho.

Sympathizing with the stranger, I shook my head and continued the long walk home with Farhad.

I couldn't help myself. I continued to lecture him on how important it was for him to focus on his studies, as he was so close to earning his engineering degree from a top university. His involvement with unrelated psychological and philosophical issues distracted him from his objectives. Controlling my voice to stay calm was an effort, but it felt necessary. Without giving him a chance to reply, I further preached to him that hurting himself was not a brave thing to do.

He shook his head. "You don't have a clue, do you, Vahid? This is about life, about how we live and what we live for. About who we are and what we can be." After a short pause, he continued. "We've grown apart so much that we've lost any commonality."

Another long silence followed, creating a time continuum that took me back to how I met him the first time …

It was about twelve years prior when the loud thump of our heavy door knocker interrupted my daydream on a hot summer's afternoon before my fourth-grade year. The huge doorknocker on our old wooden door made such a loud sound that our neighbors could always tell when we had a visitor. The house was about eighty years old, and was designed as most old houses were in Iran. An old wooden door opened up into a short hallway with a room at each side. A few stairs lead visitors into a sunken courtyard with a large utility pool in the middle. Every summer, we set several wooden platforms under the peach trees in the courtyard and covered them with Persian rugs. The wooden platforms served as an extension of our rooms. On hot days we ate, played, and entertained guests in the courtyard, under the shade of the peach and apple trees near the pool.

I jumped off the wooden platform and rushed to open the door. A muscular kid about my age, with an oval face and mop-styled dark hair similar to the Beatles, greeted me at the doorstep. Puzzled by the appearance of a strange kid, I asked who he was. He introduced himself as Farhad and asked if I recognized him. He claimed he was my classmate in the third grade.

"No." My attempt to shut the door on him was negated by his foot blocking the door.

He blamed my forgetfulness on his skinny body during the third grade, and asked if he could play with me. Still baffled by a stranger showing up at my house, I asked how he knew where I lived. He admitted following me home after school a few times during the school year. His answer intrigued me. Curious to get to know him, I asked my mother's permission.

With my mother's blessing we played and played. That day cemented a long-lasting friendship. We became best friends and had many adventures together.

Toward the end of that summer, I remembered confessing to him that I couldn't remember him in any of my classes. He didn't mind, and thought it could be because he was a "skinny, wimpy kid" during most of the school year. He remembered vividly, that during our war games, I had beaten him numerous times. Toward the end of the school year, he had started lifting weights, as he thought it would be the best way to earn my respect.

Frankly, I never remembered him being skinny. As second and third graders, with about thirty of us in a classroom, we enacted the ancient Romans vs. Persians battles during recesses. Typically, I played the role of a general and never picked any skinny kids to be my soldiers.

Fifth grade was different. I became a calm, patient kid who avoided fighting or participating in any war games. Perhaps it was because of the reality of my father's profession, and how others perceived it had become more visible to me; others didn't find it as cool as I did. The awakening moment was when I overheard the school's principal say to a teacher, "This kid, despite his father being in the dirty charcoal business, is always dressed well and clean."

At first, I felt gratified that the principal spoke well of me. However, his comment bounced around in my head for a while, and I knew something wasn't right. The heavy and sad realization hit me a few days later. They considered my father's business to be of a lower class. The black soot of charcoal gave the impression of a filthy business.

It saddened me to remember all that. There is no denial that my father's business as a charcoal retailer and distributor in Tehran brought me embarrassment. During my adolescent years, I was sensitive to how others perceived my father's profession. Perhaps it was the side effect of a predatorial culture that thrived on competitive behavior and glorified bullying. How was it that they ridiculed his honest living, a small business owner with much longer work hours and higher risks, as being less worthy than a government employee, a teacher, or a military officer?

In my twisted teenage mentality, I was angry at my father. His job humiliated me in our society. I was the son of a charcoal business owner.

"Do you think any of this actually matters?" Farhad's voice brought me back from my childhood memories.

"Any of what?" I asked.

"Weren't you listening? All the stuff I mentioned, about who we are, what we are, why we are."

"Of course it matters," I replied. "What we do with our lives defines who we are and what we are, and in some cases, even why we are. But I don't need to burn myself with a cigarette to discover who I am. I believe my body is my sanctuary, and I am in charge of protecting it. My mind and body form a vessel for me to travel this turbulent stream called life!" I preached passionately as if I were saving Farhad's soul.

Farhad didn't reply. We continued our brisk walk in silence again. Soon after, we approached the fork in the road where one of us usually chose to accompany the other one to his house, about a twenty-minute detour. Among friends, a twenty-minute detour is a small price for finishing a story, resolving a heated argument, or just to enjoy a further dose of friendship.

But that night, once we arrived at the dividing point, for the first time we each went our separate ways without a word. He turned left and I continued straight.

After a few steps, I turned my head and saw him one more time before he disappeared into the dark of the warm Tehran night.

3
NERVOUS SOLDIERS

> *Congress shall make no law respecting an establishment of religion, or prohibiting the free exercise thereof; or abridging the freedom of speech, or of the press; or the right of the people peaceably to assemble, and to petition the Government for a redress of grievances.*
>
> — The First Amendment to the United States Constitution, (December 15, 1791)

A phone call interrupted the otherwise boring morning. The caller, Zeinab *khanoum*, a distant cousin of my mother, warned me about a large demonstration forming not far from our house. The postal workers' strike had crippled the country. It also had debilitated my efforts on completing the acceptance process for schools in America, as I was waiting for the result of my TOEFL, an English language test required for admission to American universities.

As my day felt otherwise unproductive, I decided to go to the demonstration, despite the warning to stay off the streets.

I grabbed my camera and jumped on my ten-speed bicycle.

Nobody saw me leave, and I didn't bother to let anyone know my whereabouts. It was going to be a short outing, or so I thought.

The sky was clear and the sun's rays felt pleasant on my face. The streets were as busy as ever. People were moving about their business as usual. The road to my destination was a slight uphill grade. I pedaled north for about six kilometers.

My destination was a major intersection of two main roads. The north-south one started from Tehran's central train station at the south and extended over twenty kilometers north, all the way to the skirts of the Alborz Mountains. The other road stretched many tens of kilometers east to west, connecting the sprawling west of Tehran to the east. The intersection of the two roads, known as Pahlavi's four-way, was a hub of activity, featuring retail stores, boutiques, schools, and business offices all around it. On the southeast corner, a large park housed the largest theater playhouse in the city.

A rush of adrenaline pumped through my veins upon seeing the military's fortification blocking the east-west road. I had never seen such a build up for a blockade before. Heavily armed soldiers in full combat gear stood bunkered and poised, manning several heavy machine guns. Behind them, tanks and armored vehicles had formed an impenetrable barrier against any westward movement. Admittedly, this scene was exciting.

Were they expecting a worthy enemy?

On the bank of the *jube*, not too far from the soldiers, I found a place to park my bike. The rushing flow of water in the *jube* coming from the mountains in the north toward the south added an interesting mix to the ensemble of busy street sounds. My body shivered with the thought of what horror could occur there in the next few hours. I prayed that the blood of innocent people would not flow in the *jubes* to the south of Tehran that day.

Police had diverted the traffic as the military had blocked the entire west stretch of the road, facing east. Drivers were not happy; their shouts of cussing mixed with heavy traffic noise signaled an inevitable chaotic eruption.

My curiosity urged me to get closer to the soldiers, even though my sense of reason issued a warning to stay back. My camera had a strap, so I put it around my neck and moved the camera to my back, hidden from the soldiers' view. Then I inched myself close enough to hear them. The wide sidewalk was busy with pedestrians in the rush of their morning commute, ignoring the presence of the soldiers and a few onlookers who, like me, were curiously staring at the blockade.

Some of the soldiers were pacing back and forth and every few seconds gazed east, biting their lower lips or touching their chins. Some were joking around while others seemed preoccupied, and not in the mood for jesting. The tanks stood silently behind them, lurking like huge, ugly, unstoppable beasts, waiting for the kill order.

Most people in Iran were not satisfied with the existing regime. All political parties except one were outlawed. The only party allowed consisted of staunch supporters of the king's regime. Liberty only existed for people loyal to the regime, as long as their actions, expressions, and businesses were in sync with what was prescribed from the autocratic ruler. The gap between the "haves" and the "have-nots" was wide and getting wider. Economic prosperity was only for a small group of elites who were closely tied to the shah's court and the state. Iran was in violation of many human rights laws and agreements. Dissent was rising rapidly. The U.S. and several European countries were putting pressure on the Iranian regime to improve its crumbling human rights position. The shah, in an attempt to earn public trust, had replaced his prime minister, along with the cabinet, several times in the past few months, always blaming his puppet ministers for the country's predicaments. Instead, he was adding to the very instability he hoped to tame.

The path for the demonstration march had been announced in advance a few days prior by the organizers, according to my mother's cousin. The size of the crowd, however, was yet unknown. Iranians were barred from possessing guns and switchblades. The military's fortified position was indicative of their anticipation of confronting a rather large, aggressive crowd. Curious to see how far these two opposing forces would go, I awaited the encounter. Would protesters disperse once they saw the heavily trenched military? Or perhaps the military would back off once they saw the demonstrators' iron will?

Was I going to witness bloodshed?

A faint sound of rhythmic chants from a far distance reached my ears—a deep, eerie sound that reminded me of the warning grumbles of an approaching thunderstorm. Except, this was the synchronized sound of collective human voices—the voices of the protest marchers. I was certain that the soldiers heard it too. Facing east, they stared at an empty four-lane road that continued beyond the incline of a bridge five hundred meters ahead of them.

As the demonstrators moved closer, the chants became louder. But the rise of the bridge blocked the soldiers' view of what was coming. All the soldiers stood fixated ahead, listening to the eerie sound with no visual reference point.

"Check your weapons!" ordered the commander.

"Load and get in position!" barked the sub-commander.

Were they really intending to shoot? I questioned the wisdom of my up-close position. But not wanting to attract the soldiers' attention, I remained frozen in place.

Initially, a few flags waved over the rise in the road, and then the first row of demonstrators appeared on the crest of the bridge.

The commander shouted an order. Soldiers on the front line fell to their knees, weapons aimed on the demonstrators. The second row stood behind the first row and aimed east.

More and more people steadily appeared on the bridge, chanting and moving west. A massive wave of people emerged on the crest of the bridge, feeding the downpour. Soon, the street, like an endless river, was filled with marchers.

The commander shouted another order and the metallic clang of cocking weapons in unisons echoed. Some soldiers appeared edgy. I couldn't blame them. The targets at the end of their rifle sights were real people: brothers, sisters, cousins, not enemies.

A soldier from the second row walked over to his commander and said something. The officer slapped the soldier's helmet and shouted,

"Get back to your line and get your weapon ready!"

The soldier obeyed, his head hanging. Was it from shame or regret?

The chanting grew louder. The crowd was getting closer and I saw women and children marching as well. All ordinary people. Opposite them, the soldiers appeared ready to engage, their monstrous tanks quietly imposed their presence behind them.

Was I to be a witness to the birth of a revolution? A unique place to be. I didn't know if I was lucky or doomed.

Rumors were, that in order to manage the psyche of the soldiers, the army had mobilized soldiers from faraway regions. Forcing the soldiers from Tehran to shoot and arrest family and friends had increased desertion incidents. I wondered if the soldiers in front of me were locals.

Adrenaline rushed through my body again. All my senses were at high alert. Two weeks ago, I felt the same when two soldiers had aimed their rifles at me.

It was outside of a local hospital where I had noticed the unusual military presence of guards with automatic weapons wearing military fatigues. My curiosity aroused, I stopped and studied the situation. My camera was dangling on my neck and ready. I lifted it to my eye and removed the lens cap. After a few clicks, the soldiers noticed and signaled me to leave. I ignored them and continued taking pictures.

Two agitated soldiers aimed their weapons at me. It was only when I heard the unmistakable cocking sound that a strange sensation overtook me. Cold sweat suddenly covered my body as I took my eyes away from the camera and saw their high-powered rifles pointed at me. I dropped my camera. Luckily the strap caught it, although it swung furiously from side to side as I pedaled away at top speed.

Proactively, just like in the movies, and in an attempt to avoid any incoming bullets, I maneuvered my bike rapidly left and right. I heard a shot and then a high pitch whizz by my ear. My feverish pedaling didn't cease until I arrived home out of breath, my body fully soaked in sweat. The memory of that incident became a repeating nightmare for me, and I relived it again as I watched the standoff.

The demonstrators were getting closer and their chanting, louder.

From where I stood, the wave of the forward-moving crowd seemed endless. It wouldn't have been difficult for the front-row demonstrators to see the military blockade. Would they stop and disperse?

The crowd moved forward steadily. No change in the direction of the demonstrators was apparent, not even a hint of intent. Perhaps it was trust. Trust in the great Divine, the one and only God. Or maybe trust in the will of a nation to earn the long-sought-after freedom they well deserved. Once again, the military might fail to intimidate. But what if they don't? Soldiers are to fight the enemies of the state, not peaceful, unarmed citizens.

A sea of people continually moved west toward the blockade. Eager to see these people closer, I jumped on my bike, crossed the wide and busy north/south street, and moved toward the demonstrators.

The entire width of the four-lane east/west avenue was crammed with a mass of people. I pedaled my bike east, opposite of the crowd's flow. A military helicopter hovered over us. The mix of people formed an impressive tapestry of gender, creed, and race. Women covered with *chadors*, women dressed in western clothes, men, teenagers, children holding hands with their parents--they were all there.

Many smiled and chanted about freedom. A young child sang loudly while riding high on her father's shoulders. The front row demonstrators each carried a single long-stemmed carnation. The flowers were to be placed in the barrels of the soldiers' guns as a peaceful gesture of kindness to the armed forces. In the past few months, the images of soldiers smiling with a flower in their gun barrels were plastered all over the media.

As I rode my bicycle, hopeful and determined, faces of ordinary Iranian people marched in front of me. A colorful mix of cultures and humanity were represented. Distinctive features of many ethnicities were familiar on many faces. South Iranian Arabs; northwest Azaris; east Baloochies; Kurds and Lors from western regions; and Turkmans from the northeast—they all were there.

A few of them, taking a break from chanting, walked along and were discussing politics. From what I heard, I presumed the mixture also included socialists, Islamists, nationalists, Marxists, Maoists, liberals, republicans, monarchists, and many other political affiliations. Many of my non-Muslim friends also regularly attended demonstrations, and this one wasn't an exception. I'm positive that other than Shiites, one could also find Sunnis, Baha'is, Christians, Jews, Zoroastrians, and atheists. All marching together, bound by a single purpose.

It was an epic scene. What had unified such diversities? They all called themselves Iranians. Was it the geography that defined them as a nation? Or perhaps it was the language, collective vocabulary, culture or shared history. I wondered what cemented such a diversified people as a nation. Was it possible that the very struggle a group of people experience together make them a nation, a unified force? As a nation, they all suffered from the attack of the Mongols in 1219; the Arab conquest of Iran in 651; and Alexander the Great's brutal occupation of Persia in 330. And what of the future? Will this mysterious bond continue to keep them together as one nation? Or will this movement, similar to other revolutions, prosecute and devour its children? Could this uprising become a revolution, or would it wither and disappear from the pages of history by the substantial force of modern weaponry and brutality?

Observing those people in their mass diversity, yet purposeful in their strides and solidarity, shook me to my core. Was I making a mistake by leaving the country? As a Muslim, I was taught my presence as an individual was subservient to the will of the *ummah*, the community. As an Iranian, it was understood that my obligations were first to the country, its integrity, its future and its prosperity. The culture that nurtured me, conveyed consistently that the family in a larger sense, the tribe, is a revered bond worth fighting for. The extrinsic influences were piling up in signaling me to stay. But inside, my lonely sense of individualism, the fire that encouraged me to explore, was burning high. An internal battle ground was forming.

How could I not join the battle for freedom, democracy, and liberty?

Heavy in thought, I pedaled back to the area near the soldiers' bunkers. The demonstrators endless mass with all its might was closing distance with the soldiers in a steady forward movement like thick, burning lava. Behind the barricades, the front row soldiers tinkered with their helmets, mumbled to their comrades, and gently tapped their fingers repeatedly around the triggers. Watching the soldiers felt comparable to witnessing the uncloaking of a deep layer of anxiety fog that had settled upon the soldiers' area.

The officer in charge paced back and forth, then suddenly paused and shouted an order.

The demonstrators lead row was only one hundred meters away from the soldiers. Their deep collective chant resonated through the air stronger than ever, vibrating my eardrums. The endless mass of people did not change its pace. Hadn't they seen the soldiers? I wondered if a representative would approach the commander to negotiate for safe passage or a detour.

The steady flow of the forward procession indicated otherwise. No sign of a slowdown. Momentum for conflict was rising. My heart's thumping came faster and louder in my chest.

Some soldiers wiggled, some rubbed their foreheads, their eyes glued to the sea of people approaching. The commander stood erect and focused, as he was unfazed by the magnitude of the task ahead.

The tempo of the crowd stayed the same. Who would blink first?

"It's not your battle. Your journey is your mission," said my inner voice, the voice of reason I had previously ignored. "Experience freedom before it's too late," echoed in my head.

Yes, I had to see the new world. The stakes were simply too high for me to take the risk of staying. My battle was the fight to exit Iran.

The crowd steadily moved closer, step by step. The soldiers stayed put.

"Guns ready!" The officer shouted.

The rapid, united sound of metal intimidated many onlookers, including me. My time there was up. I jumped on my bicycle and peddled as hard as I could away from the conflict zone.

My heart pumped fast and a surge of blood rushed to my head, making me feel dizzy and faint. But I pedaled faster, maneuvered obstacles the best I could.

I knew if they opened fire, thousands of people would run in every direction. Roads would be blocked. Helicopters would hunt anything that moved. There would be massive arrests. I had to get away.

Pedal faster, pedal faster, I yelled at myself.

A few short moments later, hell broke loose.

Bam! Bam! First a few single shots, then machine guns, followed by the sound of chaos, screams, helicopters, sirens, and ambulances. But I only heard the chaos, I didn't see it. My bicycle had carried me away from the slaughter. I thanked God for letting me hear the voice of reason. And that I had lived to see another day.

The moment I reached home, I ditched my bike by the door and ran to my room in the basement. Jumping onto my bed, my chest heaving, my heart pounding, my hands shaking, I could only stare at the ceiling.

I stared for a long time.

Friday, September 8, 1978 (Black Friday), Jaleh Square, Tehran (a similar event in a different location and a few weeks later)

4
LIKE THE WIND I GO

> *In your light I learn how to love. In your beauty, how to make poems. You dance inside my chest where no one sees you, but sometimes I do, and that sight becomes this art.*
>
> — Rumi, Persian Poet (1207 – 1273)

The tone in her voice made the hairs on the back of my neck spike. After all my hard work planning, plotting, and organizing, after days—no, weeks—of dreaming about that very moment, was she mocking me? Maybe I had misunderstood.

I asked for a bit more clarification in my best calm voice.

She was distressed, I suppose. I could detect frustration in her voice. She emphasized again that it shouldn't make so much noise! And immediately blamed me for not doing it right.

How was I to react to such a comment?

Perhaps I should tell the story of that day from the beginning.

~

My body lay flat on the bed, serene. My arms were bent over my chest, allowing my hands to hold each other, covering my heart as if they belonged to lovers. My eyes were closed and my breathing restful.

Suddenly my eyes opened wide and my chest thumped in panic. My left arm stretched in search of the alarm clock. Relief flooded over me when I saw the time. It wasn't five a.m. yet. I had awakened fifteen minutes early that Friday morning. It never failed.

My internal clock always beat the alarm on important occasions. That summer's day was an important one for me. If everything were to go according to the plan, I believed I would remember it for the rest of my life.

The fresh cool air of the pre-dawn morning and the significance of the day yanked me to my feet. The sky was still dark. I took a deep breath and began my daily exercise routine: push-ups, sit-ups and some calisthenics. Energized with renewed vigor, I went upstairs to the kitchen.

The scene in the kitchen surprised me in a pleasant way. A pot of freshly brewed hot black tea awaited me on top of our *samovar*. A soft-boiled egg, bread, feta cheese, butter and jam for breakfast, and two egg sandwiches for my lunch, had been placed on the table for me.

My mother would be the only one behind this kind of a spread. She must have gotten up before me and prepared all that. What an angel.

In haste, I crammed down a few bites of breakfast, grabbed my lunch, filled my canteen with water, picked up my backpack and headed out the door, taking care not to slam it as I so often did when leaving in a rush.

The morning sun had not yet lit the streets. Driving on roads with no traffic was a treat rarely experienced on a typical day in Tehran. In Iran, Friday is the last day of the week and is considered a sabbath; a day of rest and prayers. Schools, government, and most businesses are closed. I was on my way to pick up Neilu, my sweetheart, from her house on the west edge of Tehran, about half-an-hour's drive from where I lived.

The sky had turned lighter as I arrived at her neighborhood; dawn approached. There were no activities on her quiet street at that time of the day, and plenty of spaces in front of her house to park the car.

The front door of her house was ajar. Cautiously, I pushed the door open and peaked inside.

Neilu's younger sister, Pooneh, was frantically packing her backpack. Yes, Neilu had an entourage. Her younger sister and brother were to be our chaperones for the day. Square-faced Pooneh was a fourteen-year-old brat. She immensely enjoyed being the spy of Neilu's family. Her big eyes, amplified by a pair of thick glasses, followed every move we made, and she regularly eavesdropped on us. I'm sure she reported every detail of our activities to her mother when we weren't around.

Pooneh noticed me peeking in. She stopped for a second and gazed up at me. I waved hello to her with a friendly smile. No words or reaction came from her; she just continued her packing.

I entered the living room and stayed near the door. From the corner of my eye, I detected a person walking into the living room. I turned my head and my eyes were rewarded with Neilu's graceful entrance. A big smile covered her face the moment she noticed me.

My heart pounded faster, and my eyes warmed with welcome.

As she approached me, she signaled me to remain quiet by putting her index finger on her nose. Her tight jeans outlined her slim body, and a white short-sleeve cotton blouse pointed out that she expected a nice summer day. Her thick, jet black hair had been pulled under control by a headband.

Her lips gently approached my left ear and with a whisper she commended me for being on time and asked me to stay quiet as her aunt and mother were asleep. She smelled like jasmine flowers. A strong temptation teased me to pull her slim waist toward me and plant a kiss on her inviting lips. But, I couldn't. We were not allowed to touch each other, especially not in front of her siblings. That was just one aggravating part of our cultural code. I was in love with her.

Our relationship was moving forward, despite my preparation for leaving Iran to study abroad.

She gently pulled away, looked into my eyes and smiled. Her playful, deep black eyes melted me, and I found myself mesmerized by her confident and self-controlled presence.

Khashayar, her skinny, twelve-year-old brother, walked in half asleep. He rubbed his dark, long face with his hands and yawned. When Neilu found out that he wasn't packed yet, she turned him around and with a gentle slap to his rear and sent him back to his room to finish the job.

A few minutes later, they all lined up to get in the car. As I opened the front passenger door for Neilu, I felt I was being watched. It was Pooneh, the spy. She asked sarcastically if I would open the door for her as well.

"Yes, of course," I answered, hoping that she would become more sympathetic toward me and relax her spying. Once everyone got on board, I took command of the vehicle and drove away.

The air was chilly and clear, a perfect start for a great outdoor adventure. The rising sun was casting its magnificent rays across the slowly revealing blue sky. Impressed by its glory, I pointed to the rising sun. Neilu ignored my excitement and asked if we were going straight to the mountains as it was planned.

We had a quick detour to make to meet up with my friend Davud and his girlfriend, who were waiting for us in a park nearby.

Davud and I met in the second year of college. We had nothing in common. Many people viewed our personalities more opposite than similar. However, for some odd reason, our friendship grew stronger through the college years. In our senior year, we decided to travel to the U.S. together for our master's degree. We became comrades in the quest to seek and experience personal freedom outside of Iran. But, in the back of my mind, I harbored some reservations about him following through.

After explaining about the quick detour, I found myself describing the beauty of the splendid sunrise again. My voice and enthusiasm dissipated in the silence that followed. For a moment, I felt lonely in my admiration of nature's beauty. How could she ignore such a glorious display? Was she nervous? I'd never seen her nervous before, so I had no point of reference for that behavior. She looked calm and in control as usual. Perhaps she couldn't see. Not all of us are blessed with the ability to see little flowers on the side of the road or even a display as large as the entire sky. Perhaps, that was a sign that I should have not ignored.

Davud and his girlfriend, Fariba, were waiting in his car in a parking lot of a small park by his apartment. I pulled the car next to his, rolled down my window, and knocked on his fogged over passenger-side window.

The window rolled down and Fariba's face appeared. She glanced in my car, scanned the passengers, and then turned to me with a knowing smile. "Yeasssss!" she exclaimed.

Nervously, I bit my lower lip and widened my eyes at Fariba, who was fussing with her wavy red hair. She was teasing me and letting me know she was aware of my plot. Neilu was very sharp, and I didn't want anything to jeopardize the plan. She was not to discover my surprise prematurely.

People often mistook Fariba's soft spoken and quiet personality as shy or even submissive. Quite the opposite was the case. Her well balanced self-esteem and will for independence, spiced with a touch of stubbornness, made her quite a challenge for Davud. She had been our classmate in college. That morning, she looked fit and healthy in her light blue jeans and yellow cotton blouse, which set off her hazel eyes and even tan.

My wink acknowledged her smile. Davud explained in a groggy voice that we would meet with our friends Hamid and Mahmood at the rendezvous point by the foothills of the Alborz Mountain, about forty-five-minutes drive to the north.

Davud's blond hair was puffed up, fuzzy and thin. His big square glasses with black frames magnified his already large, round hazel eyes. He was on the border of being chubby. Come to think of it, he was a funny-looking guy. He resembled a puffer fish.

We started our trek. I followed Davud's car headed north toward the mountains on the freeway. As the dawn broke, the view of the majestic Alborz Mountain range north of Tehran became more prominent. Villages abounded with stunning sycamore, elm and mulberry trees. Streams and rustic rural scenery hugged the foothills of the mountain range. The cooler air and serene surroundings provided a welcome refuge from the hot and smoggy Tehran. People who felt trapped in Tehran's hectic metropolitan life always found our final destination, *Kolakchal* a great weekend retreat. *Kolakchal* is at about

2,400 meters elevation, on the way to the actual *Kolakchal* summit (about 3,300 meters elevation), where there were a few structures including a large restaurant, a shelter, and a sizeable playground.

My hope was that the beautiful surroundings of our trip to *Kolakchal* would help me to execute my well-rehearsed arrangement.

As we traveled north toward the mountains, the sun's golden rays gave us the good news of a clear and gorgeous summer day. I turned my head and glanced at Neilu. She sat like a queen, with an upright posture, graceful and content. Her posture wasn't alarming, she usually walked and sat very straight. She noticed my glance, turned her head charmingly toward me and returned my smile.

The car's manual stick shift on my right gave me the excuse to reach for her left hand. With the motion of moving the gear from third to fourth, my right hand subtlety departed from the gear handle and gently landed on her left hand, which was resting at her side.

Her skin felt soft and warm, and it comforted me. I sensed connection with her body and soul.

Pooneh cleared her throat forcefully as a signal that she had spotted us holding hands. I detected a small jolt on Neilu's hand but, unwilling to grant that rascal an immediate satisfaction, I tightened my grip on Neilu's hand and held on for a bit longer.

It was frustrating. Our culture as a whole was in a social quagmire. We Iranians were caught between imposed Islamic rules by Arab conquerors (around 650 AD), millennia of traditions and western values budding from a relatively newfound paradigm of individual self-respect and actualization. Neilu's family was much less traditional and more Westernized than my family, yet we had to have chaperons watching every move we made on our dates.

A few moments later, I used a gear change as an excuse to gently let her hand go. A glance in the rearview mirror helped me to see how alertly Pooneh was watching us. A sneer appeared on my face. It had begun.

Ever on high alert, Pooneh pointed our attention to the road where a large military caravan was traveling south. Many trucks carrying soldiers, tanks, and other armored vehicles passed us. She asked if we were at war.

My explanation was that we were not at war with any foreign powers per se, but, we were at war with ourselves. That didn't sit well with Neilu. She immediately corrected me and hypothesized that either the soldiers were going for a military exercise somewhere or were transported to a location to establish order, keeping people safe.

I shook my head in disagreement, tightened my jaws, and took a deep breath. It wasn't a good time for an argument or heated political discussion. My plan for that day called for a calm and positive start. I remained silent.

Forty minutes later, we arrived at Shemiran, the city on the foothills of the Alborz Mountains immediate north of Tehran. Small business owners were hosing down the sidewalks in front of their stores, getting ready for the Friday rush of visitors escaping from Tehran's hot weather. The city bustled with hikers. Canopies of luscious sycamore and maple trees covered the streets. Many of the trails there wound along the streams that fed melted snow water to thousands of *jubes*, which spread out like veins in the lowlands of the south.

Davud, who was ahead of us, entered a parking lot. I followed him in and we both parked our cars and everyone got out. Davud explained the path to the rendezvous point with our friends and walked off, leading our little group with his hand firmly locked with Fariba's.

My longing to do the same with Neilu was foiled by the necessity to distract Pooneh and Khashayar. I waited till the two, eager and young, naturally followed Davud. Once that happened, my right hand found Neilu's left hand and gently held it as we started our stroll.

I cherished every second of Neilu's presence near me. We celebrated our closeness with silence and a gentle swing of our held hands. That simple act of affection carried a magical sensation beyond words for me. For a moment, I remembered what Farhad had said about the silent communication among close friends. Without a doubt, I was feeling it just then with her.

It didn't take long for Pooneh to realize that we were walking behind her. She did a double take when she turned back and found us hand-in-hand, slowly strolling behind everyone else.

She stopped and asked us to move faster, shooting us her disgusted gaze. Neilu reacted to Pooneh's comment and tried to pull her hand away from mine, but I tightened my grip on Neilu's hand again and claimed that the mountain wasn't going anywhere, and we were not in a rush.

Neilu's reaction wasn't because she was embarrassed. She reacted based on our old cultural barriers of suppressing natural desires to display any romantic affection. This was yet another element of our cultural oppression, which undoubtedly had contributed to the numerous cases of desperation and abuse. Heavy chains of traditional, cultural, and religious demands on individual behaviors or even thoughts, resulting from superstitions, ignorance, or plain vicious manipulation have lowered the backs of Iranian people into blind submission.

My journey out of the country was, in part, to challenge these chains to the breaking point in a society that would allow me to do as I wished. Could I survive without them? Would I lose my authenticity in the process? How important it is to hold on to traditions if their very nature is to suppress exploring new boundaries. Doesn't progress stem from exploration?

The crisp fresh air, babbling brooks, and the everlasting canopies created by the tall sycamores, elms and mulberries felt good to me. Sparrows flitting from tree to tree delighted us with their chirps while fragrances of jasmine and wild roses perfumed the air.

I caressed Neilu's soft hand with my thumb in a slow and deliberate motion as we gently swung our arms back and forth. I wouldn't have minded if time stopped there forever.

This tender start, I hoped, would be like foreplay for the promise of what the day had in store for me--for us.

We passed a bridge to cross the stream, we met up with everyone at the rendezvous place by the traffic circle. After the initial introductions, all nine of us started our climb.

Mahmood, our college mate, was the tallest person in our group. His always immaculately cared for black hair and a well-groomed beard glistened in the morning sunlight. Mahmood brought his sister, Maryam, along. She was in her early twenties, tall with long, light brown hair. Her good sense of humor made her a delight to have around. The ninth person, Hamid, also went to same college as Davud and I. In contrast with Mahmood, Hamid was the shortest of the adults. A talkative fellow with fuzzy, short brown hair and a high-pitched voice, he reminded me of a court jester. He was a goodnatured fellow, much wiser than he looked.

Mahmood, Maryam, and Hamid were meeting Neilu for the first time. The twinkle in the two boys' eyes gave me the nonverbal sign of their approval. A pat on the back accompanied by a wink from Hamid and then Mahmood gave me assurance of their knowledge of the plan and the comfort of their willingness to help.

We all decided on a less-travelled trail that followed a long, curving creek for a few miles before it made its sharp climb to *Kolakchal* station, our destination. This secluded trail with numerous boulders proved to be the perfect one for my plan. I was nervous, but encouraged by the prospects of the help of my good friends.

The sheer beauty of the scenery mesmerized everyone. The two teenagers in our group, just as two freed birds, jumped up and down the rocks and boulders.

Mahmood asked me if Davud and I were still pursuing study abroad. I went over the long and sometimes complicated process. After lengthy review of our English-translated college transcripts, we had received the Higher Education Ministry's approval stamp. After the approval, we took the lengthy TOEFL English proficiency test and were both waiting for the results.

Hamid's high pitch voice came from the other side. "What if you don't get accepted in any college? What'll happen then?"

My reaction to Hamid's question was a nervous chuckle and clarification that besides a major devastation, we would be drafted into the military. Which was not what either of us wanted.

Hamid didn't like my answer and took an offense to it as both he and Mahmood had completed their two years of compulsory military services before starting college. He claimed it wasn't a big deal.

Maryam shook her head in disagreement and jumped into the conversation, defending my position. She brought up a point that it was the worst time to serve in the military. Soldiers who were assigned to patrolling cities were shooting innocent people. Military bases were in turmoil and discontent. Insubordination and desertion were at their highest level. She compared getting drafted to receiving a death warrant.

Mahmood accused his sister for being over dramatic.

Maryam's opinion was correct in my mind and worth defending. I pointed to the treachery of the time at hand, especially for the security forces. They were more confused than the civilians. The last thing I wanted was to join a military force in disarray.

Suddenly, Maryam stopped, turned back, faced her brother and demanded him to tell us what happened a week ago to their cousin. He initially resisted and came up with some excuses about how it does not relate to our conversation until she threatened him with her version of the incident.

We were all curious by then and everyone asked repeatedly for Mahmood to share the story.

"All right!" he disgruntledly agreed.

His cousin was serving his two-year mandatory military service in an army base north of Tehran. A week prior, he ran away from the base. He wanted to desert. But his family convinced him to go back and continue his term to its completion.

Hamid's high-pitched voice interrupted Mahmood and questioned the silly notion of the cousin, claiming that everyone knows that deserters would be court marshaled.

Apparently, that day, two soldiers from his cousin's unit refused to gear up for city patrol, Mahmood continued. Their officer was very forceful, and the soldiers snapped and shot the officer dead. The incident created a chain of shootouts, and five died. His cousin was on the scene and became so frightened that he ran away from the base and hid in his house.

Fariba leaned over to look Mahmood in the eye. "Oh God, is he okay?"

"He is terrified!" Maryam interjected.

Fariba shook her head and corrected herself, "No, I meant physically, is he injured? You know Davud's father is a doctor."

Mahmood waved her off and claimed that his cousin is okay. His family made him sneak back into the base the next day. Apparently, through the confusion, nobody noticed he was missing.

At that point, I saw an exchange of looks between Mahmood and his sister. He immediately furrowed his eyebrows and looked down on the ground. She stared at him for a few moments longer.

It seemed to me that he might not have told us everything. But at that point, Davud opened a new dialogue about the frequency of these episodes throughout the whole country and how they were becoming a norm instead of the exception.

The opportunity was too good for me not to take it. I brought up the international politics, our favorite intellectual treat, into the discussion. One positive effect of the recent unrest was the courage people felt to carry on open conversation about politics. Past whispers about the government activities had now become the preferred topics of conversation in public places among people.

My worries were in regard to the internal infighting among the security forces. If the problems became epidemic, I warned, our neighboring countries, with their lust over access to our oil reservoirs and other vast natural resources, wouldn't miss a chance to invade. Like a mini commercial, I concluded this was a very bad time to serve in the military.

"Thank you, Mr. Carter," Mahmood exclaimed.

Davud widened his already large eyes. "What's all this got to do with President Carter?"

Mahmood went on explaining that, it was the president of United States' pressing the Shah on human rights issues that caused the tremendous chaos in Iran.

"I'm with President Carter. Good for him." I remember responding. "Someone needs to show some guts and put pressure on our government. Iranians have been under dictatorships for thousands of years. It is time for us to get some basic human rights."

Davud looked at me and gestured his head very slightly, signaling me to stand near him. As I positioned myself near him, he said out loud to Mahmood, "My friend, President Carter's administration is brand new. Their influence in our internal affairs is not that powerful and immediate. This soup has been cooking for a while."

He compared our country's mayhem to a pot of soup. What an odd sense of humor!

Hamid jumped into this discussion and claimed that it was all the work of the Brits. His opinion, in line with the older generation of Iranians, held the British government responsible for all political unrest in the Middle East. When something was not benefiting them directly, the sneaky Brits would change it. He thought the British government was revengeful because they lost Iranian oil revenue a couple of decades ago.

"Their commission from our oil exports went to nothing the day Shah cut off their hands from our oil." Hamid summarized.

Mahmood defended his position of American influence and claimed that Carter and Sullivan's flip-flop policies would eventually tear Iran apart. He warned of internal and external opportunists that would soon devastate the country.

Davud's large eyes stared at me and he gestured with his head again, a bit more pronounced this time, signaling me to go near him.

Pooneh, tired of chasing her brother, slowed down and walked with our group. She heard the last part of our discussion and asked with her brows arcing high, "Who is Sullivan and why are he and his friends going to tear our country apart? What is happening to our country? Are we going to die?"

Following Davud's gestures, I inched myself near him such that he could whisper in my ear, "Did you see that spot?" I nodded my head in agreement. He continued whispering, "Do you think what I think?"

"It's not safe here. Let's keep going. I'll give you a signal when we're at the right spot," I whispered back.

He gave a quick nod and walked away.

Neilu's concerned voice explained, "Mr. Sullivan is the new American ambassador to Iran and no, our country is not at the whim of foreign powers, Pooneh. We are strong and we will pull through."

Then Neilu turned toward my friends and me and warned us that the conversation was getting too deep and was scaring the children.

She suggested that we change the subject.

At that point, Hamid, who was walking ahead of the group, turned around, faced me and shouted, "Let's hear some poetry!" "Poetry?" Neilu asked, her eyes bulging in surprise.

I apologized for failing to tell her that I was known as a poet among my friends.

Neilu shook her head with an amused smile.

"Yes, an off-the-cuff poet. He can create poetry anytime, anywhere," Hamid announced.

With a sudden enthusiasm, I jumped on top of a small boulder, stretched my arms out wide, and with a shout, invited my friends to submit to the beauty of the surrounding and become poets for a while.

Davud turned his head toward Neilu. "Fake poems, not real ones."

"Improvised, my dear Davud, not fake. I can improvise poems on the spot. However, before you hear my impromptus, I challenge the brave ones to a game of poetry."

Khashayar's ears perked up and he asked me to describe the game.

The poetry game was among the more delightful old Persian traditions. One person starts with a verse of a well-known poem, the next person will continue with a new verse that begins with the last alphabet character of the previous verse. The first person unable to recite a new verse is taken out and the game continues. The last person standing would be declared the winner.

Khashayar complaining that it was too hard, excused himself from the game, and walked away. Pooneh also complained about the game being too hard for her and that she doesn't care about stupid poetry anyway.

Her last comment didn't sit well with Mahmood who softly scolded Pooneh, "You don't have to play, but you can't call Persian poetry stupid."

He went on describing how Persian poetry had brought enlightenment, encouragement, and entertainment into every aspect of people's lives for over two millennia. Being oppressed by dictator kings during the nation's long history, intellectuals used poetry and animal personification to criticize the power-thirsty and often ruthless government officials.

Impatient Hamid had enough of talks, so in his rusty, high-pitched voice, he started reciting the first verse from *Omar Khayyam* and the poetry game began.

"With them the seed of Wisdom did I sow / And with mine own hand wrought to make it grow; / And this was all the Harvest that I reap'd-/ I came like Water, and like Wind I go."

Then Mahmood used the last letter of Hamid's poem and recited a poem that started with that letter. He finished his poem with the letter "a," which in Farsi it pronounced more like "ye." The time was perfect for my mood-setting poem from Rumi, I jumped in and seized the moment:

A moment of happiness,/ you and I sitting on the verandah, / apparently two, but one in soul, you and I. / We feel the flowing water of life here, / you and I, with the garden's beauty / and the birds singing. The stars will be watching us, / and we will show them / what it is to be a thin crescent moon. / You and I unselfed, will be together, / indifferent to idle speculation, you and I. / The parrots of heaven will be cracking sugar / as we laugh together, you and I. / In one form upon this earth, / and in another form in a timeless sweet land.

The game went on for a while as we moved forward on the trail.

Davud was the first person to disqualify in the first round of the game, then Mahmood's sister. There were three people left in the game when I ran out of memorized poetry. Slickly, I recited some of my own on-the-spot creations. The first one passed undetected.

On the next round, after the second of my on-the-spot creations, Neilu turned toward me and said, "What? I don't..." I quickly placed my index finger on my nose and she went silent.

Neilu's protest nearly exposed my scheme. Her curious look was replaced by a smile. Good, she was amused. After a few more rounds, Mahmood noticed my little secret and raised an objection. Needless to say, they disqualified me. A few moments later Hamid declared victory.

After the game, Mahmood, who was a bit taller than me, put his arm on my shoulder, pulled me aside and asked if I needed letters of recommendation for the U.S. colleges. He was a manager at an export/import company at the time.

He was surprised to hear that both Davud and I had already

received and translated into English letters of recommendations from our law and economics professors and one from our chancellor.

"The chancellor?" he asked.

Hamid was listening to our conversation and interjected his warning that our chancellor would be arrested if the unrest turned to a full revolution and the subsequent regime changed.

Alerted, Davud asked why she would be arrested.

We all knew our chancellor had close ties to the royal family. Hamid reminded us that a typical side effect of political revolution is mass execution of people close to the toppled dictatorial regime.

Neilu didn't appreciate the political history lesson from Hamid and particularly wasn't pleased that Hamid described Iranian monarchy as a dictatorship. She, being a pragmatic, corrected him.

Hamid took a double take. "Come on, you must be kidding me! We don't have a monarchy; it's a farce, a pretend, a fake monarchy. This nation has been under dictatorship for thousands of years."

Mahmood's sister, in an attempt to preventing a heated political argument, jumped in and explained that history had taught us that after a revolution the oppressed layer's revenge is brutal. Her comment ended with a cautionary note that we should be prepared, as often, revolutions turn into new periods of dictatorship of the oppressed.

"So, our chancellor may get executed," Hamid clarified.

Preventing further stress and argument, I closed the discussion with rooting for the chancellor's keen awareness of the situation and hoped that she would get out of the country before it becomes too late for her.

We arrived at a perfect spot. The trees and boulders formed an ideal set up for phase two of the plan. I gave a wink and a nod to Davud. He acknowledged the signal.

Davud rubbed his stomach and in his loudest voice announced it was ten-thirty and he was tired and hungry. He invited everyone to rest, eat, and play a few card games.

Hamid and Mahmood looked at him in disbelief. Usually, we took a short, five-minute break right before the steep climb, about another thirty minutes of hiking. But not where we had stopped and certainly not for a long stay. Food and games were saved for the actual rest station *Kolakchal*.

My friends' stares quickly changed to a smile the moment they saw Davud's wink.

Fariba pulled out a sheet from her backpack and spread it on the ground. Everyone gathered around and sat on the sheet to play cards. Pooneh complained as she grabbed her sandwich. She didn't want to play and used her brother's lack of understanding card games as an excuse.

Hamid gave me a worried look. Mahmood winked at me and put his arms on Khashayar's and Pooneh's shoulders and said that he would be more than happy to be their teacher.

Neilu was about to sit and play cards when I pulled her close to me and whispered, "Let's climb those boulders to the right and check the view."

She smiled and nodded. A quick scan of the group showed everyone engaged with the card game, and that to me was the green light. Hamid had everyone gathered around him intensely listening as he explained the rules.

My eyes searched for the two spies, Khashayar and Pooneh. I found them heavily engaged with the group with their backs to a big boulder.

Neilu and I gingerly stepped away. We climbed up a few boulders and stopped when we found a private location on top of a large one. From there, we could see the green tops of many trees, but it was the presence of tall aspens lining the trail and the rushing sound of water in a distance that added to the serenity of the surroundings.

Finally, a few moments of privacy. We sat close to each other and held hands. She sat tall and erect, as usual, on the boulder. She closed her eyes and let her face and hair be caressed by the sun and the wind. Her calm demeanor made her charisma even more spectacular. I intended to cherish every second of those precious private moments.

The time, the location, and the set up created just the right atmosphere for the big moment. The one that I had fantasized and replayed over and over in my mind, the moment that every cell of my body had longed for, the next step.

After what seemed like hours, but was only minutes, she slowly opened her eyes. Turning her face toward me, she found me studying her face, fascinated by her beauty. In that very moment, she became so unbearably attractive to me, far more interesting than the nature surrounding us.

Our faces slowly neared each other. Those dream-like, unhurried moments felt eternal. Time froze and the outside world became irrelevant, as if we sat somewhere in the kingdom of clouds.

My heart pounded so fast I could feel the rapid drumbeat of my pulse behind my ears. I didn't know what to expect. My virgin lips had never kissed a girl before.

Neilu closed her eyes and moved closer to me. My senses were on the highest alert, my mind in a peculiar state, and my desire longed for those moments to last forever. Afraid to spoil the moment, I held my breath. And then . . . we kissed. Soft, heavenly soft.

Never had my lips experienced that kind of touch. Nerves from all over my body happily transferred their sensory power to my mouth so I could celebrate every fraction of the contact. My first kiss. Our first kiss.

In a culture that forbids romantic contact between men and women outside of marriage, this was an important event for us. A big step toward defying repression. A rare moment of closeness that was void of guilt and ill intentions. Just simply, two human souls connecting in a way they had never before.

Gradually my barely open eyes lay sight on her tranquil face. Her eyelids were relaxed as if nothing about the outside world mattered anymore. All that mattered was there, within a few inches.

Our faces slowly separated. Her eyes were still closed, but a slight tightness in her eyebrows appeared. She opened her eyes with a puzzled look. "It shouldn't make this much noise."

The tone in her voice made the hairs on the back of my neck spike. After all my hard work planning, plotting and organizing. After days —no, weeks—of dreaming about that very moment. Was she mocking me? Maybe I misunderstood. Utterly confused, I asked for clarification, doing my best to sound calm.

Neilu explained, "Our kiss, Vahid. It shouldn't make this much noise! You're not doing it right."

How was I to react to such a comment?

It felt like a free fall from where I was sitting in the clouds all the way down to the ground. I had to swallow my injured pride. Acting curious, I asked if her determined criticism was coming from experience. Had she kissed anyone else before?

"No, but in the movies, it doesn't make any noise," she replied. A small knot appeared where her eyebrows would have met if they weren't plucked. Her tone first felt like she was accusing me of ruining the moment, and it hurt. But then, a split second later, I reasoned that perhaps her tone was more curious than accusatory. So I went with that idea and replied, "The noise is natural, I think." Then a flash of a brilliant idea hit me.

"Could we try again? Perhaps we could get rid of the noise by practicing it more."

She agreed, and we kissed again. After a few more tries, she insisted, "There is still something wrong. It shouldn't make so much noise."

I was stunned. Never in the thousands of rehearsals in my mind had I come across these objections. What am I supposed to do now? I didn't know, so I just stared at her face studying every line and nuance. Perhaps they could tell me what to do.

A sudden movement about ten meters behind her distracted me. Not wanting to alert her, I moved my head slowly into a better position to survey the area.

To keep her occupied, I philosophized, "Well, we know it doesn't make a noise at the start. The only noise is when our lips part. I am sure this is a natural sound."

I prepared myself for possible intruders. She looked down and then turned her head toward the area where I sensed movement. She must have heard some noise also. To avert her attention, I reached for her chin and turned it toward my face. I asked for one more try and this time, we both would try to depart very slowly.

She agreed and with a determined voice ordered me to start. Her directive sounded more like a command, which seemed strange to me —not as I had imagined. And not very romantic.

I was distracted by my sixth sense, warning me about a possible stalker.

She closed her eyes and gently brought her lips close to mine. It had become somewhat mechanical and too complicated now. I had to make sure the landing and most importantly, the parting of our lips happened perfectly without any sound, otherwise, she might never kiss me again. At the same time, I had to solve the mystery of the suspicious movement.

My eyes stayed open. As our lips touched, my body began to relax and enjoy the sensation. Suddenly, I noticed movement behind the bushes. My ears perked up, my eyes zeroed in the area while kissing. And, yes, I saw it. It was the abhorrent little spy, Pooneh, hiding there and spying on us.

I jerked my head in reaction, forcing me to detach my lips quickly.

Unfortunately, the dreaded noise happened again, loud and clear.

"Didn't you hear that? This time was even louder! I can't stand that noise!" Neilu screamed.

I inched back from her, put my elbows on my knees and held my face with my hands in a thinking posture. Not able to find a solution, I suggested we both do some research about it and recommended returning to the others.

Giving Pooneh the satisfaction of catching us in the act was not an option. Her report to her mother could cause embarrassment and more restriction to our dating. Dating in public was already challenged by law and cultural codes. We didn't need additional parental disciplines.

From the corner of my eye, I saw Pooneh moving from boulder to boulder. The little spy used evasion techniques to get closer to us. Surely she had planned to surprise us.

Neilu, intensely involved with the mystery of the noise, did not notice my change in posture, nor did she seem to care.

Soon the little weasel called out to her sister. Pretending that she had not seen us, I'm sure.

Neilu turned away from me and called out. The two sisters hugged each other. I smiled with the satisfaction of depriving Pooneh of catching us kissing.

Pooneh stayed close to her sister for the rest of the day, therefore eliminating any chance for Neilu and I to continue our courtship. We climbed for another hour up to the *Kolakchal*, had our lunch there, played more card games, and decided to return as the sun began its slow descent.

On our way back, we ran, jumped and skipped down to the base of the mountain. From there, we took the same trail back to the parking lot. Somewhere in the middle of the trail, I felt an arm on my shoulder. It was Mahmood. He asked if I was having a good time.

My response was a resounding affirmation, of course. After thanking him for coming along, I asked if he enjoyed the day as well.

He winked at me and said that he did, but not as much as me. We laughed. Then he asked if I was firm about going abroad.

"Like wind I go." I quoted *Omar Khayyam's* poem with a smile. However, his question seemed odd to me. After acknowledging my intentions, I asked the reason for his concern. He paused for a few moments, then instead of answering me, he asked if I was serious about Neilu. Slightly offended with his line of questioning, I confirmed my intention with Neilu with confidence.

He immediately responded, "Then you are creating a dilemma for yourself, my friend."

My confused face encouraged him to continue. "You may have to choose between the two."

He went on and gave me a sermon on the importance of intention in a relationship. His concerns were my earlier comment about leaving the country in a few months. "What about Neilu?" he asked. "You know, in this country women are not as free as the men. Is she going with you abroad? Are your feelings serious about her, or is this a just little summer fling?"

I didn't know how to reply, so I didn't. It wasn't a summer fling for sure, but I wasn't sure if I had any answers to his other questions, which were good questions. Where was my priority? I loved her, but what did that mean for my future? Was I prepared to forego my dream of studying abroad in order to have a relationship with her?

We walked together in quiet for a few moments, and then he continued. "I don't mean to put a damper on your exciting day. Apparently, whatever you two kids did back there today lightened both of your spirits."

In his view, that day, Neilu and I entered into a more serious relationship. He advised me to make up my mind about marrying her sooner than later. As the country was heading toward chaos, no one could tell what the future had for us. He warned me, "You need to think seriously about the future of this romance. Don't lead her toward an unnecessary disappointment and heartache."

I nodded. He left me in my thoughts. I felt as if I had crashed into a wall. I loved Neilu, and the last thing in the world I wanted was to hurt her or create hardship for her.

We were all speed-walking the downhill trail. When Pooneh ran ahead of us to chase her brother, Neilu came close to me, held my arm tight and asked, "You know that I have another year and a half until I graduate from college, right?"

I felt her heavenly warmth melt my heart. Hugs and close bodily contact were not common in my family. The sensation of another human embracing me, even for a few moments, was a welcome gift. I gently gave a few short nods. After a split second of thought, I turned to Neilu to explain how much I cared for her and that my intentions for her were real and honorable. I wanted to tell her, no matter what happened, we would find a solution to stay together; and that she was the most important person in my life at that time. But Pooneh had already run back to her sister and locked arms with her.

At that moment, all I could say was, "Yes, I know."

Alborz Mountain range north of Tehran.

5

TOOT

> *The heart is a Ten thousand-stringed instrument That can only be tuned with Love.*
>
> — Hafez, Persian Poet (1325-1389)

"The air whooshed by my ears as I sprinted across the flat rooftops made of dried mud and straw. My eyes scanned rapidly for the dangers ahead. Another rooftop approached fast. This one was higher, much higher. I jumped as high and as far as I possibly could."

My uncle Raahmat had come to visit his mother, my grandmother, who lived with us. He had moved to Orange County, a desirable area south of Los Angeles in the United States, four years ago, and returned to Iran every other year for a few weeks. Mostly to collect his retirement payments and his rent. I loved his storytelling, because he made the events come alive with his expressive gestures and colorful descriptions. On this day he told the story, which I hadn't heard before, of his adventure collecting fruit from the mulberry tree, *toot* in Farsi.

My mother had two brothers. Raahmat was the younger one. We called him *daijune koochikeh*, dear younger uncle.

He was telling me about the world before I was born. The irony was, he had come from a world that soon would become my future, I hoped. With his beady eyes wide open, and his arms mimicking his jumps across the rooftops, Uncle Raahmat continued:

"Done, I said out loud when I landed on the taller roof top and continued my run without a pause. I turned back a few times to see if my two younger sisters were in pursuit. Your older uncle continued running ahead of me without looking back.

"Running on roof tops was a risky business. The prize was not too far away though, just a few more rooftops and then the mighty jump. The last roof top was a meter lower and two meters farther. It was a much more difficult jump. I was worried about the return jump, as it was even a bigger challenge for my ten-year-old body.

"And then suddenly, there it was. The magnificent white mulberry *toot* tree, in all its glory, became visible. Oh, I could already taste those delicious *toots*."

I had to interrupt his story, as he forgot to tell me where the tree was. He didn't mind, nodded his head and continued the story.

"The tall *toot* tree had emerged at the other end of the last roof, right after the great jump. Growing tall and wide from the yard below, its large canopy created a glorious presence. At that point, I was already imagining climbing up and picking those deliciously ripe white mulberries.

"'Remember! Don't jump,' I shouted to my sisters when I was about three meters away from the jump. 'Just sit on the edge and we will bring you *toot*.'

"Then your aunt, who was holding your six-year-old mother's hand, shouted back, 'Don't worry, brother. Naji and I'll sit and wait for you. Just bring us a lot of *toot*.'

"'I see it!' Uncle Asdollah shouted. 'I am going for it! Ahhhhhh,' he screamed while in the air on the mighty jump.

"I wasn't far from my brother when I saw the mighty jump. I stopped at the edge and examined the distance. I went back four steps and checked to see if my sisters were all right. Then, I mustered all my power and ran as fast as I could, jumped right on the edge and stretched my body as far as I could. Missing the landing zone was not an option, as the drop to the ground would be fatal."

Just then my mother walked into the room carrying a tray of cold summer drinks in tall glasses. We were sitting in my grandmother's room, a small, sparse space containing only a double bed in the center, two chairs, and a small coffee table. The room had two doors, leading from the inside hallway and the other opened up to a balcony leading to the back yard. One entire wall of the room was made of glass and metal frames, which allowed ample daylight and a handsome view of our small garden in the backyard. My grandmother rested on the bed with her head turned toward my uncle, listening to his story. She had been basically bedbound for over a year.

I was sitting on the edge of the bed. My mother offered each of us a glass of the much-desired drink, halting uncle's story. The drink was called *sekahnjebean*. My favorite part of it was the grated cucumber and a few fresh mint leaves as a garnish floating on top of white vinegar syrup diluted with sugar, water, and ice. What made my mother's drink so different than others was the few drops of lemon juice she would add to it.

Mother sat down with us and explained how important the white mulberry tree had been in our Iranian hearts. And how my grandmother, like many other Iranians, had donated funds on several occasions for white mulberry trees to be planted in Tehran's southern ghettos. The idea was that the tree's magnificent canopy would provide much-appreciated shade in the summer heat. And, its delicious fruit could be consumed as a sweet feast. Also, its leaves, the food source for silk worms, could help the people make silk.

Each individual benefit of mulberry trees was not unknown to me, but I never considered its combined good to the local people as a socioeconomic benefit. Its fruit fed hungry stomachs, its canopy relieved stress from the hot summer sun, and its leaves helped people nearby to create silk from which they could either make clothing or sell the silk. The brilliance of it was how a small and affordable act by a middle-class grandmother with limited resources could help strangers for decades.

Anxious to hear the rest of the story, I asked my uncle what happened next. Did he break his legs?

My uncle shook his head. "No, I stumbled on the other side and the velocity of landing threw my legs out of control, but I managed to keep my balance. Without any hesitation, I propelled myself toward the tree and jumped on the first branch I could reach. Immediately, I grabbed a fistful of the mulberries and rushed them into my mouth.

Mmmm, they were delicious and sweet.

"Asdollah's legs were dangling from the branch above me. I moved from branch to branch, and with every stop I crammed as many berries as I could into my mouth. I lost track of time, and it was only when my stomach felt full that I thought of my waiting sisters."

My uncle looked at my mother, who was smiling. Their eyes tangled for a bit. He smiled back and fidgeted in his chair. The delicate wooden chair creaked, and after a short pause, he continued.

"My eyes found them standing on the edge of the big jump. They were whispering in each other's ears. I shouted to Asdollah that they were going to jump, but he didn't respond. So I called out to the girls, with my mouth full of *toot*, 'Sit on the edge! We will bring your *toot* very soon. Do not jump!'

"Sisters looked toward my direction trying to locate me among the branches and leaves. Naji sat down, but your aunt did not. That worried me. I looked for my brother and found him on a couple of branches to the right, unconcerned about his sisters, continuing to feed his face.

"'Asdollah,' I yelled. 'Tell them to sit there and wait for us!' But he ignored me and kept eating. I called out to him again, pleading that they would listen to their older brother.

"'SIT DOWN!' Asdollah shouted in a thunderous voice. Your aunt Mansoor obeyed immediately, and sat on the edge.

"After I saw our sisters safely sitting, my mind eased and I moved up to a higher, farther away branch for even juicer and bigger *toots*. A tiny voice reached me a few minutes later. 'Brother, have you forgotten us? Where are my *toots*?' It was little Naji. She was persistent, even as a child.

"I filled my pockets. Once my pockets were all full of the delicious white mulberries, I took a final mouthful and climbed down the tree. Big smiles appeared on my sisters' faces when they saw me jumping off the tree and running toward them with pockets full of *toots*.

"Approaching the mighty jump, my eyes on the target, I stopped to secure my feet and prepare myself to propel with a strong sprint. The upward jump was a complicated one as I had to leap both high and away. Since there was a strong possibility of a fall, I hoped my older brother was right behind me. I turned my head and looked for Asdollah. No, he was still on the tree busy picking and eating.

"'C'mon, Asdollah.' I yelled. 'Sisters are waiting. I don't want to jump back alone.'

"'Don't be afraid, go ahead and jump,' he replied. 'I want to stay on the tree longer. I'll watch you from here.'

"Your uncle Asdollah often lost his temper quickly, so I didn't dare argue with him. To avoid losing *toots* from my pocket during the jump, I pulled out my large handkerchief and filled it with the *toots* from my pockets. Then I tied the four corners of the handkerchief together and tossed the bundle onto the other rooftop where our sisters were sitting.

"The bundle landed on the roof top right behind my sisters. They rushed to the bundle, opened it right away, and devoured the berries. I liked it, because it kept them busy, and I could go back to eat more *toot*.

"We brothers played on the tree for a while longer. It was only after several complaints from our two sisters that we both filled our pockets again and headed back home."

The story had played like a movie in my mind. My mouth could taste the sweet white mulberries. We usually offered a dish of them to our summer guests, but not that day.

My uncle had moved to the United States in 1974 with his wife and two sons, soon after his retirement from the Petroleum Ministry. He was a great source of information about life in the U.S. My correspondence with him was mostly about the details of life in California.

My younger uncle was a calm, gentle man of average height with a square, clean-shaven face and a dimple in his chin. He favored American classic-style clothing. That day, his dark brown wingtip shoes and pastel pink oxford shirt intrigued me. Wingtip shoes were not common in Tehran; he was the only one I knew who wore them. Popular men's shoes in Iran were mostly handmade in imitation of European fashion. I was especially fond of his wingtips.

In my mind, I was only a few months away from being in the U.S. Understanding that as a student I would not be allowed to work, budgeting had become an important concern of mine. After patiently waiting for his story to end, I asked my uncle about the price of a hamburger sandwich in Los Angeles.

"What? you want to go to L.A. so you can eat a hamburger?" His thick eyebrows parted as he smiled. Everyone laughed as he mocked me.

I chuckled in pretense, but in reality, his comment wasn't funny. I had imagined, if I would eat out in the U.S., it would be either a hamburger or a hot dog. For me and my friends, a hamburger was a fun and relatively new western sandwich. Without a doubt, I could eat hamburgers three meals a day for many consecutive days.

My mother shook her head and apologized, complaining that I asked thousands of questions from anyone who visited us from the U.S. or Europe.

He smiled and turned his head toward me and asked if I had applied to any colleges yet.

I had been eagerly waiting for him to ask that question. I explained where I was in the process--that I had taken my TOEFL exam, my transcripts were translated to English and approved by the Ministry of Higher Education, and I had applied to Hartford University in Connecticut, University of Kansas in Lawrence, Texas Tech University in Lubbock, Syracuse University, Loyola, and UCLA.

Our conversation continued over many different topics as my mother served a bowl of cooled watermelon and cantaloupe slices, a refreshing summer treat. I admired my uncle. He spoke with a soft voice, but his genteel demeanor emitted a false impression about his abilities. He was among those strong-willed, quiet men whom no obstacle could stop.

Occasionally, a burst of humor showed his lighter side. His confidence, self-discipline, and ability to focus, derived from his athletic youth, were commendable and attractive to me. He had managed to become a successful and prosperous man, despite all the difficulties life threw at him, and he had retired as the head of security for oil pipelines in the Iranian Petroleum Organization. The oil business was the lifeline of the country. He worked closely with SAVAK, the feared secret police, and other security and intelligence organizations as part of his job.

But he never said anything about his work, and I never asked. However, whenever I looked deeply into his dark brown eyes, I saw a tortured soul. (Direct eye contact is discouraged in Iranian culture, but once in a while, among the close family members, one can sneak it in.)

During our conversations over the years, he had told me many stories. But that day, for no apparent reason, without any warning or introduction, he launched into another one. This time it was the story of the cigarette factory and his first adventure into earning money; it was a story of resilience, hard work, and having good work ethics. For me, it was a treasure chest of information about the world of the Iranian people before and during WWII.

A bowl of White Mulberry (Toot)

6

UNCLE RAAHMAT AND THE CIGARETTE FACTORY

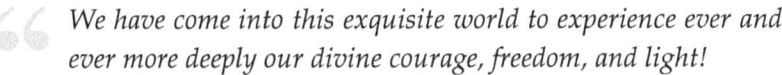 *We have come into this exquisite world to experience ever and ever more deeply our divine courage, freedom, and light!*

— Hafez

His gaze was pointed at no particular place, although his eyes were telling a different story. He was at a place and time far away from my grandmother's room in our house in Tehran. Then without any prompting he launched into the story:

"The last school day of my ninth grade was a glorious one for me. Until I went home. I had participated in a national track meet event at my school and won first prize for the one-hundred-meter dash, and four-hundred-meter race. That day, I was named one of the fastest runners in the country for my age group. A few days prior, I had turned fifteen, which was a big deal for me.

"In the afternoon, on my way home from the race, my hunger, a nuisance, did not diminish the excitement over my win. It was past lunchtime, and the last meal I had eaten was the dinner the night before. My father, our only breadwinner, had been sick in the hospital for a few months. We had used all our savings to pay for his treatment, and the daily expenses of our family of four. We had just moved to my aunt's (my mother's sister) house, and all of us, my mother, two sisters and me, lived in one room. My older brother was boarding in a military school.

"Upon my arrival that afternoon, I asked my mother," my uncle nodded toward my grandmother lying in the bed, "if there was anything to eat. I might have hinted at my extreme hunger due to lack of neither lunch nor breakfast.

"Mother abruptly became hysterical, screaming and hitting herself, crying and calling out to God, '*Khoda, Khoda*, what am I to do with no money and no food in the house for my dear, tired, and hungry son? My husband is half dead in the hospital and my kids are hungry! God show me a way, a solution or something!' Her loud screams were accompanied by the repeated beating of her chest. My sister, Mansoor, ran to assist my mother, calling out, '*Khanoum*-jon! *Khanoum*-jon! Why are you hitting yourself?'

"To our surprise, my mother passed out and crumpled to the ground. Mansoor screamed, becoming hysterical, believing our mother was dead. A cold sweat covered me. Little Naji," he pointed to my mother who was sitting on the skinny wooden chair next to me and listening, "was frozen in dismay and watching all this come about.

"I ran outside to look for my mother's older sister. Her room was across the courtyard from our room. She was washing up by the utility pool, getting ready for her daily prayers. I begged her to come to my mother's rescue right away.

"'Aahhh, she is acting, leave her alone, she will get up soon. I have to do my prayers.' My aunt said, refusing to assist my mother. But how could she pray when her sister was in need of help, lying unconscious in the other room? What kind of God accepts that attitude?

"Frustrated by my aunt's reaction, or lack of it, I decided to run to my grandmother's house a few blocks down the road. Every second was crucial, speed mattered, all my energy went to my weary legs. The image of my dead mother haunted my thoughts as I ran. I shook my head vigorously a few times to get rid of the image.

"If both of my parents die, who would raise my two poor little sisters? I wondered. I was sad, mad, hungry, scared and tired. Once I reached my grandmother's house, I could hardly breathe.

"'Mother is dying…' I gasped.

"My grandmother immediately picked up her *chador*, covered herself, and we both rushed back to my house, where my sisters were fanning my mother's motionless body. My grandmother immediately took my mother's head in her lap and asked for water and a towel, while cursing my aunt for being so mindless and cruel.

"A minute or two later, my mother responded and gained consciousness. Her first words were, 'Mother, I am desperate. My kids are hungry. I have no money, no food and my husband is still in the hospital.'

"Caressing her daughter's thick black hair, my grandmother assured her of help. Her calm and kind manner helped my mother feel better. A few minutes later, she asked me to walk her home, and to help her carry groceries back to our home.

"On the way to her house, she explained about life's ups and downs, and assured me that our downward spiral would soon pass. Her positive talk helped me to visualize a successful life for myself and eventually a handsome family of my own, despite all the difficulties. My grandparents were kind and positive people who never hesitated assisting those needing help. People loved them; I supposed that's why this street that your house is on is named after them.

"Anyway, her words soothed me, but the incident shook me. I could no longer tolerate the situation. I believed the solution was for me to find a job.

"I loved to run in the early mornings when the streets were quiet and empty. So early the following morning, during my run, I came across a large crowd gathered in front of the cigarette factory in our neighborhood. Curious about the crowd, I inquired about the cause of the gathering and learned that the cigarette factory was going to hire kids from fourteen and older the next day.

"Finally! The sun was peeking out from the clouds of my gloomy life. I ran home nonstop and prepared my documents. The next day I was at the gate of the cigarette factory at 6:30 a.m. sharp.

"A large crowd had already gathered at the gate. I fought my way to the front and gripped my hands tightly on the metal bars of the gate. There was no way I would lose that opportunity.

"The appearance of a few men on the other side of the gate caused the crowd to move like a wave, side to side, back and forth. Applicants in the back pushed and shoved to get to the front of the gate. My arms locked, I held fast to the metal rails. Everybody wanted to be the first to get in.

"On the other side of the gate, several men, unfazed by the commotion, set up for the opening. Two men brought out a small table, and then a chair. A notebook, a black ink bottle, a pen, and a stamp set were placed on the table.

"A moment later, a skinny man wearing a suit and hat arrived. Ignoring the crowd, he sat on the chair behind the desk, spent a few minutes flipping pages on a notebook, moved and organized some paper, and checked the stamp and his pen.

"When he was ready, he nodded to the two men. The crowd pushed forward again and pressed me against the metal rail. The two men held the gates firmly and only allowed one person at a time to enter the courtyard.

"I managed to get in. At the table, the skinny man lifted his head slowly and looked at me. He sported a thin mustache on his narrow face and wore spectacles. He extended his hand and asked for my documents. He adjusted his spectacles and reviewed the documents for a few minutes. He then picked up a form, wrote my name on it, and stamped it. 'You are hired,' he said, 'Come tomorrow morning at seven. You will get paid six *rials* per day.'

"It was unbelievable! That day was a very happy day for me. I decided not to tell anyone. A feeling of maturity and adulthood came over me. My new job would help my mother and my sisters; I could take care of them now. No more going to bed with a hungry stomach.

"I ran all the way home. At home, Naji, your mother, was the only one who detected a change in me. She thought I was happy because I had brought home food. But I told her that I had hope. Hope that soon our troubles would go away.

"The next day, dawn broke just as I was running to my new job, with my best clothes on, and my dampened hair perfectly combed to one side.

"They let me in on the factory floor, since I was half an hour early. I had to wait till all the new recruits showed up, then they gave us a tour. The factory was cleaner than what I expected. Many men were wearing lab coats. The man who showed us around handed us each a yellow lab coat. My coat was rather large; it hung all the way to my ankles. Coats were all adult size and I was a short teenager. But I didn't mind it. The whole experience was extraordinary for me. I was in heaven.

"At the end of the tour, he took us to our work area and assigned each of us to a different work group. The only break I had was a onehour lunch, but the cafeteria on campus was closed. It was the month of Ramadan and all the adults were fasting, so it was inappropriate for the cafeteria to prepare or serve food.

"Boys were permitted not to fast if they had not gone through puberty yet. However, fasting was much easier in my situation. The only meal I ever had was dinner.

"Fasting while working full time during hot summer days was hard at the beginning, since in Islam, fasting means no food or drink between sunrise and sundown. Hunger and thirst were my nemeses in the first week. Soon, I learned how to distract myself by immersing in the work.

"I loved my work and became very good at it. There were a few other kids my age working there, so whenever I finished early, I assisted the others. My helping attitude and newly acquired skills helped me win many of my co-workers' admiration.

"My pay at the end of the first week was thirty-six *rials*. My hands trembled when my boss handed me the money. I inhaled deeply. Every cell of my body was in celebration. I closed my hand and put the money in my pocket. Finally, my earnings could help the family.

My sisters no longer had to suffer hunger. My mother didn't have to ask for help from her pitiless sister anymore.

"I ran back home with the great news. My mother was on the floor praying. The proper etiquette was to wait till she finished her prayer. So, I did. The moment she ended her prayers I burst out with, 'Mother, Mother, here are thirty *rials*. Go ahead and buy groceries for the family with it!'

"My mother suddenly and swiftly grabbed my wrist, squeezed it hard and said, 'Come here, you rascal!' She yanked me closer to her. 'Tell me, where did you get this money?'

"Her action caused the money to be thrown on the floor. I struggled to release my wrist from her strong grip. But she was strong and I didn't want to hurt her. Her worries were that I may have been under the influence of some toxic friends and had stolen the money. Her teary eyes sunk my heart. I admitted to her that I couldn't accept our situation anymore, and that I was old enough to get a job and help. The cigarette factory was hiring and I got a job there. Her next worry was about me ditching school. My promise of returning to school in the fall eased her mind.

"My mother's wet eyes stared at me, penetrating my soul, reaching deep inside to see or to gauge my pain. She dipped her head, and I dropped my gaze to the ground, not wanting her to penetrate that deep. After a moment, she smiled, pulled me to her breast, squeezed and hugged me, and then let me go. My heart filled with warmth. A sense of accomplishment and purpose came over me. I now provided for my family.

"Going to work was pleasing. My obsession with performing the best job possible often caused me to skip the lunch break.

"One day, while everybody else was on lunch break, I took a short break and returned to my workspace. The workshop was empty. I was the only person in the factory floor at that time.

"'MONSIEUR MALEK!' The thunderous call shook me as it was so loud and low it carried all over the shop, bouncing off the walls. I stopped and looked up in search of the source of the powerful voice.

"In the middle of the factory floor, like a tower, stood Mr. Herman, the German general manager of the factory. My intense focus on the work had diverted my attention from noticing his arrival. The person he was calling, Monsieur Malek, was the Iranian manager in charge of our department. He was educated in France and fluent in French. Since Mr. Herman's French was better than his Farsi, he spoke French with Monsieur Malek.

"'Monsieur Malek!' he shouted again.

"My rapidly pounding heart felt as if it were jumping out of my rib cage. My quick scan to spot Monsieur Malek was fruitless. No one except me and Mr. Herman were on the shop floor.

"I was frightened, but Mr. Herman's third and agitated shout made me jump off my stool. I ran toward Mr. Herman and automatically in French asked him if he wanted me to find Monsieur Malek. It was unclear to me if I was shaking, or if it was the adrenaline that made my voice jittery. My slight body in front of the exceptionally tall and muscular Mr. Herman was an interesting scene, I'm sure.

"Mr. Herman looked down and found me, a small factory boy in an oversized yellow lab coat, standing in front of him. My fright kept my head down. I felt his eyes penetrating my skull, and then heard his determined voice say, '*Oui.*'

"Hoisting my lab coat, I ran fast. Monsieur Malek ate his lunch at the executive's lounge on the second floor at that time of the day. I climbed the stairs and flew toward the lounge. My forceful opening of the door turned everyone's head toward me. In my excited state, I forgot Monsieur Malek was Iranian and could speak Farsi perfectly.

"I rushed toward him and, in French, told him that Mr. Herman was in the factory floor asking for him. I didn't even wait for a reply or a reaction. The moment the message was delivered, I turned around and ran back to my station and continued my work.

"A few minutes before quitting time, my supervisor came to me and said that Monsieur Malek wanted to see me. I was worried that my theatrical entrance into the executive's lounge upset him, and he wanted to discipline me. Fearfully, I approached his office.

"Monsieur Malek wore his usual bow tie. His nicely oiled and carefully combed hair was a deliberate but unsuccessful attempt to cover up the prematurely bald part of his head. In his early thirties or so, he had the demeanor of an educated and cultured man. He was sitting behind his desk writing something, his shoulders stooped as he leaned over the paper.

"My hands were shaking as I knocked on his opened door and went straight to his desk. After a few moments, he looked up and stared at me through his round eyeglasses.

"He asked if I spoke French and I said that I did. Then he wanted to know where I learned it. At that point, I realized my little knowledge of French could be considered strange, as in those years, it was an anomaly for a poor young boy like me to know any foreign language. Frankly, I never thought the little French I knew was of any importance.

"'My older brother and all my uncles know French. Also, at school, I study French as my second language. I got the best grade in my French class,' I replied enthusiastically, my fear subsiding.

"Then he asked if I could write in French. Of course, he didn't believe my affirmative answer so he asked me to write my name in French. He passed me a piece of paper and a pen. This was the kind of pen that you had to dip in ink before writing.

"I dipped the pen in the inkwell and wrote my name in my best handwriting. He sat back in his chair and examined it carefully and gave me a deep look. I dropped my eyes to the floor out of respect and shyness. After a few second's pause he said, 'Well, then, you will start in my office tomorrow, early morning. You'll be preparing reports in French and create tables in a neat and clean manner for these reports.'

"Without waiting for my reaction or reply, he called his assistant and asked him to set up a desk, a chair and office supplies for me. Then he dismissed me. Before I could step out of the doorway he shouted, 'Don't wear that hideous coat tomorrow. You don't need it here in the office.'

"I stepped out of the office with a huge smile. The sensation of butterflies fluttering in my stomach was with me the rest of the day. At the end of the day, I ran all the way home to burn off my cooped-up excitement that had been gathering all day. At home, I kept the promotion to myself.

"The next day, early in the morning, at the office upstairs, I froze by the doorframe at the sight of my new work area. There was a desk with a clean surface, a small bundle of clean white paper, an ink jar, a pen, and a chair waiting for me. Was this real or just a dream? I slapped my face. No, it's real.

"I gingerly approached the desk, gently pulled out the chair, and sat behind the desk. It felt good not to wear the silly oversized coat. I thought that maybe it was a mistake, and when my boss saw me behind that desk, he would throw me out.

"The little voice inside me bothered me all day, sending unsettling messages to my mind. As the morning progressed, other clerks trickled in. Some tightened their brows and made a serious face when they saw me there, some pushed their lower lip upward and raised their eyebrows in a gesture of approval. Others ignored me.

"'*Bonjour garcon*,' Monsieur Malek said as he whizzed by my desk in mid-morning.

"'*Bonjour, monsieur. Mon nom est Zibah*,'" I politely reminded him of my last name, thinking that perhaps he had forgotten.

"'Not bad,' he replied in Farsi.

"So, that had been a test. His speaking in Farsi put me at ease because I didn't have to talk in French anymore. Frankly, my vocabulary in French was extremely limited.

"The next day, my old supervisor asked for the return of my cafeteria card. I had to muster everything within me to ask him why.

"'Let me see it,' he said, his face set in a stern, serious expression. I thought perhaps he was going to revoke my cafeteria privileges.

"Slowly, I reached into my pocket and handed him the card. He examined it, raised his thick curvy eyebrows and pushed his lower lip upward. Then, he reached in his pocket, pulled out another card and gave it to me with a smirk on his face. He then turned and left without a word.

"I inspected the new card and couldn't believe it. The card was a supervisors' cafeteria card. That meant higher clout and better food. I was only fifteen! Allowing me to eat among the supervisors was considered an acknowledgment of my recent promotion.

"My enthusiasm about the new position was seeping through my eyes, my skin, and my whole demeanor. Often, I stayed late. It didn't take long for the other clerks to figure out how easily I could be persuaded to do their jobs. But it was a fair trade. They enjoyed going home early or taking a longer lunch break, and I enjoyed learning how to do their work. Soon, my knowledge of the work in that office grew so much that I could easily function as any of the clerks.

"At the beginning of fall, when school started, I received another promotion and raise. My new responsibilities were to train the newly hired clerks. My new promotion, raise, and status helped me to support my family better. My father was recuperating but his fragile condition disallowed him to work fulltime. I didn't sign up for school that year. My parents didn't say anything about it. By their silence, I knew they had accepted the harsh reality.

"A year later, the factory was absorbed by the Ministry of Manufacturing, and they downsized my division. The chaos of the merger left no one paying attention to the payroll. Many employees didn't receive their paycheck, which upset the workers. The ministry bookkeepers didn't understand the factory's payroll. The situation was becoming intense with factory workers threatening a walk out. The new boss from the ministry asked if I could help. Of course, I jumped at the opportunity.

"Several long working days helped me to finish the entire payroll. Everyone was paid one week later. I was promoted to the accounting office in charge of the payroll. Shortly after that, I learned how to do most of the payroll math by memory. My dedication was noticed and rewarded with an upgrade of my cafeteria card to the ministry's executive's cafeteria."

My uncle paused, looking out the window at the horizon. A few seconds later, he chuckled and added, "The executive's cafeteria was across the courtyard from my office. It was hard for me to walk across the yard, because the workers who started with me clapped and greeted me as if I were a hero. I wasn't. I was just doing what I loved to do with the best of my abilities."

His story had taken me to a time in our history that I couldn't relate to. It was only forty or fifty years prior, but to me, it felt like several hundred years ago. The Tehran I grew up in was a modern city with all the hustle and bustle of any major metropolitan city in the world. It was remarkable to see how a few decades of prosperity and stability could change a nation. I asked my uncle if he ever finished his schooling.

A smile appeared on his face, with a nod he explained that he completed high school by going to night school classes.

Here was a man sitting in front of me, who despite the difficulties life threw at him, bounced back and pushed forward. A sort of quiet, urban hero. As long as I remembered, he had always lived in upscale, modern properties. His family had the best of everything, far from what his childhood was. Once he retired and moved to the United States, he bought a house in Orange County and enrolled his two sons in local public schools. Without any fanfare, he amassed a comfortable fortune and never stopped improving his standard of living.

He even smelled like progress. It seemed that whatever he was wearing carried a fresh fragrance of success and freedom to me. It was too bad that his wife and my mother had had a falling out. The result was we were cut off from visiting his family in Tehran. The tiff was especially unfortunate for me, as I never, even for a moment, thought of requesting to stay with them once I reached Los Angeles.

Uncle's story about his first job explained his contact with Europeans early in his life, but never explained his involvement with the Iranian Petroleum Organization, where English was the preferred second language. I was also curious about this part of his career, so I asked.

He answered, "Yes, two years later, I was offered a job at the Petroleum Ministry by my brother-in-law when I was visiting your aunt in a small town near the city of Shush, where the prophet Daniel's tomb is located. The Petroleum Ministry was a prestigious organization, and the salary he offered me was five times the salary I had with the cigarette factory, and the world of petroleum was a promising, brand new world."

Based on my calculation, that must have been in the early '40s when he went to that small city. World War II was in full swing at that time. I asked if it had been a dangerous time in a dangerous place.

He looked up and gazed toward the horizon again, perhaps into the past. Who knows how many faces and events he viewed in those few moments?

He exhaled and acknowledged that the time was certainly a turbulent time. Iran was becoming a major hub for the Allied forces. Through Iran, Allies transported supplies and weapons to the Russian front. My uncle Jafari, his brother-in-law, was in charge of a refueling station for Allied trucks in that city.

He stayed quiet. I decided to lighten things up by asking about uncle Jafari's eccentric behavior in those days. He must have been in his late twenties, stuck in a small town in the middle of nowhere.

A smiled appeared on my uncle's face, and with a nod he agreed on Uncle Jafari's eccentric behavior. Apparently, a group of them formed a drama club and put on many shows in that small community.

Uncle Raahmat was a staunch supporter of the monarchy. Since his thoughts were traveling through the era of WWII, I used that moment to insert a little political commentary. To my knowledge, Reza Shah, the old king, tore down many religious walls during his reign, forcing women *not* to wear the traditional cover *chador*, dismantling religious schools; forcing people to wear Western attire, to name a few. I asked if he noticed discontent in the social climate during that time, for example, among religious people. Had they been extremely upset?

He pointed to the increased political uncertainty caused by the chaos of WWII. The old king was forced to abdicate by occupying Allied forces and a new king, his son, was taking over. The country was in a state of pandemonium. He cleverly avoided a direct political discussion.

My own father was a truck driver, transporting Allied supplies from the Persian Gulf to the Russian borders during that time. I asked uncle Raahmat if he ever came across my father, or if he remembered seeing him.

He shook his head, chuckled and said, "Oh, that was a crazy time, and we didn't know each other then."

In my history courses, I had learned a covered-up version of World War II and its impact on Iran. One of the advantages of the 1978 dissent and turmoil in Iran was the availability of many otherwise-tabooed literatures and documentation, revealing different points of view.

But hearing it from a person who was actually there during the years of the World War II was fascinating.

I continued probing him for more information. In one instance, I asked if he knew that the code name for the Allies' invasion of Iran in 1941 was *Countenance*.

He took issue with the term "invasion." He said, "Well, I wouldn't call it an invasion. That was our way to help the Allied forces." He fidgeted in his chair, clearly uncomfortable with the conversation.

Observing his nervousness, and craving more information, I decided to hit him with more facts and launched into a lecture about the Iranian king at the time, Reza Shah, who declared Iran's status neutral in World War II. But, since the Persian Corridor was vital for the survival of Russia and the security of Iranian oil fields, Allied forces invaded and occupied Iran. I explained that I had read somewhere that over one thousand Iranian soldiers and civilians died during the invasion. And, since Reza Shah was not cooperating, he was sent into exile by the occupying powers, the Allies. His son, Mohammad Reza Pahlavi, was placed on the throne with the agreement that the new king would not interfere with Allied activities.

Uncle Raahmat's eyes widened. He sat up in his chair and basically regurgitated the official historical teaching that we all had read in our school's history books. That Iran was a crucial supply route for Allies, and we facilitated the delivering of millions of tons of war materials and supplies to Russia, and that is how Russia turned around and kicked Hitler's forces out. Also in 1943, Iran declared war on Germany and became a member of the United Nations. Then he asked if I had read about the Tehran Conference in November of 1943, when President Roosevelt, Winston Churchill, and Stalin, in their historic secret meeting in Tehran, called Iran "The Victory Bridge" and committed themselves to Iran's independence and territorial integrity.

He was clearly agitated. I didn't want to upset him, so I faked a chuckle and shared with him that to me, the most interesting aspects of that era were the personal stories of how ordinary Iranian people were affected by WWII. To lighten the situation I said, "Even Iranian bears have stories to tell."

He raised his eyebrows at me and asked, "Bears! What are you saying?"

He had taken the bait. With a smile, I went ahead and told him about a recent story I read in a publication about the Polish soldiers who were stationed in Iran during WWII. They rescued an Iranian bear cub and became quite attached to it. When it was time for them to move to the war zone, they requested to take the bear with them. Apparently, the only way to do so was to enlist the bear with a complete name, rank, and serial number in the Allied forces. The bear moved with the soldiers, carried heavy mortar rounds, and took part in the Italian campaign.

After a short snicker, he admitted that he had never heard of that story and thought that I made it up.

Reassuring him that the story was true, I referred him to a zoo in Scotland where a bronze statue of the bear is on display.

"Scotland?" he challenged me. "You just said the bear went to Italy with the Polish regiment. What does Scotland have to do with it? Was it because it was shot while saving some Scottish soldiers?"

I clarified that the bear survived the war. After the war, the Polish soldiers didn't know what to do with the bear, so it was sent to a zoo in Scotland. The statue commemorates the bear's bravery and contribution to the Allied troops. The bear died of old age in the mid 60s in the zoo.

He looked at his watch and admitted that the bear story was a great story. The bear could be the only Iranian who served in the front during WWII. Then he stood up and declared that it was time for him to leave. But as his last advice of the day, he warned me that life in the U.S. was not an easy one. I would be in a strange land with a culture so different that in some respects, it would be totally the opposite of what I was used to. He reiterated the fact that I needed to learn and respect the American way of life; and unlike Iran, there would be no large extended family to protect me.

I would never forget his final words: "Often, fantasy makes us forget the harsh realities and difficulties of living in a different world, Vahid. Call me if you make it to America."

My mother and I exchanged a look. We knew this could only be his wishful thinking, for in reality, there would be a slim chance that his wife would allow any contact between us.

The statue of Wojtek (the Persian Bear) at the Edinburgh Zoo in Scotland.

7

TRIP TO SHIRAZ

> *That until the philosophy which holds one race superior and another inferior is finally and permanently discredited and abandoned; that until there is no longer any first-class and second-class citizens of any nation; that until the color of a man's skin is of no more significance than the color of his eyes; that until the basic human rights are equally guaranteed to all, without regard to race—until that day, the dreams of lasting peace and world citizenship and the rule of international morality will remain but fleeting illusion, to be pursued but never attained.*
>
> — Speech by H.I.M Haile Selassie I – California (28 February 1968)

My fingertips traveled evenly and smoothly along the surface. Softly sensing every curve, the contact ignited my imagination, taking my mind back thousands of years to the height of Persian Empire. The wall carvings of the ruins brought many ancient stories to life. Horses, chariots, soldiers with their long beards, foreign dignitaries, and all the hustle and bustle of life twenty-five-hundred years ago in the great city of Persepolis, raced through my mind like a motion picture on fast forward. What an amazing place! Persepolis, the center of the glorious Persian Empire, the capital of the Achaemenid Empire. And then, one day, it was all destroyed by a young Greek, Emperor Alexander the Great, in 330 B.C.

The ruins of once majestic columns, imposing stairs, fantastic architecture, priceless art works, and many magnificent carvings on walls were a horrific reminder of the end story, a lesson for all its visitors. The Persian Empire, with all its might, one of the largest military powers of its time, with hundreds of thousands of men, beasts, and modern weaponries, was totally destroyed and devastated by the hands of Greek conquerors.

"It's sad, isn't it?" said a short man standing near me staring at the ruins. I didn't notice his presence till he spoke. I guessed him to be in his forties. He wore a pair of aviator sunglasses.

Nodding my head, I acknowledged him, and in return, I posed to him a rhetorical question on what happened to the vast network of intelligence, great strategists, infrastructure, knowledge, financial resources, and years of experience the Persians had.

The man shrugged his shoulders. Recognizing my observation, he raised his own query on the puzzling matter of how an army of a young, inexperienced emperor, thousands of kilometers away, could reach and devastate the place so rapidly.

I looked down at the ground and shuffled some dirt with the tip of my shoe. His questions and investigative outlook compelled me to share more of my thoughts on this concern with him.

Glorification of the ancient times when Persepolis was at its height was a popular exercise among people. The same with expressing sorrow about the destruction of it. My wonder was that no one talked about the misery and devastation ordinary people had to go through. The tens of thousands of girls and women that the soldiers of Alexander raped and killed just in that region alone.

The man turned his face toward me. "What do you think caused the Persian Empire's demise?"

"Who knows? Some say pride made them vulnerable, and some say it was corruption," I replied.

The man shook his head. "I don't think so. History tells us about many corrupt and proud powers that stayed in control regardless."

Curious to hear his opinion, I asked about his view on the cause of the demise.

"My guess is that they became too rigid," he replied. "They convinced themselves that they were invincible. They set too many unbending and absolute rules, disallowing changes and challenges to the system. Just like a dry and rigid branch of an old tree, it easily breaks during a storm. The surviving branches are the ones that can bend."

Intrigued with his fresh angle on the subject, I asked, "So, you are saying that it wasn't corruption or becoming lazy?"

"My friend, these are all symptoms. Universal laws teach us that change is constant, perpetual, and necessary for survival." After a short pause, he continued. "Recognizing that fact, and allowing for adaptation and evolution, is a key to success. Stagnant water becomes toxic or evaporates."

I nodded my head in understanding and started to move on, when the man suddenly began reciting poetry.

"Ah! My beloved, fill the cup that clears / Today of past regrets and future fears / Tomorrow? Why, tomorrow I may be / myself with yesterday's seven thousand years." I smiled at him. "Omar Khayyam."

He returned my smile and nodded.

I walked away and continued my exploration of the ruins. But his comment "the surviving branches are the ones that can bend" echoed in my head the rest of the day. I had a strong impression that this was a message intended for me—and about my future.

The visit to the Persepolis ruins, about fifty kilometers northeast of the city of Shiraz, was a side excursion during my unexpected trip to Shiraz with my mother. I needed a break from her, as I had been compelled to accompany her there.

. . .

Four days prior, my concerns over the unusually belated TOEFL exam results were mounting. Strikes were spreading like a wildfire, engulfing many government organizations, such as banks and postal services. Schools in the United States required TOEFL scores with each application. Without it, I could not get accepted. Every additional day of delay added to the uncertainty of the outcome, and my increased stress level.

Fall came early that year. Leaves changing colors, rain, wind, and cooler temperatures were signaling the change of season. This made me more nervous. Time was passing fast, but my processes to study abroad faced delay after delay and the progress was slow.

Passing by in the hallway, I had noticed my mother in her room packing a suitcase. For a moment, I thought to ignore it. But I couldn't. The urge to learn why she was packing was too strong.

Without taking her eyes off her suitcase, she responded to my inquiry. She was packing for a trip to the city of Shiraz.

"Shiraz!" I stared at her. Then I noticed something highly unusual.

She was quietly weeping. I asked her about it.

She wiped her cheeks with her hand and said nothing. The only person my mother knew in Shiraz was my younger brother, who was a freshman in the University of Shiraz. He had started there early in summer. I asked if something happened to him.

Her quiet weeping turned into a pronounced crying when she explained that he hadn't called or written for a while. She wasn't sure if he was all right.

My attempt to calm her by blaming his lack of communication on his youth and that he would have contacted us if he was in a trouble didn't work. She continued packing, but I didn't see any of my father's belongings. It was odd, as usually she would pack for both of them. She was traveling by herself. The answer came with continued quiet weeping.

Now she had my attention. She couldn't go alone! I lowered myself to make eye contact with her and told her so. She ignored me, turned her face away from me and continued packing her suitcase.

Just in case that she had believed all the recent hype about women's freedom in Iran, I reminded her that in our society women's freedom was all pretence. We had a long way to go yet. No hotel would rent a room to an unaccompanied woman. Also, during the sixteen-hour bus ride, there could be many crazy and precarious people who would try to take advantage of her. It was dangerous for a woman to travel alone.

She continued her silence. I paced back and forth in the room. Her silence was not comforting. My mother had an independent soul, but I was worried. Our culture wasn't tolerant of lone woman travelers.

My concern was turning into anger toward my father. Why wasn't he traveling with her? She was his wife!

This was the second marriage for both my parents. My father's first one failed due to his first wife's loss of interest in him. Despite his devotion to her, she found someone more ambitious than my father. My mother's first one was a disaster. Apparently, her family didn't approve of her love interest. To avoid a possible fiasco, her parents forced her to marry someone she abhorred at age seventeen. She begged her first husband for two years to divorce her, which finally happened. Both my parents brought a child from their first marriages into this one. I knew my parents were not in love with each other, but they respected and tolerated each other. Together, they provided a stable and amicable family environment for their children.

She explained that my father wasn't convinced traveling to Shiraz was wise in such a difficult time.

I took my father's side and asked if she could delay her trip and even perhaps ask my brother to come and visit her.

She threw her clothes into the suitcase with rage and looked me in the eyes with her eyes flooded in tears, affirming that she had delayed the trip long enough. She knew since my brother had just started his fall semester, he would not be coming back for a while. She was desperately in need of seeing him and making sure he had all the help he needed.

She slammed closed the suitcase and lifted it from the bed, pushed me aside with her other hand, and left the room.

"Help? He hasn't asked for your help. He is not a baby anymore. He is eighteen and free!" I exclaimed, following her out of the room. The last sentence echoed in my mind a few times. *He is eighteen and free.*

She stopped in the hallway, put her suitcase down, and started weeping again.

I couldn't take it anymore. I gave in, but as a last attempt to change her mind, I asked if she would give me enough time to follow up with universities in the U.S. and wait a couple of days to see if my TOEFL results arrived. While awaiting feedback from colleges in the U.S, I was in the midst of plotting my plan B, in the case the TOEFL results never came. But of course, I told no one about this possibility.

She said, like my father, that I was full of excuses and declared that she was fully prepared to go alone. She was all choked up when she said that. The guilt she put on my shoulders was unbearable. I couldn't let her go alone.

My father was a stubborn man who despised traveling. I knew he wouldn't change his mind. My mother had both an iron will and the patience of a saint. When she said she was going to do something, she would.

I gave up, but not without negotiating terms. I had two conditions. One, I asked if she could give me at least a day to organize my affairs. Two, on the way back I wanted to get off the bus in Isfahan and visit Neilu for a few days. The trip from Isfahan to Tehran was relatively shorter and safer for her to be alone.

She raised her head up, looked at me with a smile, and agreed with a satisfied nod.

My brother was ranked twelfth in the country's college entrance exam from among 110,000 participants. Basically, he could choose whatever university he desired in Iran. He had selected the University of Shiraz, which was among the top universities in the country.

My mother missed him immensely. She had cried every night since my brother left the house. My father wasn't worried about my brother; in his view, my brother was eighteen and able to handle his affairs. However, he did try to discourage her about the trip without giving up his position. A cop-out in my opinion. It didn't work anyway; she was adamant to visit her son.

A day later, we started our trip. The bus station was in a busy section of downtown where lots of people, motorcycles, vehicles, and large trucks were moving in every direction, adding toxic exhaust to the already polluted air. The bus left on time at 4:00 p.m.

Inside the bus, which seemed less hectic than outside, I sat by the window. From my window, the chaos outside was comical. Carts pulled by donkeys, bicycles, vehicles, and motorcycles carrying two or more passengers rushing, interweaving amongst each other, willfully ignoring the traffic rules, missing each other by a centimeter or two. All highly entertaining.

Strangely, I felt detached. Even though I was part of that crazy system, looking at it through a window in the bus felt bizarre, but not unfamiliar. The feeling of detachment in general wasn't strange to me. Unlike many I knew, I never felt comfortable with disorder. Perhaps another attraction of the western world to me was the idea of citizens respecting the law and therefore creating a more orderly world. Perpetual chaos and constant arguments of bending civic rules and ordinances was exhausting to me. In my view, ignoring the rules for self-satisfaction and disregarding the cost it imposed on others was a form of bullying. Often, I thought about the root of this behavior. Whether it could be a form of aggression? Did it come from lack of trust in the system, or is it in the DNA of our culture? Would Westerners do the same if put in the same environment? Would Germans break the rules if they could?

My mother's elbow poking into my side distracted me from my thoughts. She offered a wrapped candy as she always did when we traveled and said, "I don't know what he eats in that God-awful apartment that he shares with his roommates." She sat next to me in the bus, her legs tucked in front of her and her small body sunk into the seat.

I teased by asking if she was going all the way to Shiraz to see what he ate. She didn't find it amusing, and further blamed her heightened worries on the daily flood of bad news about college students' demonstrations, uprisings, arrests, and deaths from the confrontations with military. "I just want to see my son," she summarized.

A ferocious flow of cold air suddenly hit my face. I looked up at the source. The air conditioner nozzle was completely open and a rush of the cold air blew when the driver turned on the air conditioner. After getting my mother's agreement, I turned the knob on the console above our heads and shut the blasting air vent.

My fortune didn't last that long. The assistant driver, a seventeen-year-old boy, was patrolling the aisle. He noticed my air vent was shut. Acting like an officer of a slave ship, he ordered me not to touch the nozzle and twisted it opened to full blast. He then walked toward the front of the bus, ignoring my complaint about the uncomfortable, cold air.

Three hours later, we had cleared Tehran and were on our way to the city of Ghom. The assistant took his second walk, tossing cans of cold colas to the passengers. He noticed my air nozzle was shut again.

His violent temper was unleashed on me, while twisting the nozzle open again. Yelling his last warning, he said that I would be tossed out if I tampered with the nozzle again. The driver heard his assistant, and in support of him shouted, "Do I need to stop this bus?"

Picturing myself alone in the darkness in the middle of a vast desert in the central part of Iran, magically made the discomfort associated with the blasting of the cold air much more tolerable. One would not dare to challenge such a warning. People like him often deliver what they promise without even the slightest prick to their conscience.

A few hours later that night, we arrived at the city of Isfahan for a quick unloading and loading of passengers. A few people got off and a few new passengers got on board. We were not on the road again for more than twenty minutes when the bus slowed down and pulled over to the shoulder in the dark of the desert.

I wiped the condensation off the glass and cupped my hands around my eyes to look outside. Flashing red and blue lights illuminated the road and a few armed men in uniform approached the bus.

My mother nervously prayed to God asking for a trouble-free passage. Hiding my own worries, I assured her of the strong possibility of just a routine inspection.

The driver turned on all the lights in the cabin. A man in civilian clothing and two soldiers with automatic weapons got on the bus. The man talked to the driver as the soldiers walked up the middle aisle toward the back, inspecting the passengers.

My heart raced. Lately, with the increased activities of the underground freedom fighters, the Iranian security forces were more edgy and unpredictable. The murmuring of people on the bus replaced the initial quiet atmosphere.

The man in plain clothing asked everyone to get their IDs out, and to exit in an orderly fashion through the front door.

My mother's eyes were wide open. She was sitting erect, extending her neck and moving it rapidly to see what was happening beyond the seats in front of her.

Other passengers around us were doing the same thing, sitting up and craning their necks to figure out what was going on. The ones in the front of the bus obeyed, and with their IDs in hand, quietly exited the bus. No one complained loudly; just some whispers could be heard.

Progress was very slow. The two soldiers in the back of the bus were watchful of every move we made. My mother stepped down the steep stairs at the front of the bus with difficulty, as she was trying to hold her *chador* to cover herself with one hand, and with the other, hold the rail and her ID. I followed her.

The desert night sky was clear and carpeted with stars. Two men in plain clothes were checking the IDs with flashlights. A soldier holding a submachine gun at the door pointed his gun at every passenger who stepped down from the bus. Several flood lights illuminated the bus and the area near it.

They lined us up next to the other people alongside the bus. We all stayed close to each other, the cold temperature of the desert's night was biting. The fifth person after me was a young man of about my age, tall and skinny. The moment he started to hand his ID to the plain-clothes officer on his left, he grabbed the officer and threw him toward the soldier with the submachine gun and ran.

"Halt, halt!" a soldier yelled. And then I was jolted by the loud clatter of several machine guns rapidly firing. People screamed and everyone ducked or dropped onto the ground. I tried to cover my mother as best I could. I felt her trembling beneath my arm.

Two soldiers stood in front of us with their guns pointed at us. One of them ordered us to stay put. The rest rushed toward the front of the bus. They picked up the lifeless body of the skinny young man and threw him in a military truck.

My throat tightened, and I was about to throw up. My hands were shaking, and not from the cold. A flood of questions bounced around in my head. Was he a criminal? He was awfully young to be a hardcore criminal. Or was he just a poor student who dared to stand against the regime? It was only during my last two years of college when I became aware of the regime's relentless pursuit of underground freedom fighters.

My mother's shaking voice reciting prayers nonstop brought my attention back to her. I put my arms around her again, comforted her and soothed her trembling body.

People were whispering questions to each other. A few moments after they took the body away, the officers ordered us to stand up, and one by one they questioned us. Nothing special--just our complete names, where we were from, where we were going, and if we knew the ill-fated young man. An hour later, we continued our trek to Shiraz.

I turned this way and that in my seat throughout the night, working hard on tolerating the discomfort of the long ride, the blasting cold air, and the awful images of what I had witnessed. Once a while, the sound of someone's weeping reminded me that I wasn't alone in absorbing the horrors of the night.

Had the fellow truly been a student running away from agents of the regime? Or was he a freedom fighter on the way to his next assignment? Either way, at that young age, he stood for something. Was it for his people, or his own pride? Did he pay the ultimate price for something he believed in, or was he tricked into it? Was that what Farhad wanted me to do? Stay and help the resistance? And be hunted like this? How many of them were hunted like this? If I would stay, could I save any of them?

Before long, the darkness of sky gave way to light. Dawn was welcoming news. And soon the city of Shiraz's gates appeared on horizon. I nudged my mother, who barely opened her eyes and leaned over me to see out the window.

She smiled and praised the beauty of the view.

Although this was my first time visiting the most romantic city in

Iran, somehow, I felt very close to it. People of this city were known for their friendliness. And Neilu was originally from Shiraz.

As soon as we arrived at the bus station, my mother, with the determination of a mother in search of her lost son, stood up in the aisle, anxious to exit. With her handbag clutched to her chest she moved forward one step at a time until she stepped down from the bus.

As we walked out of the bus station, I suggested the order of business to be first locate a hotel, place our luggage in the room, and then look for my brother. She argued that she could not bear one more moment of not seeing her son. The previous night's horrors made her even more anxious. However, after a few more minutes of discussion, she relented with a terse nod.

The city was busy but not as crowded as Tehran. Tall cypress trees lined the streets. Their pointy tops gently waved with the wind against the clear blue sky, creating an exceptional imagery. The air felt cleaner and warmer than Tehran. According to my mother's side of the family, there was a small possibility that our lineage was from a dynasty originating from this region several hundred years ago. Knowing that, I felt somewhat connected to the city and anxious to explore.

I spied a motel near the bus stop—a three storied brick building with a smallish entrance. It seemed clean and respectable enough. My mother didn't object, so we went inside.

The man in the front desk asked for our birth certificates. Every motel and hotel registered guests and inspected guests' relationships, especially when the guests were male and female. Only men and women who had a legal relationship such as parent, children, or husband and wife were allowed to stay in a room together.

The room we rented was small with two beds, but it was clean and tidy. There was only one sink in the room. The toilet was in the hallway. For bathing, guests were supposed to use public bath houses in the city. As soon as I put the luggage on the ground, my mother opened her suitcase and pulled out several bags of boiled eggs, tomatoes, cooked potatoes, cucumbers, a few pots and pans, and a kerosene burner for cooking. She basically had transported a small kitchen.

I couldn't help but laugh at the situation. Far away from home, about to reunite with her beloved son, the first thing she does is to make sure my brother would have a warm, homemade meal when he first arrived. It was hard not to tease her about it. I knew this was her way of expressing love to my brother, but I teased her anyway.

She wasn't amused and gave me the task of peeling cucumbers. She went on a rant about how her young boy had been suffering the terrible cafeteria meals all these weeks and expected to see him as nothing but skin and bones. I couldn't handle it anymore. I set the dish with peeled cucumbers on the bed and left the room to find my brother and bring him to her.

Perhaps it was a bit of sibling rivalry, or maybe my young mind couldn't understand parenthood. Outraged by her behavior, I hopskipped the stairs in a rush to get to the street and fetch a taxi to my brother's address.

His building was a clean, modern structure. His apartment was on the second floor. After a few knocks on the door, his roommate opened it. My brother wasn't home. I left our hotel information with his roommate and asked that my brother go to the hotel as soon he returned.

My feelings for him were a mixture of jealousy and pride. At age eighteen, he was already living in a different city, and there I was at twenty-one years old, graduated from college and very much longing for independence, but still living with my parents.

Returning to the hotel and witnessing my mother's insane preparation for the prince, my brother, was not an option at that time. Instead, I decided to explore. Shiraz University was nearby. It was considered among the top three universities in Iran, and by many accounts number one.

The campus was expansive and well groomed. Tall cypress trees lined the walkways and pools with fountains and colorful roses set among other flowers added color and serenity to the campus landscape. Inside the library, I found an inscription about the history of the university. In 1960, Gaylord Harnwell, the president of the University of Pennsylvania, was commissioned by the Iranian government to evaluate Iran's higher education system and subsequently was asked to assist the Iranian government in transforming Shiraz University into one of the very few institutions in the Middle East that was based on American-style higher education.

Suddenly it dawned on me that Farhad also studied there. Had he signed up for a summer session? This should be his last year. With so many strikes among all higher education institutions, it was hard to say what college was open and what wasn't. My brother would know. However, after our walk together from the music store, I wasn't sure if I wanted to see Farhad again.

On a bench under the shade of a large maple tree, three students were arguing over a mathematical problem. I found myself standing near them and listening to their argument. Oh, how I loved and already missed my college days! Those long hours we labored on heated discussions about something or another. One of them noticed me hovering. I collected myself and asked if they knew Farhad. One of them nodded his head and said that he lived off campus, spending most of his time with his girlfriend.

"His girlfriend!" I repeated. I didn't know that he had a girlfriend. He never told me. Was it because he had realized life had taken a different path for each of us and that our friendship had reached its end? Or could it be my self-absorbed narcissism that didn't allow me to ask about his life?

After an hour of a wondrous walk and exploration of the modern campus, I went on foot back to the hotel. The urge of discovery and absorbing the pulse of the ancient city was strong with me. Its natural beauty, historical monuments, mosques, palaces, libraries, and gardens had made the city a destination for many millennia. Shiraz was and still is known as the most romantic city in Iran because of its poets, gardens, flowers, singing birds, and wine. I read somewhere that archeologists had found seven-thousand-year-old wine in a clay jar near the city. Some people claim that Shiraz is the true birthplace of sherry wine.

The explorer in me enjoyed making all the new discoveries. But every other thought was about Neilu. This was the city where she was born and spent her childhood. I felt closer to her with every turn. It was sunset when I finally returned to the hotel.

In the room, I found my mother sitting on the floor, her white *chador* covering her body completely. She was deeply engaged with her daily prayers.

My brother sat on the bed, submerged in pages of a newspaper. The fragrance of the food my mother managed to make with the little resources she had was divine.

After a hug and the two customary kisses, one on each cheek, my brother and I caught up with the news on each other's life. After her prayers, my mother dished out our dinner with a wide smile on her face.

During the next few days, my mother cooked food, washed, ironed, and repaired my brother's clothes. I, on the other hand, devoted my time to immersing myself in the natural and historic beauty of the region, including the excursion to Persepolis.

The last day of our stay in Shiraz was the emotional pinnacle for my mother. After many hugs, kisses, and tears of farewell with my brother, she got on the bus and we started our journey back to the capital city. The driver and assistant driver on this bus were more tolerable than the previous ones.

During our return trip, a nagging voice in my head argued against getting off in the city of Isfahan. One side of me wanted to remain in the bus and not leave my mother alone; the other side had an uncontrollable urge to visit Neilu.

I missed Neilu terribly. The battle in my mind was in full course. It felt like a trial; my conscience was the judge, my morals the district attorney, and my love, or perhaps lust, was the opposing counsel. This created an exhausting debate during the return trip for me.

A good son would not leave his mother alone on a bus trip, especially after what had happened on the way to Shiraz. A good boyfriend would not pass up the chance of being with his long distance love when an opportunity presented itself. But also, one other issue was looming in the background—the sanity of my urge to get closer to Neilu when I was about to leave the country. The nearer we got to Isfahan, the stronger my temptation became. Finally, the forces of desire prevailed.

I brought up the subject to my mother, hinting about whether she needed me to stay on the bus. I needed her confirmation of our initial arrangement in order to ease my conscience.

She gave me a long look. Her eyes and facial expressions were adequately expressive; I didn't need to hear her words. Her eyes said, "Stay on the bus."

But after a few moments of silence she said, "You know she is not the right girl for you."

I turned my head away from her and gazed out the window. Her words were not what I expected.

"It pains me to see you spending so much time and emotional energy on this relationship," she continued. My mother never hid her feelings.

However, it was my life and my decision. Neilu challenged and comforted me. I also needed my mother to be on my side, it was natural for me to defend our relationship. I turned toward her and went over Neilu's positive attributes and her effect on me.

"Comfort you? Like what? Name two?" my mother countered.

"She is smart, calm, confident, and very independent. How is that for a start?"

She tried to argue back, but I cut her off and explained to her that I didn't want to continue that conversation with her. The bus had entered the city, and I really wanted to get off the bus and visit Neilu for a few days. I asked again if she would be okay.

She turned her head away from me. "It's okay. If you really want to do it."

Her tone gave my conscience a chill. It was the typical passive-aggressive maneuvering that I witnessed among many women in my upbringing. Men bullied their way around and women manipulated passively. Perhaps a clear cultural line. A behavior I hoped not to face often in my new world.

However, I was used to all her games and didn't budge. I explained that her discomfort was not my intention, and if being alone on the bus frightened her, I would stay on the bus.

"No, unlike your relationship with this girl, staying on the bus alone won't frighten me. I will stay on the bus. Your father will be at the station to pick me up. And if he doesn't show up, I can get a taxi," she replied. It was kind of her to end it there and not to make a big deal about it. She knew well that she could manipulate my conscience with heavy guilt and force me to stay.

The bus stopped. With a quick farewell to her, I grabbed my bag and got off.

The excitement of visiting Neilu and breathing the fresh air of an early morning in a new city energized me. I inhaled a large gulp of air and waved good-bye to my mother, who was sitting in my seat by the window as the bus drove away.

Persepolis

8

ISFAHAN

> *We do not admire the man of timid peace. We admire the man who embodies victorious effort; the man who never wrongs his neighbor, who is prompt to help a friend, but who has those virile qualities necessary to win in the stern strife of actual life.*
>
> — THEODORE ROOSEVELT, TWENTY-SIXTH PRESIDENT OF THE UNITED STATES OF AMERICA

The city of Isfahan was waking up. Some shopkeepers were washing and sweeping the front porches of their stores. Trucks were delivering fresh daily produce, and birds were jumping from the branches of one large tree to another in search of a morning meal.

The sense of independence gave me joy. Here I was in the big, famous, and historical city of Isfahan for the first time, all by myself. The city had appeared over and over in my readings from literature to history throughout my intellectual growth. Admired by historians, scientists, politicians, clerics, and poets alike, the city of Isfahan had always kept a special place in the heart of Iranians. Now it was my turn to discover it. I knew only one person in that city, Neilu. She didn't know I was there. I had kept it a surprise.

The first order of business was to secure a hotel room for myself. However, I couldn't wait to hear her voice. It was about 7:30 a.m. when I called her from a public phone. She was renting a room from a family near her school. A woman answered the phone, I spoke slowly and in a low tone to prevent nervous trembling.

The sound of slippers shuffling on a hard floor faded out. A few moments later, Neilu's sleepy "hello," like a sought-after melody, caressed my ears. Her voice sent shivers through my body. My heart was pounding loud with excitement. "Hi. It's Vahid."

Her voice went to a higher pitch. She wasn't expecting my call, as I wanted my visit to be a surprise to her. But the unusual timing of the call worried her immediately. After a moment of pause, not knowing where I was, she asked if I was all right.

"Oh, yes. Can you guess where I am calling from?"

"I don't know, on a street somewhere near your house? I hear the sound of traffic."

"Yes, I'm on a street but not in Tehran. I'm in Isfahan!"

Her excitement transmitted through the phone line. I closed my eyes and enjoyed the image of a thrilled Neilu. We decided to meet around noon at the main gate of the university.

I loved making her happy with surprises. Her reserved lifestyle, imposed by her need to control and plan everything, didn't allow for much spontaneity. She had a loving mother and a kind and devoted aunt who lived with them. But the divorce, departure, and eventual remarrying of her father had taken a toll on her life. I wasn't sure if it was her military father, or lack of a father, that made her such a tough, independent woman on the surface, and such a vulnerable, sensitive, and a delicate person inside.

I closed my eyes again and let my imagination take me to her. I saw her serious and controlled face first, and then a slow hint of a smile with a twinkle in her eyes.

A heavy knock on the telephone booth shattered my daydream. The man outside, who was waiting to use the phone, lost his patience when he saw me closing my eyes while holding the receiver. I hung up the phone, opened the folding door of the telephone booth, and exited with a sheepish smile and an apology.

Soon, I located a small hotel with vacancy. A few moments later, I turned the brass key in the lock and opened the door to my room. It was a small, windowless space, but I entered with joy as this was the first room that I had obtained with my own funds, independent of my parents, relatives, or friends. I inhaled deeply and jumped onto the bed. I had time to rest.

Three hours later, at the university's front gate, the presence of soldiers in full battle fatigues and carrying automatic weapons were chilling reminders of the turbulent time. The military was not there to fight the foreign enemies of the nation or to protect the students, but to contain students who dared to voice their opinions in forms of strikes or demonstrations.

The guards did not let me in. I waited outside for Neilu's arrival. A few minutes later, a tap on my shoulder turned me around and there she was standing with a big smile. Her lush and long jet-black hair framed her narrow face perfectly. Her dark black eyes displayed twinkles of joy. The desire for a big hug and many kisses was strong, but our culture forbade such a display. I smiled and we briefly held hands. We decided to go to the campus cafeteria for lunch. She cleared me through the gates.

Happy to see each other, we held hands on the walk toward the cafeteria. The path was a pleasant road lined by large Plane trees forming a long canopy protecting pedestrians from the hot, direct sun of Isfahan.

She asked about the occasion for the unannounced visit. Once I explained, intrigued by the coincidence, she said that she had been in Shiraz two weeks prior. And if she had known I was coming, perhaps she could have arranged to meet me there. She added that her meeting with Farhad in Shiraz was enjoyable.

Farhad? She met with Farhad in Shiraz? I couldn't help but repeat his name in disbelief. She confirmed it, but her eyes weren't looking at me. Rather, she was staring at the ground. I felt a twinge in my chest.

Something didn't seem right.

"What did you guys do?"

"Talked, he played his guitar. I filed his right-hand nails and showed him how to do it correctly," she explained.

My immediate reaction was to inform her that he had been playing classical guitar for several years and knew how to file his nails.

"He asked for it. He's such a silly boy." She smiled, seeming to be reminiscing about her time in Shiraz with Farhad and ignoring my comment and my feelings about the matter.

Her confession bothered me. I let her hand go. I felt hot and confused. Farhad knew that Neilu and I were together. What was he doing, another test? What had really happened in Shiraz between those two? I pictured them alone in his room and shivered.

"I play classical guitar too. How come you never filed my nails?"

"You never asked!" she replied playfully, looking at me with her big smile.

A motorcycle was heading toward us from the opposite direction on the same road we were walking. There were two men riding it. As a precautionary move, I switched sides with Neilu and put myself between her and the oncoming motorcycle. Learning to be vigilant and suspicious of strangers had become second to nature for me. It was a necessity for survival in a crowded metropolitan city such as Tehran.

When they came near, the driver swerved toward us. In a rapid movement, the passenger riding on the back of the motorcycle, extended his left arm in an attempt to hit me with a shiny object. I bent away from him in an automatic reaction to avoid the shiny object. Then I felt a strange sensation on my face. Immediately, I touched my face. It was wet.

I turned back toward the motorcycle and saw the passenger was turned around and watching me. Then he shouted, "Traitor!" I moved to chase them, but Neilu thrust out her arm to stop my attempt to run after them.

"Did you get hit? Are you okay?" Neilu exclaimed.

"He spat at me!" I answered.

"Are you hurt?" Neilu asked, raising her voice.

I checked and noticed that my shirt was cut. "No! But he cut my shirt. Why did you stop me?"

"Just ignore them! You couldn't catch them anyway."

Angrily, I retorted if it wasn't for my fast reflex, I could've been cut by his knife. I wiped my face with my sleeve.

"There is no use going after them. It could also be a trap to lure you to an ambush. They are very strong on the campus." For the first time, I saw her worried face.

I asked if she knew them or had seen them in the school before. She surmised from their appearance that they looked like members of the conservative Muslim student group, which was becoming a strong force in the student movements on the campus. She thought that was a warning to us.

Not familiar with the culture of large university campuses, I wasn't clear what she meant by *warning*. "Warning about what? What do they know about us?"

"Probably they didn't like what you are wearing, or that we were holding hands," she answered like an expert on the subject, but still holding my hand firmly. I enjoyed her strong grip. It felt as if she wanted me to stay close to her.

What was wrong with what I was wearing? I stopped and glanced at my attire, a bright orange shirt, tight blue jeans and a pair of bright blue sneakers that I bought from England the year before.

She encouraged me to continue our walk toward the cafeteria by putting her arm around me and pulling. "You look like what they call a 'West-toxicated' person. That's why he called you a traitor. West-toxicated people are—"

"I know what that West-toxicated label is about. I just can't believe how aggressive those conservatives have become. God have mercy on us if they get the majority of power in the future government. They will take us back to the Stone Age. Intimidation and bullying are not the way to shape people's opinions and behavior. It's a prescription for hatred and despair."

"I know. I know what they are about. They want women to cover themselves and become second-class humans, not much higher than slaves."

I detected anger and irritation in her reply. But she quickly changed her tone and assured me that Iran will never go back to a primitive status of oppressing women and imposing hardcore religious orders. To her, it was impossible to even imagine it. She saw the future as a more collaborative and progressive form of government. Listening to her added more concern to my nerve-wracked state. She was a progressive and independent girl. I questioned how she was coping with those clowns and asked if they were giving her a hard time in the school.

"I just ignore them and don't engage them. They are like a bunch of brain-washed people. Logic evades them," she replied and pointed her right index finger toward a building. "Here is the cafeteria."

The place looked melancholy to me. A large concrete building with a few broken windows and many revolutionary slogans sprayed all over the outer walls. I asked if she knew what happened there.

Again, like an expert, she explained that the smaller holes were from bullets and tear gas canisters that security forces shot. The big ones were from students throwing chairs to jump out of windows, evading arrest. Apparently, there had been a demonstration there a few days prior.

It was discouraging and sad to witness what our higher education institutions had become. I suggested we dine in a nice restaurant away from the university, not wanting to spend any more time in such an atmosphere.

She agreed on the condition that I concede to the fact that she was not running away or hiding from anyone. I agreed.

She gave me a smile, and that twinkle I so adored appeared in her eyes again. Immediately, she suggested that we go to *Naghsh-e Jahan* Square, the second largest square in the world.

The anticipation of seeing such an important historical place improved my mood. We picked up our pace. Outside the campus, we stopped a taxi and jumped in.

Naghsh-e Jahan Square, meaning "image of the world," was built during the reign of the *Safavid* Dynasty in the sixteenth century. The west side of it is called, *Ahli Qapu*.

Neilu asked, "Did you know that *Ahli Qapu* means Exalted Port?" I shook my head.

She went ahead and explained that the name was chosen by the

Safavid dynasty to rival the Ottoman Empire's celebrated court's name. The great monarch used to entertain noble visitors there. She further explained that archeologists found artifacts dating back to the Stone Age in Isfahan.

"This is such a fascinating city. It has history, culture, art, modernity, and a great climate," I said.

Neilu turned her head toward me and stared at me. Her look was different. I saw playfulness and joy in it. When I asked the reason for the stare, she replied, "I think you should stay."

"You mean stay here in Isfahan?"

"No, silly, here in Iran. You get so excited about history and culture. You can get your master's here and even your PhD if you want."

It was intriguing that she was asking me to stay. I turned my head around and looked out the taxi's window in silence. For the first time, I didn't immediately react by opposing the idea.

She tapped my elbow with hers. I turned around and saw just a slight smile on her beautiful face, but her eyes were showing a bigger, playful smile.

"You said modernity. What do you mean by that? This is not a modern city! Far from it. It's a historical city."

It was no secret that many Westerners lived and worked in Isfahan as professors, military advisors, teachers, and employees of foreign companies such as Bell Helicopters, which had over a thousand employees just in the city of Isfahan. I explained that in my view these Westerners had brought with them the elements of modernity.

"That is not called modernity, my dear. Modernity usually refers to the infrastructure, technology, and architecture."

"Well, I call that modernization. To me, the term 'modernity' has much more significance. It questions tradition and prioritizes individualism, freedom, and equality. It includes a social climate that allows easy and free access to modern thought, culture, and way of living. Westerners represent modernity to me. Not because they have the latest technology or modern infrastructures in their own country, but rather their thoughts, what they believe and the way they see the world is refreshing, and it represents openness and that is modern to me."

"Even their traditionalists?" Neilu asked.

"Yes, even them. They may be traditionalists in one aspect of their thoughts, but in general, they believe in democracy, respect individual liberties and human rights. But most importantly, it is their collective hunger to push the boundaries in all aspects of their lives that make them progressive. To have tens of thousands of them in this city, so easily accessible, is wonderful and modern to me."

Neilu raised her narrow, black eyebrows and claimed that the discussion was getting real heavy.

My stomach gurgled. It was embarrassing, but it helped to change the subject to food. I rubbed my belly and said, "All this talk of modernity is making me hungry for some traditional food. What about a restaurant that serves *ahbgoosht*?"

"Wow, what a departure! I thought after all that talk, you would ask for a Western meal like hamburger or pizza! But, you love to keep me off balance, don't you?"

Her teasing words and smile were a welcome sign of relief from any possible tension. She knew of a traditional restaurant in *Naghsh-i Jahan* Square. She extended her long, slim neck to look outside my window in search of the restaurant. "By the way, there are a lot of Russians and Eastern Europeans here too. They are oppressed behind the Iron Curtain and don't have any of the stuff you said earlier about freedom." She pointed as we just arrived at our destination. She ordered the taxi driver to stop.

There was no need to argue with her. As I stepped out of the taxi, the vastness of the square overwhelmed me. The view was breath taking. The area was an incredible rectangle easily half a kilometer long and nearly one-sixth kilometer wide. In the middle was a large park and a long rectangular turquoise pool with multiple water fountains in the center and on the sides displaying a festive water show. Surrounding the park were buildings of magnificent seventeenth century architecture consisting of mosques, royal palaces, glorious domes, minarets, bazaars, shops, restaurants, and hotels.

I was mesmerized. It would take weeks to explore it all.

Neilu chuckled, pointed to my torn shirt, and warned me that the restaurant would not allow me to enter with such clothing. The tear was so large that I couldn't hide it. So, I rushed to a nearby souvenir shop. A few minutes later, I walked out wearing a khaki paisley print shirt, a specialty design of the Isfahan region.

Neilu tried but couldn't hold her explosion of laughter. With her whole body shaking, she said, "Now you look like a tourist! I don't know which look is funnier—you as a victim of a thug attack or you as a tourist!"

Laughing, she pointed her hand toward the path to the restaurant. "Go ahead. Tourists first."

In the restaurant, my eyes took a few moments to adjust to the darkness inside. The rays of sunlight sneaking through the painted glass windows were delightful helpers for illuminating the space. The large brick ceiling was low with many small, inverted domes. The smell of burning incense mixed with the fragrances of Persian food welcomed visitors to a traditional Middle Eastern setting. Large cushions were placed along the walls and on the floor for customers to sit on. Customers who preferred to use western seats could use tables and chairs in the center of the restaurant. A small water fountain in the middle of the restaurant added charm to the atmosphere. The tablecloths were the handmade, paisley print design similar to my new shirt.

We sat on the cushions, folded our knees and studied the menu. After a few moments, I spotted my favorite food, Persian lamb stew, on the menu. Neilu lifted her eyebrows upward and made a comment about how usually people don't order *ahbgoosht* in a restaurant unless they are tourists.

"Well, I am wearing a tourist shirt so I may as well order tourists' food. Did you know, in ancient Persia, *ahbgoosht* was an easy traveling food and shepherds would take a pot of the tasty lamb stew into the fields with them?"

Neilu was not amused. Since *ahbgoosht* is also considered a blue-collar food, I asked her if she was worried about her social status—sitting next to a guy who ordered this traditional stew.

She thought I was being ridiculous about the social status. Claiming that I like modernity, yet ordering the most traditional food, in her opinion, was some kind of erratic behavior.

To me, the most delicious part of *ahbgoosht* was the *goosht-koobideh* which means pounded lamb. But it isn't just meat. The lamb is mixed and pounded with tomato, potato, garbanzo beans, white beans, onions and spices. The pounding part starts after the juice is separated. The juice is either eaten like a soup or with pieces of bread thrown in the bowl, soaked and then scooped out and eaten with a spoon. The remaining ingredients stay in a metal bowl. The lamb is so tender that it easily mixes with the other cooked ingredients to create a delicious mash that is eaten with bread.

"My dear, tasty food is good no matter what you believe. I like to be free of these chains," I said.

She placed her fork down on the plate and looked at me. "What chains?"

"All the unwritten, unproductive codes that we tie ourselves into in this society are chains."

She asked if the chain had a name and went back to preparing her appetizer, a piece of flat bread and feta cheese. Then she gave me a look with a cute spark in her eyes and her special undetectable smidgen of a smile that only people who knew her could see.

Understanding her interest in continuing the dialogue, I played her game. "I call this the protocol chain. Why should I feel bad that I like *ahbgoosht*, a food that is loved by most hard-working people, the working class, or the proletariats, as some of your college friends may say? I'm trying to rid myself of these chains."

"Oh, so we are socialists during lunch time! By the way, communists are not my friends," she continued, still in a teasing tone.

I slipped a bite of feta cheese and bread from the appetizer plate in my mouth. Still upset from the earlier incident, I reminded her that the idiots who spat on me and tried to knife me earlier that morning did it because they thought my clothes betrayed our culture and religious values. To them, I had sold myself to the West. Yet, they had enslaved themselves with a rigid belief, chains that will cause their demise. History has repeatedly reminded us of this truth.

The waiter brought our main courses and set it before us with a display of fine presentation.

Neilu playfully ordered me to stop talking and eat my food.

Traditional folk music was playing softly in the background. I took Neilu's hand and covered it with both my hands, then praised her patience with my ongoing rant.

She squeezed my hand then pulled hers away and started eating her meal. I enjoyed her playful behavior. On rare occasions, when she laughed, her whole body would move. Her smiles were short lived and often dissipated into a more serious face. But that day she was happy, an unusual occurrence in her lonesome life. It wasn't that she didn't know anyone. On the contrary, she had a lot of acquaintances, including many Americans and Europeans, but I never saw or heard of anyone she called friend. That day, we ate, talked, laughed, and let the jovial atmosphere take us away, momentarily, from the unpredictable political storm that was forming.

The next early morning, on a bus to Tehran, the sunrise caught my gaze and my thoughts began rambling over my recent impressions of Shiraz and Isfahan. A warm sense of belonging enveloped me momentarily, until my mind reeled over the image of the young man's lifeless body tossed in the truck. How about him? How about his aspirations and hopes? He is also part of my heritage. His death and the deaths of hundreds or possibly thousands like him was forming a history that would shape my future heritage. Did I want it? Can a man change his tribe? And by doing so, will his future become a new history for his clan? Is it allowed? Do we form the history, or is it the history that forms us?

Then the appalling images of the motorcyclist who spat on me took the place of the dead young man. And then, his knife. What would have happened if his knife had cut me? What about his hopes and aspirations? Is his reality going to be the future of Iranian society? Would I, or *could* I, make a difference if I stayed and became one link in a chain of thousands of links? I shook my head rapidly to lose the images. My body shivered with the thought of staying in Iran.

The surviving branches are the ones that can bend. It was only a few days prior that the man in the Persepolis ruins spoke those words. But his voice kept echoing in my head. She had said, *stay*. I chuckled at the humorous word play my mind did with Neilu's voice. *Stay and make a future with me.* If I could decode her encrypted message, would I find that sentence? Does she want me to stay and make a future with her? Very tempting, but, what about her curious visit to Shiraz and meeting with Farhad? He knew I had strong feelings for her. Do I need to worry about them?

As the bus traveled through the central desert, making its way to Tehran, I turned my head to the left and let my eyes gaze toward the west. My thoughts traveled to America, the land on which I was about to bet my future.

City of Isfahan

Naghsh-e Jahan Square

9

PASSPORTS

> 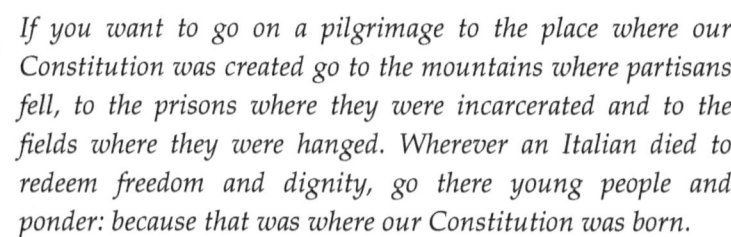*If you want to go on a pilgrimage to the place where our Constitution was created go to the mountains where partisans fell, to the prisons where they were incarcerated and to the fields where they were hanged. Wherever an Italian died to redeem freedom and dignity, go there young people and ponder: because that was where our Constitution was born.*
>
> — Piero Calamandrei, excerpt from speech to the young held at the Humane Society Milan, (January 1955)

To others it may have looked like another miserable, late fall morning, with trees mostly naked, a sky covered with dark clouds, and the air frigid—all sad excuses for ingredients of a day.

However, that day was different for me. It was a day that could potentially take me significantly closer to getting out of the hell of my life in Tehran in 1978. The difficulties were not just political oppressions or continuous social unrest, it was the entire fabric of social culture.

It was the culture of favoritism, passive-aggressive behaviors, systematic use of intimidation, and the use of fear to impose its values.

The second hand of a large round clock on the wall of our living room moved ever so slowly. Seated on the couch, staring at the clock hanging above our red color TV, I literally counted the seconds awaiting the arrival of my friend Davud.

It was his turn to drive that day. We were going to the Passport Bureau, the central organization for processing all such matters, to pick up our passports. This was a crucial step to finalizing my long ordeal of getting out of Tehran.

The sound of the door buzzer jolted me off the couch. I grabbed up the intercom handset. It was Davud. My briefcase stood ready on top of the coffee table. I grabbed it and rushed toward the door.

But alas, my mother had heard the buzzer. She yelled from the kitchen, asking if I was leaving.

"Momon, I'm in a rush. Davud is waiting in the car and we're late. I have to pick up my passport, and I will be back in the afternoon." I replied.

I could hear the annoyance I felt in my tone. And I felt sorry about it. But my resentment was driven by the fact that at the age of twenty one, I still had to explain to her where I was going, why, and when I would be back. Like a schoolboy. In the back of my mind, I knew her concerns were legitimate, as the time was full of uncertainty and turmoil. People were disappearing or ending up in hospitals with bullet wounds. But still, it agitated me.

She rushed out of the kitchen and asked if I'd return for lunch. Bothered by her question, as it slowed me down, my eyes tangled with her eyes to reply. My heart dropped. Her striking, almond shaped eyes were scanning my face and I saw sadness there, as if it were the last time she would ever see me.

I lowered my eyes out of respect for her and replied, "No, I will be back in the afternoon."

"Then don't skip lunch. Eat a good meal somewhere. You are such a skinny boy. May God protect you. *Khodahafez*, good-bye."

We were not a hugging or kissing family. But her expressive eyes revealed her emotions explicitly to me. Her gaze gave me the sensation of a loving embrace. She stood there in the hallway and watched me rushing out the door. I jumped down the five short steps and opened our heavy metal and glass door to the street.

The smell of exhaust fumes hit me the moment I stepped out onto our short street. I could easily hear the honks and beeps of car horns coming from nearby roads with the usual accompaniment of the low hum of a bustling metropolis.

Oddly, Davud's dark gray sedan struck me as the color of our times, dull and dirty. I never liked the color of his car. Nevertheless, I got in and shook his meaty hand. His quick, firm handshake gave me a warm feeling of a determined and strong friend. Just the right kind of a person to have beside you when you don't know what the next hour may bring.

The traffic was unusually heavy on the main road. We were both excited and nervous. The excitement was because our passports were ready, a major step toward achieving our goal. The past few months had been long and difficult. Every small step of progress was a result of many attempts and setbacks. Unstable political situations, long strikes of public organizations, and rapid changes to every aspect of life were making daily life unbearable. Especially to anxious people like me and Davud, whose dreams of a future free of the heavy yoke of oppression were on the line.

Our nervousness was due to the uncertainty of life in our city. Soldiers were everywhere, crowds of demonstrators could pop-up on any corner. You would never know what hit you—rocks from demonstrators, bullets from soldiers, or with any luck, bird droppings which would be considered a good omen!

The only thrill people had was in the dynamics of the change. The political chaos brought relative openness of the press, for example. Or gave ordinary people such as taxi drivers, bakers, and shopkeepers the chance to voice their opinions freely without fear of reprisal. Just a hint of the possibility of freedom in a nation that was oppressed for thousands of years felt like the sweet fragrance of spring flowers after a hard winter.

Davud expressed his frustration with the traffic by cussing. I shifted in my seat. It was an untimely gridlock for us. Davud cranked up the stereo. But after a few minutes of sitting still, I turned the music down and asked him to tell me about the nightlife in the big hotel where he worked.

Davud was a food and beverage supervisor for the room service of the Sheraton Hotel in Tehran. Sheraton was among the top luxury hotels in Tehran, hosting many international clients. According to his stories, life from midnight to morning in a large international hotel was full of adventures. His stories, some erotic, some funny, seemed more like life on another planet. Who knew how much of it was true, but, they were entertaining.

Music, jokes, and stories were good only for the first half an hour. There were no signs of the traffic opening up and time was flying. A fog of nervousness settled on us. I looked at Davud's face, his big fish-like eyes were getting bigger and rounder. His sad gaze to the horizon bothered me. It gave me the feeling of helplessness and despair, when only minutes before his presence instilled confidence and hope.

In a quick move, he turned off the music and rolled down his window. I rolled down my window too.

"Listen!" Davud said. "Do you hear that?"

The cracking of multiple gunshots and some rapid firing of automatic weapons in the far distance broke through the noise of the traffic. Sadly, this was not unusual, and I was nervous, but not scared. Yet.

Every morning, as a new routine in our daily lives, we listened to the radio announcements for any road closures or planned demonstrations. That day, the radio had not announced any particular problem for that part of the town.

Time was not our friend. There was not much flexibility left for coping with long delays in getting our passports. Rumors about rapidly deteriorating political conditions and the fall of the government were getting stronger every day.

"I know what it is, I don't need a radio to tell me," Davud said, his red face displayed anger with failure of accuracy of Tehran's radio reporters.

Getting stuck in traffic jams caused by conflicts between security forces and the demonstrators was dangerous. Soldiers, flooded by adrenalin, typically would chase demonstrators, shooting and hitting them with absolutely no regard for the life of people who got caught in between.

Davud turned his face toward me and whispered, "Look, if I get hit by bullets, you take over the wheel and take me straight to the children's hospital where my father works. I will take you there if you get shot too. My father can treat us without reporting it to the authorities."

I nodded my head in acceptance. I knew the address. His father did not have a surgery room in that clinic, but if the wound was not really serious, he could handle it. Doctors were ordered by the government not to treat any gunshot wounds without permission. Civilians had to pay a one thousand *toman* fine (about $320 in 1978) for the removal of each bullet, whether alive or dead. Hospitals were not to release wounded or dead bodies until the fine was paid and interrogation of the family had been completed.

I had a lot of respect for Davud's father. When he was a young doctor, despite having a family with small kids, he chose to serve in the nomadic villages. It's admirable to provide medical care to people with little or no money, when he could have easily stayed in a big city and moved up in the world.

Davud's breathing became heavier and his puffy, round eyes wider. He accelerated the car with sudden and rapid, forward and backward movements. He repeated it several times, back and forth, back and forth.

I held tight to the door handle and objected to his erratic maneuvering. The last thing we needed to delay us forever was an accident.

Heavily engaged in his maneuvering he said, "I'm not going to sit here and wait for the bullets to find me."

With five short reverse and forward motions, he expertly managed to make a real tight U turn and drove on to the northbound road, the opposite direction of the gunfire. A few cars coming at us had to swerve and honked their horns announcing their dislike of Davud's dangerous maneuvers.

"The new plan is to go north about a mile, then turn east on

Shahreza Avenue and use another road to get to the passport building, getting us out of this mess," Davud explained.

It actually felt good to move. Getting the passport was not the last step in our process, but it was an important one. Once we had our passports, we could apply for a visa from the American consulate. Obtaining a visa was not easy either. Iran's unstable political situation had created a huge rush to exit Iran. Lines were getting longer and the approval processes were becoming more difficult.

He turned right into *Shahreza* Avenue and then slammed on the brakes and came to a quick stop.

We looked at each other in disbelief. The large, four-lane street was empty. We had never seen it like that before. Where were all the cars and people?

Davud shook his head. "I have a bad feeling about this. What if the road is closed on the other side of the bridge?"

There was a one-way bridge about two hundred meters ahead us. The bridge was built to provide a continuous flow of eastward traffic over many streets. The steep angle of ascent was blocking our view of the other side. We could only see up to the crest of the bridge. The height of the bridge must have been around seventeen meters.

I sat up in my seat. We had to quickly decide. There would be no way of returning once we were on that bridge.

Davud wasn't moving. He had his two hands on the wheel and his eyes fixed on the road ahead. A few moments of silence felt like hours. Time was running out. Strikes were spreading like a cancer. There were no telling what group would go on strike next. The passport organization's employees strike could delay our plans for weeks or months. We must proceed. Davud gave me a look asking what to do.

"We have lost so much time already. Let's go on. Maybe we'll get lucky. Go, go!" I gave him the nod.

He turned his head and his eyes back toward the road. With a determined look and both hands firmly gripping the wheel, he inhaled deeply and sped the car forward.

Climbing the bridge, we were anxious to see what was on the other side. There were no cars ahead of us. It was eerie to be the only car on a normally busy street. Davud shifted the gear to a lower gear for more power on the uphill climb. We were fast approaching the crest of the bridge.

Multiple gun shots cracked the air as we reached the top.

"Oh my God!" we both screamed, and he stopped the car.

At the bottom of the bridge, about hundred meters ahead of us, was a large four lane traffic circle. A large statue surrounded by a small park was in the center of the circle. What we saw was a mayhem of tanks, military vehicles, cars, and many soldiers chasing and shooting hundreds of people on the run.

We looked at each other. We both knew what needed to be done. I gave him a nod. He inhaled visibly and proceeded driving downhill. Once we cleared the bridge and were on the street, he maneuvered expertly between cars, people, and tanks. There were no rules. It was chaotic. People, vehicles, and bullets were coming from every direction.

Sitting on the edge of my seat, I was poised and ready to take the wheel in the case Davud got hit by a bullet. In my mind, I quickly mapped the direction to his father's clinic, not too far away. He was a solid man and a trustworthy doctor.

BOOM!

A man angrily hit the hood of the car with his fists and cussed. Davud maneuvered away from him. A moment later, someone yanked the passenger side's door handle of the car and tried to get in the car. But it was locked. He hit the window and shouted, "Let me in. Help me escape!" Davud maneuvered away from him too. We couldn't let him in the car. The moment we would open the car door many others would flood in. It could also bring in a downpour of bullets and other troubles. Our mission was clear. We were to focus on getting to the passport office.

My heart was beating out of my chest. I thought about my mother and the look in her eyes. Maybe I should have paid more attention to it—to her motherly instincts. Would it really be the last time she laid eyes on me?

"There!" I shouted at Davud and pointed to a small opening a few meters ahead of us to the left. I asked him to turn into that alley. It seemed to be our ticket out of that mess.

Davud acknowledged my directions and turned the car toward the alley. At that moment, a few men jumped in front of the car and signaled us to stop. But Davud didn't stop. He continued driving the car slowly, heading into the ally. The men hovered over the car, striking the hood and yelling.

"We have an injured man. Stop!" they cried.

At that moment, we saw two men emerge from behind one of the other men. One was holding a man who was barely able to stand. Davud drove the car steadily forward but very slowly. Suddenly a man hit the front window with his bloody hand, smudging a bloody tracing on the glass. "STOP! Didn't you hear? We have an injured man! Open the door!"

Reacting to the sudden bloody exposition, I jumped in my seat and looked at Davud. His face was pale and hands were gripping the wheel tight.

"We must help him," I said.

He nodded and stopped the car. I reached and unlocked the back door. A man jumped in the back of the car and then very carefully he and another man slid the injured man into the back seat. The injured man was screaming. As soon as the third man got in the back he shouted, "Go! Take us to a hospital! Fast!"

Davud turned on the head lights and the flashing hazard lights and with his hand on the horn he weaved his way among people and other moving things. I looked back and checked on the injured man. He was bleeding from his left lower abdomen and was loudly moaning. The other two men were applying pressure to the wound trying to slow the bleeding.

"Did he get hit by a bullet?" I asked.

"Yes, brother, can you believe these criminals?" said a man sitting to the right of the injured man.

The other one cut him off. "Damn these soldiers, they are supposed to fight the enemies of our country, not shoot us, the citizens!" He had a Turkish accent from Azerbaijan province northwest of Iran, next to Turkey. Davud's parents were from the same region, and Davud himself was fluent in that dialect.

The injured man screamed. One of the men said something to him in Turkish. I looked at Davud to check his reaction. He took a quick glance at them through the rearview mirror.

I asked quietly if he was taking them to his father's clinic. He shook his head and, while maneuvering the car, said that he was taking them to the nearby hospital two blocks from there. Every time he swerved, the loud cry of the injured man filled the car. The man who held the injured in his arms was sobbing and once a while saying something in Turkish. I asked him if the wounded man was related to him and he said, "Brother, he is my dear younger brother." He then broke out again and kissed the head of his brother. The smell of blood and sweat was overwhelming inside the car.

Davud finally turned into the street where the hospital was located. The car stopped and he froze.

A sea of people covering the entire street was moving toward us. A man in the back seat shouted with excitement, *"Allah-O-Akbar, Allah-O-Akbar,* praise the Lord." He rolled down the window on his side and pushed out half his body, swinging his arms and waving his bloody hands and continued shouting, *"Allah-O-Akbar."* The other man also rolled down his window and waved his one free hand that was drenched in blood, screaming *"Allah-O-Akbar."*

People on the street saw us and some pointed at us, repeating, *"Allah-O-Akbar."* Noticing the blood and the injured man in the back of the car, the crowd opened a path for us to pass, just like the Red Sea parted for Moses.

I couldn't contain myself any longer; the magnitude of the moment besieged my entire self. I was surrounded by hundreds if not thousands of people praising God in unison chants, for giving them the courage to fight a powerful and brutal regime. While busy with chanting, the crowd opened a path for the injured comrade to reach a medical facility. Emotion overwhelmed me. I got up, turned back, covered my hands with the injured man's blood and thrust myself out of my window shouting as loud as my lungs could handle *"Allah-O-Akbar, Allah-O- Akbar!* Yes, open the road brothers, we have a wounded man."

Davud slowly drove through the opened passage, the hyperexcited crowd chanting and peeking into the car to see the wounded man. A few minutes later, we arrived at the hospital's emergency entrance. I jumped out and opened the door. A couple other men rushed to our help and swiftly moved the injured man into the hospital.

Davud, holding the wheel, was ready to depart. He leaned over onto the passenger side, and through the opened door, shouted at me, "Don't go anywhere. We have to leave immediately."

"I want to wash the blood off my hands and get a rag to clean your car!"

"Forget it. We have to leave now, before the security forces storm this place!"

After a quick scan of the area, I saw a faucet outside the hospital's walls. I rushed to it and washed my hands hurriedly. Then, I took a handkerchief with my initials on it, which my mother had made for me, out of my pocket, soaked it with water, and dashed back to the car.

The door on the passenger side of the car wasn't completely shut when Davud stepped on the accelerator. The car's tires spun, and with a small burnout we drove out of the hospital's driveway and away from the mob.

He checked the rearview mirror several times as he drove away. I cleaned the blood from the windows and back seats with my soaked handkerchief as he drove us away from all that craziness.

About fifteen minutes later we finally arrived at the passport building, parked the car, and entered the building. The building was full of people waiting in several lines. Shaken from the experience, I focused on finding the right office to pick up our passport.

Davud, however, was more upset about the crowd in the building. He made a comment that it seemed to him half of the city was out on the street yelling and the other half trying to get out of the country.

And maybe he was right. There were long lines at every clerical window. The staff seemed overwhelmed. Overall, feelings of uneasiness and anxiety were everywhere.

Usually, Iranian people make the best out of the long lines with jokes and fun stories. Not that day. Our line was moving very slowly.

Quietly, we inched our way forward.

"There are two types of people here," Davud whispered in my ears. "The ones who are in the line, anxiously getting closer to their final steps toward the great escape. And then, there are the ones who are stuck behind those dreaded windows, facilitating the escapees," he continued.

"It seems the second group is getting a dark joy out of making the first group suffer. Ingeniously, they come up with new twists and road blocks to delay the process," I replied.

He mimed to my sarcastic comment about the clerks' revenge on each other.

We chuckled, not maliciously, of course, but in an attempt to reduce the boredom of waiting.

What seemed like hours later, we finally collected our passports without any further incident. Pleased with this progress, I tossed my passport into my briefcase and wrapped my blood-crusted fingers in a tight grip around the handle.

No one was going to take that briefcase away from me.

10

MUSIC GROUP

> *So long as the people do not care to exercise their freedom, those who wish to tyrannize will do so; for tyrants are active and ardent, and will devote themselves in the name of any number of gods, religious and otherwise, to put shackles upon sleeping men.*
>
> — Voltaire, Francois Marie Arouet (1694-1778)

The telephone rang five times before I answered it. I relished the luxury of not having to race my mother to the phone. She was out visiting her cousin for a "strategy meeting." Her cousin's son, a freshman in the prestigious Meli University in the north of Tehran, had shown up earlier that day drenched in blood. It wasn't his blood, but he had been badly bruised. The blood belonged to a couple of his friends who were bludgeoned by the campus police during a protest.

I picked up the receiver. The girl on the other side of the line said she was Leila. I repeated her name in disbelief. Hers was a voice from the past. She had been my apprentice and was now the new head of the Student Music Appreciation Group in my former college.

Reminiscing those days, brought a smile to my face. The last time I spoke with her was a month before my graduation. Her voice was an instant messenger of good feelings about one of my greatest achievements in college--my burgeoning, and now sprawling, Student Music Appreciation Group movement.

In her typical soft and polite manner, she started with the customary inquiries. She asked about the status of my quest for study abroad.

"It's going too slow to my liking," I replied, and then explained how the postal workers' strike had slowed the process. Further, I clarified, that despite taking the TOEFL exam for the second time, I was considering applying to a language school in the U.S to speed up the process. It was my plan B, in the case postal service never delivered (or lost) my test results. At that point in time, this seemed like a strong possibility.

She was politely quiet on the other end of the line while I rambled. A few moments later, I realized that she really didn't want to hear about my process in such a detail. She called because she needed something. I stopped talking about myself and asked how I could be of assistance.

After a bit more polite small talk, she revealed that her call was about an urgent matter. I noted the change in her tone—she sounded stressed.

I wondered if her call was about the music group.

I remembered vividly what a difficult and complicated task it had been to convince the college president to allow me to form a music appreciation group two years prior. The school's administration had become wary of strong anti-government sentiments among the students. My college had strong ties to the Pahlavi ruling family. Specifically, the college president was proud of her close relationship with the queen and did not want any student group jeopardizing it. Clubs such as the poetry club, literature groups, and similar organizations were deviating from their original purpose and becoming more political, putting up posters and other displays of antigovernment sentiments.

Leila began to tell me about the recent meeting of all the student club leaders. Apparently, Mr. Abaassian, the head of the Muslim Students' Revolutionary Group of our college, was dismissive of the Music Appreciation Group and called for the dismantling of it.

This news wasn't a shocking surprise for me. Often, conservative Muslims consider music nonproductive, and some even go so far as calling it a work of evil. However, I wanted to hear it from Leila when I asked on what grounds he was dismissing the group.

She replied, "He claims music is un-Islamic and our group, the Music Appreciation Group, is not helping the revolution."

"That is absurd!" I replied, disgusted with his attitude. "Perhaps he wasn't around two years ago when our group, for the first time, changed the political climate of the very college that he is in."

The fact that we were the first group that could successfully put up posters with revolutionary sentiments across the campus did not change his mind, she explained. Even after repeated reminders, that it was our club's activities that inspired and led the other groups to become more creative in expressing their political opinions, did not change his course either. In fact, she said, he didn't want to meet with her anymore. She asked if I would be willing to meet with him.

Interesting notion, I thought. Since I wasn't a student there anymore, I wondered under what capacity she wanted me to function in that meeting. And why didn't he want to meet with her? I decided to ask her rather than keep wondering.

"I don't exactly know. Maybe because I'm a woman, or perhaps he thinks music is not relevant. That's why I think as the founder of the group, you could articulate the ideology of the group better than any of us," she replied.

As the founder. That comment felt good to hear. A compliment to what I had accomplished, however non-intended perhaps; nevertheless, it sat well with me. I also liked the challenge. We needed to educate people like him any chance we got. I agreed with her to go ahead and set up the meeting. I liked having a challenge and felt a surge of energy. Now, I had a mission to fulfill.

That phone call took me a few years back to my sophomore year.

My friends and I were all so proud of ourselves for putting the first group of posters on the campus walls. The posters were carefully created to display Beethoven, Chopin, and other composers' revolutionary thoughts.

Other student groups were banned from displaying any posters on the campus. In the name of music, we pushed the boundaries of promoting progressive thoughts in our college.

Soon, my small Music Appreciation Group became the largest student activity group in the college. In selecting the members of the group, I stayed open to all ideological and religious backgrounds. Later, to my amazement, I believed that the group's greatest achievement was that despite such diverse and, at times, conflicting backgrounds, the members remained interested in the group's goal of appreciating music as an intellectual endeavor. So much so, that it multiplied into many sub-groups. Students were actively listening, discovering, and discussing different genres of music and its impact on progressive thought.

The next morning, I was in my room in the basement, getting ready to leave for my meeting with Leila and Mr. Abaassian, when my mother shouted from the balcony, announcing a visitor for me.

"It's Hassan from the old neighborhood."

Hassan *laboo*? That was the only Hassan I knew who lived nearby. I hadn't seen him for over nine years! I couldn't imagine what he wanted.

The lower half of Hassan's face was covered with a red birthmark. He was called Hassan *laboo* by the kids in our neighborhood, because half of his face had the exact color of cooked beet, *laboo*, a popular dessert during the winter.

Hassan was sitting in the couch in our living room. He stood up when I entered the room. We shook hands and kissed each other's cheeks twice as the custom goes. His handshake was strong as always. He had turned into a muscular man about the same height as me. His complexion was darker than I remembered And his close-shaved head and face resembled a huge brown egg.

As part of the customary small talk, he complained about my lack of visits to the old neighborhood since moving to our new house.

That was true, I never went back to the old neighborhood. That place was run down and a thing of the past for me. It was there that Hassan, in a boxing game, had punched me in the face and I lost my two front teeth. It was there that I had my last bloody brawl with my older brother who was ten years senior to me. I never forgot seeing my mother on the floor, passed out, in her effort to bring the fight to an end. Not to mention the old pervert who tried to molest me when I was seven years old. I didn't care for that neighborhood.

My mother, being a proper Persian hostess, brought hot tea on a silver tray and served it to us. He took his tea and thanked my mother, with his eyes looking down, the conduct of a conservative Muslim.

In the interest of time, I decided to cut down in the traditional small talk and asked to what we owed the good fortune of his visit.

He glanced at me and his smile dissipated. He didn't say anything, but slowly put a sugar cube in his mouth, poured the hot tea into the saucer, blew it, took a sip, and then said, "After high school, I served two years in the military. At the end of my service, I worked in my father's carpet store in the bazaar. My father passed, and now I have my own store."

"God bless his soul," I said and looked down, searching for a way to get him to say why he was there. It was certainly not for the news of his father's passing as I had hardly known the man. I looked at my wristwatch. Time was flying away.

After a short pause, he said, "Look, Vahid, I'm here to ask you to join my group."

Wow. I didn't *expect* that, and inquired about more details.

He looked around. No one else was in the room. He slid closer to me and whispered, "Look, the times are changing. This regime is going to collapse. What do you think will happen when this government falls? Who do you think will take over? Who will be in power?"

I leaned back on the chair and crossed my legs. This wasn't a small matter, I had to be cautious in my response. "Hopefully, a democratic regime!" I answered.

He shook his head passionately in disagreement with me. "No, my friend. No. First it will be chaos, lawlessness, lots of looting and crime. Then we will prevail, brother. We!" He hit his chest as he finished the sentence.

I had forgotten about his fat lower lip and how fast his saliva dripped when he got excited. I stopped staring at his lower lip and looked him in eyes. "Who is the we?" I whispered.

"Conservative Muslims, brother! Who else?" He leaned back on the couch, obviously disappointed that I had to ask that question. Without giving me a chance to reply, he explained that he was in command of a group of men, brothers, as he called them. His neighborhood's mosque had agreed that during the chaotic time of the regime's downfall, his group could take over the security of the neighborhood. He added that he had guns and plenty of ammunition. Once a month he took his group to his village four hours east of Tehran to practice shooting and other warfare exercises. "I want you to join us," he repeated.

I took a deep breath. It was true that we had been neighbors during our childhood. Our houses were in a small alley and we often played soccer and wrestled together. He was pretty strong then. My jaw still remembered his punches. And the day he had invited me into his house to show me his new gun was hacked permanently into my memory. I remember asking him if I could hold it. It was heavier than I expected. I held it up and then aimed it toward a tree. He explained to me that it was just a BB gun and not a real rifle. Their rifles were well hidden underground in their village properties far from the city. Owning firearms was illegal, therefore, those few ordinary citizens who had them hid them to avoid trouble with the government.

He then, like a good instructor, took the time to go over the detailed instructions on how to aim and shoot.

The excitement sent a shiver through my body. That was the first time I had touched a gun. I pointed it at a corner of his courtyard and said, "Let's shoot targets. Do you have any cans or bottles that we can line up in the yard and shoot?"

"Forget fake targets, let's shoot sparrows," he replied and took the gun from me. Without wasting a second, he targeted a sparrow on a tree and pulled the trigger. The poor bird fell immediately to the ground. We both ran toward it. I was hoping that he missed, and the bird would fly away. Alas, the bird was hit. He picked it up and immediately twisted its head, separating it from the body.

To my dismay, he shot a few more and gave them to his mother for sparrow stew, a common dish from his part of the country.

Hassan's booming voice asking if I was in brought my focus back to the situation at hand.

"Why me? I don't live in your neighborhood anymore," I said.

"If you join, we will protect your neighborhood too."

Protect my neighborhood? I never thought of a day that we would depend on a civilian militia to provide security. What kind of a world were his people planning on?

His black eyes become wider when I told him I was planning to leave the country to study abroad. He sat back and looked away. After a moment, he turned his serious face to me and said, "Don't be a coward. Leaving the country at this sensitive juncture is a cop out. Join my group, and you will benefit far more than your study abroad."

Passion framed his serious face. His level of conviction convinced me not to argue with him and to play it more carefully. I leaned forward and whispered, "You have all the men and the guns you need. What can I possibly add to the mix that you don't already have?"

He agreed that he had men and guns. But he was convinced that the revolution was going to become much bigger than what a lot of people imagined.

"Once it begins," he philosophized, "I would need somebody like you to help me to strategize my moves. There will be many groups like mine, but only the smart ones will elevate to the top. Power, money, and glory will be ours, brother."

His face was so close to mine that I felt his spit landing on my face as he spoke. The discussion was getting out of hand. I had to stop it. Using the excuse of my meeting with the head of the conservative Islamic student movement of my college, I stood up and said that I needed to think about it.

He stood up shook my hand firmly, and with his strong arm he pulled me close to his face and said, "See, you're already doing it, brother. You're a natural leader. Don't miss this opportunity. Come and see me soon."

His approach sent a chill up my spine. I definitely didn't want to see him again.

About an hour later, I pulled into my old college's parking lot. A flood of memories raced into my mind: the first day, when I proudly walked into the building, the first disastrous lunch date with a skinny girl, my old friends, teachers, etc.

It wasn't a big campus, just two separate three-story buildings with a courtyard in the middle. I couldn't stop gazing at the far corner of the large entry terrace in front of the building, where I used to park my ten-speed bicycle, my pride and joy. That bicycle was my first large investment. I bought it with my own hard-earned money. For the first few months of my freshman year, I rode that bicycle fifteen kilometers uphill to the school and fifteen kilometers back home.

A few minutes later, I found myself in a dark corner of the college cafeteria, facing a skinny guy with a two-day-old beard wearing an old, oversized green army jacket. His unshaved face indicated his nonconformity to the clean, Westernized culture. The old green army jacket was a display of simplicity and admiration to some sort of militia action. Next to him sat a few of his similar-looking friends with unshaved faces and old army fatigues.

He was Abaassian, the twenty-year-old who was the leader of the conservative Muslim Students Group. Next to me sat Leila and a few members of the Music Appreciation Group, who incidentally, were all girls.

My few months of absence from the burgeoning college scene felt like a few years. The rapidly changing social climate had drastically impacted the campus. The grounds were no longer in pristine condition. Flyers, announcements, posters, and graffiti were all over the walls. Unlike the old times, no music was playing in the cafeteria. Most students' faces were unfamiliar to me. I was told that the principal of the school was absent, and the rumor was that she had fled the country. The official announcement was that she had gone to Europe to participate in some symposium.

The power and influence of student groups had been steadily

increasing across the country. There was a newly found sense of cooperation and unity among the various student political groups. Groups in opposing political spectrums, such as atheist Marxist groups, were working shoulder to shoulder with Muslim conservatives. The glue that bound these archenemies was no more than the single objective of toppling Pahlavi's regime, the monarchy.

"The music group is not helping the revolution. Islam forbids music. I move for the vote to dismantle the group," the student leader said right after Leila introduced me.

I intervened and asked for some dialogue before jumping to such a conclusion.

He glanced at me and looked down at his notebook. That was the sign of non-confrontation. Typical of the fundamentalist Muslims, it is impolite to look in the other person's eyes directly. In a soft tone, indicative of his demand for respect, he asked about my role there.

He listened patiently to my explanation about my role as the founder and the spokesperson for the Students Music Appreciation Group.

He kept his eyes on his notebook. After a moment of silence, in a soft and deliberate voice he explained that they were all fighting a powerful, corrupt regime and that the struggle could not afford any distractions. He believed that groups such as Music Appreciation wasted students time and energy in such a crucial time.

My face felt suddenly hot. Blood must have rushed into my head. I pressed my lips together and forced myself to be patient and not to interrupt him. When he finished, I looked straight into his beady eyes, and with a calm and yet firm voice, I asked if the poetry club and literature club were allowed to continue their activities.

He kept his eyes fixed on his notepad on the table, avoiding eye contact with me and nodded in the affirmative. He then added that many poets and writers had significantly contributed to the revolutionary movements, and their writing had elevated our knowledge and fueled our passion for the revolution. Then, he briefly looked at me.

Surely, it cannot be this easy! I thought. This must have been be a cover up for something much deeper. He wasn't taking me seriously. I decided to get to the core of his resentment. So instead of a reactionary response, I decided to approach it like an onion, peeling layers one by one.

One by one, I scanned the faces of his friends. Each one looked serious and gave the impression of self-importance. I began what became a ten-minute talk about the significant contribution of music and musicians in politics, and specifically, the impact of music during revolutionary times. I talked about the role of patriotic music and the importance of marches. My lecture then moved to the role of composers, whose work and impact influenced the direction of history. Musical works such as Chopin's revolutionary etudes and Verdi's operas helped Italians to throw off the yoke of Austrian and French domination.

"For example, Verdi used opera to show how power can be corruptive. By his time in the nineteenth century, opera was accessible to most classes of society; therefore, he easily influenced Italians with his nationalistic and patriotic songs. Even to these days, when Italians hear the *Va, pensiero* chorus sung, they excitedly shout 'Viva Italia.'" I raised my fist in the air, adding some drama to my speech.

During my talk, I noticed everyone around the table was attentively listening. For a brief moment, I felt like a professor giving a lecture on music history.

"Now, you need to understand," I further explained, "that it was this Music Appreciation Group who bravely beach-headed by putting up posters and quotes all over the campus. This may seem a trivial task to you now, but back then, when SAVAK informers were roaming around freely in this campus, it was a nearly impossible task. This was a time when your beloved poetry and literature clubs were so severely paralyzed by the college administration that they couldn't even announce their meetings. During those difficult times, members of the Music Appreciation Group were spreading the seeds of freedom of speech and other basic human rights."

A short pause gave me a chance to look around. Most of the conservative students had their lower lips pushed upward and their eyebrows raised, a typical facial impression of being intrigued. However, my sixth sense felt uneasy and wasn't convinced. It was time for the main issue to surface.

"Mister Abaassian, it seems that we have examined every angle of this matter. You and your friends," I pointed to the council members, "seem to understand the importance of the music group's contribution, yet I feel there is a deeper concern. What is really bothering you?"

Abaassian looked at the walls near him and then the ceiling and then back to his notepad. Was he annoyed or did he feel cornered? He then took a deep breath, raised his head and looked me in the eyes. "Music is forbidden in Islam. I said it before. We are Muslim and this country is becoming a Muslim country. We cannot allow music groups like this to spread the love of music to our students, corrupting their souls."

He gave me a brief stare, signaling a checkmate. Then he quickly looked at his friends, sat back in his chair, and locked his eyes to mine. It was as if he had delivered his most powerful blow, not only to me, but also to all others sitting there. He played his God card. If it is forbidden by God, then no one can reverse it and we all must obey the ruling.

I anticipated this issue to surface and had a strong hunch that this matter was the core concern for the conservative Muslim group. I'd waited a long time for him to spell it out.

This wasn't the first time I had encountered objections to music. The topic is an important misunderstanding that many fundamentalist Muslims have against performing arts. Despite their illusion, music has been and forever will be part of human culture, Muslims or non-Muslims alike. This was a hot issue for me, and I relished the opportunity to engage.

My gaze moved from him down to the surface of the table in between us. I took a moment to reflect. Slowly, I brought up my arms and rubbed my temples with my fingers. Then gently, my hands stroked my face in a contemplating manner. All that theater, in my calculation, was to give him the illusion of having the upper hand over me and therefore, to lower his shield.

"Mister Abaassian, do you practice your daily prayers?" I asked.

He sat back, furrowed his brows, yanked his neck and answered, "Of course!"

I asked if he got up before dawn every morning and prayed the way it is supposed to be done. He answered '*yes*' with an agitated voice and now he was staring at me. Then I inquired if he hears the *azhan* at dawn from his local mosque. Defending his local mosque's assiduous attention to their duties, he claimed they played it three times a day.

I asked him to describe it.

He looked at me. I detected a hint of a smile on his face. "It is the most beautiful sound in the morning. It used to be a live person making the call to prayer, but nowadays they just play a recording of it over loudspeakers."

He was coming along well with my line of questions. My next question was if listening to the singing of the *azhan* moved him.

"If it's done well, it moves my spirit and sets my mood for connecting to God. I guess that's why it's called call to prayers," he replied with ease. I felt he no longer was hiding behind a wall.

"By saying 'if it's done well' do you mean if it is sung well?"

He nodded his head up and down vigorously. "Yes."

I needed him to focus more on the quality of the *azhan* sound he had heard, so I asked him if he had ever watched the international competition of Quranic recitation.

"Yes, I saw it on TV, this year it was in Malaysia. What is this? An interrogation?" he complained.

"No, of course not. Just bear with me please. Do you enjoy the recital of the Quran in those competitions?" I continued.

"Of course, those voices are heavenly," he answered.

"Their voices and the way they embellish the sound is amazing, isn't it?" I asked.

He nodded in agreement. His friends were all nodding too.

Then I asked, if in his opinion, the quality of voice and recitation of his local mosque is the same as the competitors in Malaysia. He shook his head and with authority said the event in Malaysia was an international competition. Only best of the best were admitted there.

"Wouldn't you say each contestant's voice had a unique quality, and that they had obviously trained for years, in addition to being talented?" I asked.

"Yes, listening to them lifts me up to the heavens, and makes me feel closer to my Creator," he said.

Aha, I had him.

I put my elbows on the table and looked him straight in the eyes,. Did you know that both the *azhans* and Quranic recitations can be written in musical notes such that, a trained musician, unfamiliar with Islam, can reproduce the exact sound and words so well that you wouldn't be able to tell them apart?"

He moved his whole body, adjusted himself in his chair, and gave me a stern warning not to insult Islam. Of course, everyone knew the punishment for making a mockery of Islam was severe.

"I am not insulting Islam at all. I'm merely stating the facts. You can think of music as a form of language that one can utilize to transfer and communicate simple or complicated emotions such as love, devotion, hate, happiness, sadness, patriotism, and so on, to the listeners," I explained.

One of his friends protested by shouting, "This is crazy!"

I ignored the guy and continued. "Music is a beautiful medium that helps us humans to feel and understand life better. Music is woven into the very fabric of human cultural tapestry, including religions." I looked at every one of them, one by one as I continued. "Chants, calls for prayers, recitation of holy scriptures, and many other religious rituals have musical elements woven into them." I paused briefly to let all that seep in, but not long enough for anyone to interrupt me. "But, like other good things in life, people can abuse music and create something nasty and even dangerous."

A few of them were shaking their heads. It seemed they didn't like what they were hearing.

"Let me put it in simpler terms. The fact that a knife can cut us into pieces doesn't mean that we have to abandon its good use in our lives."

They were not convinced yet. I could tell from their faces.

I continued. "As a matter of fact, music has been used to help people get closer to God. For thousands of years, angelic voices and heavenly melodies have helped humans feel closer to the great divine. Many poems and many musical works have been and are still being created to the glory of God. If you listen to Gregorian chants, for example . . . " Suddenly I remembered that these folks wouldn't know what that is. "...which are prayers of monks, not knowing their origin or the words, you would feel peaceful and spiritual. Conversely, if a Westerner listens to the *azhan*, not knowing the purpose of it, he or she may still recognize it as spiritual and peaceful music," I continued.

Abaassian and his friends were quiet. A few of them were gazing somewhere, trying to digest what I just said. His head was down.

Judging from their reactions, I went for the close.

"What I'm saying is that when we have something good that can benefit us all, the paranoia of its potential abuse should not deter us from its gain." I closed my argument with those words, and sat back.

A few of them wiggled in their seats. Abaassian looked at his friends' faces one by one.

He put his elbows on the table, leaned forward and said, "Learning the Music Appreciation Group's history in our college and recognizing its participation and positive impact on our collective objectives as a student body movement, we agree to its continued functioning as long as the group stays on the revolutionary track."

I turned to Leila. A smile was painted across her face. Mission accomplished!

On my way out, Leila approached me and quietly said, "Are you sure you can't stay? Our battle has just begun. God knows what devastation will come to our world of art if the fanatics win. We need to protect art. Please stay and help us battle for its survival in Tehran!"

Here we go again, I thought. Two times in one day I was asked to stay in the country, to forgo my individual aspiration for the good of another group. At least, this one was an honorable cause. I was flattered and extremely grateful that she thought I could make a difference.

I felt torn. What Leila said was important. The obligation to protect art was compelling. A copious amount of misinformation and misunderstanding were polluting the minds of young and old alike in Iran. The need to stay, and to continue to educate was real and necessary. Could I make an impact? What about my own cause? At what point should one crush the longing of self-edification for the good of a society? What were the odds of success in the austere and ambiguous future of Iran?

After a few moments of thought, I said, "It's a noble and an important cause, I agree. But I have my own quest to pursue. The torch for this college is passed to you and your friends, Leila, keep it burning."

11

OCCUPATION

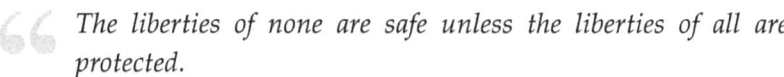 *The liberties of none are safe unless the liberties of all are protected.*

— William O. Douglas, U.S Supreme Court Justice
(1898-1980)

His eyes squinted behind the cigarette smoke, staring at nowhere in particular. My father, sitting across from me in a café, with the last ounce of breath left in his lungs before the next inhale, uttered, "It was in Gorgan, a long time ago." He inhaled deeply and exhaled. Smoke spilled out between his lips.

I waved off the smoke. I didn't have a clue what he was talking about, but decided to humor him and played along. "How long ago?"

"Oh, I don't know exactly, perhaps about thirty-seven years ago or so." His skinny face blurred every time he exhaled.

Gorgan, a city thirty kilometers to the west of Caspian Sea, was a midsize town north of Tehran that I'd never been to. However, during the forties it was small, sleepy village.

He blew out another cloud of smoke and spit a grain of tobacco that was stuck on his lower lip.

At this point, I assumed he was going to tell a story. However, I had invited him out to a café for a personal reason. Feeling manly, I was going to tell him about my serious feelings about Neilu and my next step with her. If it went well, I thought, I would break the news of us getting married. I had selected a ritzier café than what he was used to in the north part of town. But it felt strange, as this was the first time that I asked him out to eat. I did it on purpose, to keep him on edge. My hope was that he would be anxious to get away from there and agree to my plan quickly, giving me his approval. Instead, he sat back in his chair, obviously relaxed and wanting a long chat about one of his many wild experiences.

A waiter stood close by, ready to take our order, so I requested hot tea and two *kloocheh*, his favorite Persian sweet. It felt good to buy him a treat for once. He looked comfortable and pleased. That wasn't how I initially wanted him to feel, but, then I thought, why not? Maybe he's really enjoying this. He had a rough life growing up. The burden of life's reality hit him hard when he was in sixth grade. His father, the sole bread winner of a family of seven, died of pneumonia in his mid-thirties. His mother (my grandmother), and five small children were left to fend for themselves in a cold winter. My father had to quit school and support the family at that young age. His life was full of interesting and sometimes amazing stories. Like a cat, my father had always landed on his feet. Actually, I thought of him more like an alley cat—a street smart, self-made man. And true to form, he had already outsmarted me.

He took another puff on his cigarette. A small smile appeared on his clean-shaven, wrinkled face. His eyes gazed down on the coffee table in front of us as he launched into a tale that I had never heard before:

"It was a foggy, early morning in late June of 1941. Most people in Gorgan were asleep in their beds, when a strange, loud and constant humming rumbled from the main highway. I woke up abruptly and sat up in my floor mat, alert.

"My worker Mashdali, who was on his late thirties then, thought it was an earthquake. He was sleeping on the floor by the door. He rolled his body out of the bed and went to the windows. The trembling ground shook the small tea glasses lined up on the window sill. He could see tanks and military vehicles on the nearby main road in spite of the early morning fog and heavy exhaust smoke."

"Oh, good old Mashdali," I interrupted. "Did he even then pronounced his "s" like "sh"?

My father nodded. "Yes."

Mashdali used to take me to his store when I was in grade school. His workers were nice to me. I knew them all. His store was on a busy street with the hustle bustle of an industrial part of town. Industrial or not, everyone lived in a tangled, crowded way. Large trucks, sedans, horse pulled carts, donkeys carrying loads, people weaving through heavy congested traffic without fear, kids running around, dogs sheepishly searching trash for food, and cats everywhere. Even as a child I noticed how different life was in his neighborhood. Mashdali was an old, hunched-back man when I met him. An old man with a funny way of talking.

My father continued with his story. "I swiftly stood up on my mat and peeked out the window. Yes, it was a military convoy all right, and it was coming from the north toward the town. The convoy's direction alarmed me. I asked Mashdali to wake up Ali, my other worker, so we all could go to the town."

"I don't think I've met any of your workers named Ali," I interjected.

"No, you've never met him. He was a tall, nineteen-year-old kid with an oval face and short haircut. Next to short Mashdali and me with my thin, toothbrush mustache, we made a comical looking construction team. Now let me continue.

"The three of us rolled up our beds and tucked them in the corner of the large room of an unfinished building that we were contracted to finish. It was the only room that was totally finished. We lived in that room while working on the project. Outside, we used our handkerchiefs to cover our noses and mouths. Breathing was difficult with the amount of dust and smoke generated by the military convoy. As the convoy passed by us, I noticed the writings were in a foreign language.

I guessed it was Russian. We were only eight hours away from the Soviet Union's southern border.

"The city of Gorgan was about five kilometers from our building. We set out walking, and as we got near the city, we saw road blockades and observation posts being set up by the same military that had passed by our sleeping quarters. The town was under siege. Many onlookers were already outside on streets, silently watching the parade. I asked a man on the street, who was watching the convoy, if he knew what was going on. The man shrugged, scratched his bald head and replied, 'No, I don't know.'

"Unsatisfied with my conversation with the stranger, we continued the walk toward the center of the town. I needed to know what was going on, but all stores and shops were closed. Near the town center I asked another man if he had heard any announcement in the radio about this. He said the news was more about Germany's invasion of Russia and about advancing British forces from Persian Gulf, where they had landed a few weeks ago.

"A lot more people had gathered near city hall. A tank flanked by two military vehicles stopped in front of the city hall and pointed its gun at the building. A few soldiers stood guard as the rest of the convoy continued going south. We stood and watched.

"A few minutes later, the front door of the city hall opened and a bald, chubby-faced little man limped to the edge of the stairs. The cool morning air apparently wasn't helpful to him, as he had his white handkerchief in his hand and was using it to wipe off the sweat on his face. He was the deputy mayor.

"'Does anyone here speak Russian?' The deputy mayor shouted to the crowd. Someone asked why. He answered that the military units were Russian soldiers and they didn't speak Farsi. He repeated his question. People looked at each other in wonder.

"Mashdali asked me if I spoke any Russian. I put my index finger on my nose and whispered hush, to quiet him down, but he didn't obey. 'Here, here!' Mashdali yelled and pointed to me. 'My bossh does.'

"All heads turned toward me. I was surprised by this and turned my head left and right rapidly while taking a few short steps backward. The deputy heard Mashdali's shout. He walked over to me, grabbed and pulled my arm, and asked if I spoke any Russian. I looked around, all eyes were fixed on me. After taking a deep breath I collected myself and answered, 'Let's go see what they want.'

"Inside the city hall, the Russian military commander had set up a table and a few chairs in the hallway. He was shouting orders to his lieutenants. Soldiers ran around, searching every room. The mayor and two other men were sitting near the commander. All three, speaking in Farsi, were trying to communicate with the commander in vain. The commander shook his head, said something in Russian (which I did not catch) and gestured to the mayor to sit down. The deputy mayor pushed me toward the commander's desk.

"'*Privyet*,' I said. This was the familiar Russian word for hello, not the correct one in this setting, but it was all I could remember from the days I was an assistant truck driver traveling around the Caspian Sea ports talking to Russian sailors. The commander looked up and stared at me. The mayor and his men also went silent and looked up at me. Everyone stopped talking. Seconds of silence felt like hours.

"'*Vyi govoritye porusski?*' The commander asked. I guessed he was asking if I spoke any Russian. After a short pause, I nodded my head and mumbled, '*Da, porusski.*'

"'Ackh...' sighed the frustrated commander and let go a flood of words toward me.

"'*Da...da.*' I nodded my head in acceptance and repeated yes...yes in Russian, giving the impression that I understood him. When the commander stopped talking, the room became deathly silent. All eyes stared at me.

"'Well, what did he say?' the mayor asked.

"I cleared my throat and said, 'Eh... he, he said that people must go back to their daily business. Stores must open--bread shops, restaurants, everybody must conduct their business like before. They are not going to harm people if we don't resist.' Everybody sighed, smiled, and praised God.

"A faint smile appeared on the Russian commander's face after he observed people's reaction to my words. I used the opportunity to usher people in the city hall outside and give the commander space and time. And to end my duties as interpreter. One of the men with the mayor asked me if the commander explained why they were there. Thinking quickly, I said that I would ask that later, but for now we should show him some good faith and do what he asked. After all, I was hungry, and breakfast was first on my agenda. The mayor, being a politician, said, 'Mirza is right, we will get to the bottom of this, but not now.'

"The mayor had called me *mirza*, the learned one! I smiled and nodded.

"A few minutes later, my crew and I went to the nearest bread shop. It had just opened. A large crowd was gathered at the doorstep, waiting to buy their morning breakfast bread. The bread shop's counter faced the street. As with any other bread shop, the owner collected the money and handed people bread hot from the oven. We stood at the outer rim of the crowd and waited for our turn to order the bread. Someone from the crowd recognized me and said, 'Oh, look who is here! It's Mirza from the city hall!'

"Heads turned and the crowd parted like the Red Sea, opening a way for us to reach the counter. People gestured for me to proceed ahead as they stepped aside. My eyes were wide open in disbelief. I nodded in appreciation and moved forward to the counter. The fragrance of fresh baked flat bread tickled my nose in delight.

"The baker handed me two hot loaves just out of oven. I thanked him and handed him the money for the bread. The baker refused to take my payment and said, 'Oh no, Mirza, it is the least I can do for you. Please take the bread. It's a token of our appreciation for what you have done for us.'

"I was speechless. Bread in hand, I walked away briskly, thanking everyone in the bread shop as Mashdali and Ali followed. On our way to the grocery store, people on the street waved and half bowed to greet me. I didn't know any of them. When we passed a coffee house, the owner recognized me and beckoned me to enter. 'Mirza, Mirza, come inside, enter please. Let me have the honor of offering you breakfast this morning. Come on in, please.' We three stood there and looked at each other in disbelief.

"The coffee shop owner insisted by opening his arms and herding us three hungry men inside. There we found a wooden platform with a Persian carpet and sat. The interior of the coffee shop was dark and populated with wooden platforms covered with carpet. A few chairs were scattered around, and a water fountain splashed in the center of the shop. In the mix were the gurgling of *ghalyans,* and the sound of saucers and small tea glasses rattling in a rapid rhythm. A teenage waiter with a baggy, pajama-like black pants and a brown felt hat, brought hot tea and our breakfast on a large aluminum platter.

"The owner sat next to me and asked many questions about the Russians. The windows of the coffee shop rattled in sync with the arrival of a new military convoy roaring down the street. The shop owner pointed his hand to the street and said, 'What is this? More of them are coming! We thought they were done! It seems that they are about to occupy the whole country.'

Other patrons joined the owner and fired their questions at me. One of them asked if he should go dig up his rifle from under his yard and get ready to fight. I asked them to be patient and wait.

"Despite my efforts to calm them, comments continued and soon it turned to politics. At that time, we knew that the war with Germany was not going well for the Russians, but what we didn't know was why the Russians were there. Some customers hypothesized that perhaps Russians were experiencing shortages of food, ammunition, and medicine, hence their invasion to steal away our food and take our people. Talk of distrust and resistance grew wilder by the minute.

I used every excuse that I could to calm people and buy more time.

"A teenage boy slammed opened the coffee shop doors and shouted, 'Mirza, Mirza!' Then he bent over to catch his breath. The Russian commander had summoned me. It was good timing. I had finished my breakfast and was on my second glass of tea.

"People from the coffee shop followed me on the road to the building where the Russian commander was bunkered. On my walk, I wondered how I got into this jam. We were construction workers from Tehran, sent by a contractor to finish construction on a radio station. We had no families in Gorgan, no supplies, no money, and no food stored for emergencies. I questioned our survival chances.

"More people joined me and my entourage as we moved closer to the civic center. It had turned into a beautiful sunny day. Humidity was higher than what I was used to, but the temperature was pleasant and comfortable with a slight breeze gently blowing through the town. The center square in the town was filled with Soviet military equipment and personnel. The exhaust fumes from the Russian's vehicles was overwhelming. A large crowd of concerned citizens had gathered at the square. As I walked through the crowd, people asked many questions about the intruders.

"I didn't have any answers for all the questions. I asked Ali to go to the bus station and see if any bus had arrived from out of town. Ali nodded and disappeared in the crowd.

"I spotted the Russian commander on top of the stairs, standing in front of the door to the building. His arms were moving franticly as he talked to the mayor and his people. He talked with his whole body. Russian soldiers had their weapons in their hands and not on their shoulders. I sensed tension.

"The mayor spotted me and let a loud sigh. He moved his heavy round body closer to me and asked me to translate again. Despite my hesitance, he pushed me toward the commanders.

"The commander showered me with fast Russian words, his arms flying around emphasizing each and every word. I used my hands to give the sign of slow, but I actually said soft instead."

My father chuckled at this memory, took a sip of tea, and continued:

"After a few sentences, the commander put his arm on my shoulder, and gave a hand gesture to me to translate for the mayor. The commander's facial expressions had given me some clues about what he was saying. I had tried to focus on his blue eyes, which were the gates to his soul, and then on his arms.

"'Honorable people of Gorgan, this is what the commander is saying,' I shouted. I moved my feet a bit and looked at the mayor. The mayor, eager to know what the commander had said, gave a nod to me to continue. 'The commander wants you to know, that…that they are not here to harm people,' I continued. The palms of my hands were sweaty and the sun was in my eyes.

"The mayor nodded his head in approval and with confidence, as if he himself had negotiated a peace treaty. The commander observed the mayor's nods and then looked at the people. He then continued with a few more sentences and stopped.

"I took the commander's pause as my cue. I swallowed hard, cleared my throat and projected my voice so the crowd, which by now had multiplied around me, could clearly hear me. 'Commander said that they will move out of the city as soon as they get clearance. They do not want to harm anyone. Your cooperation will speed the process. Please go back to your daily business. The city will get back to normal very soon.'

"Someone from the crowd shouted at me to ask the commander if this was an occupation. I didn't know the word *occupation* in Russian, so I told him so. Then another one shouted, 'Then ask him what they are doing here in our city and in our country.' Then the crowd started arguing with one another.

"The Russian commander glanced at me, his brows were tight and he jerked his face from side to side, gesturing me for input. I shook my head in dismissal and gave the signal to the commander that the crowd's comments were unimportant and he should continue. The commander resumed talking again and the crowd went silent. The commander went on with his barrage of Russian words.

"In the meantime, Ali returned from his mission and waved his arm. I recognized him in the crowd. He shook his head signaling me that no bus had arrived yet.

"Commander stopped and looked at me to translate his words. I told the crowd that Russians intended no harm to the people. Just stay out of their way and don't cause any trouble. The mayor, satisfied with my translation, dispersed people and I decided to go back to my construction site and deal with the local laborers who might have been waiting to start the work.

"We walked back to our building on the outskirts of the town. On our way back, we saw more military trucks, tanks and soldiers pouring into the city. This did not look good to me.

"A group of local day laborers were gathered awaiting my return. I basically told them that we haven't had delivery of materials and that meant no work until the roads open. The laborers complained, mumbled, and slowly dispersed. Once they all were gone, I called Mashdali and asked him to cook lunch for the three of us from what we had left. Then I went to the back to our room. I checked to see if anybody followed me, but I was alone. So I pulled out the money pouch that my mother had sewn for me from under my shirt and counted the money I had hidden inside it. The amount was very small.

We could not survive here long on so little funds.

"Upon my return to the front room, I picked up my prayer rug, spread it, and asked the men to pray with me before eating lunch. The other two stood behind me as a sign of respect. Facing southwest toward Mecca, we started our prayers. At the end of the prayers, I stayed sitting on my knees, extended my arms up above my head toward the heavens and loudly begged God for a peaceful resolution to the troubles at hand and a safe passage home for the three of us. Ali and Mashdali repeated after me loudly. The dramatic scene finished with a loud and harmonious Amen. Ali and Mashdali rubbed their faces with the palms of their hands and stood up. Ali went and sat in the corner by the window, and Mashdali went to dish out lunch. But I remained in the sitting position. I had a private request for God.

"'My dear benevolent God,' I prayed, 'extend your vast mercy on me, your petrified subject. Give me wisdom and light my path in this darkness with your grace. I'm afraid, afraid of letting down my fellow countrymen, afraid to unintentionally impose harm on these people. Give me courage to pull through this endeavor.'

"Mashdali announced that the lunch was ready. I rubbed my face with the palms of my hands and let out a loud Amen. I hoped that if it was loud enough the angels could hear me better.

"We consumed our lunch with vigor and decided on taking the customary short afternoon nap. Each of us rolled out our bed on the ground and lay down. Close to an hour later, I woke up to the clattering of saucers and tea glasses being washed. Mashdali had woken up before me and brewed a pot of hot tea. He poured tea in a clear glass, placed it on a saucer, added two lumps of sugar cubes and handed it to me.

"Ali reluctantly got up, washed his face and joined us for the afternoon tea. He put a lump of sugar cube in his mouth and poured some hot tea in his saucer. Sucking on his lump of sugar cube, he sipped the now cooler tea from the saucer. Abruptly, he sat tall, extended his neck to an alert posture and asked, 'Do you hear that?'

"We all sat up and listened. There were no sounds from the road nearby. Only a complete and eerie silence. I rushed outside toward the main road. The other two followed me.

"The road was completely empty! Ali squinted, put his right hand above his eyes to block the late afternoon sun, and looked further up on the road. 'Look,' he said, 'it's a man riding a donkey. He's coming toward us.' When the man came closer, we asked him what he had seen. He said that there was a road block and checkpoint five kilometers to the north. But he didn't see any more convoys. I decided it was time to return to Gorgan.

"In town, Russian soldiers and military equipment were everywhere, much more prominent than before. I asked my men to each go in a different direction to investigate and meet at Hassan *agha*'s coffee shop in one hour. I went straight to the bus station. It was unusually quiet there. Two buses stood parked, but nobody was around. After a few shouts, a short fellow with his mouth full of food appeared from the office behind the counter. He said no new arrivals or departures of busses had occurred since the Russian troops arrived.

"I asked about the cost of tickets for three people and time of departure for the bus to Tehran if and when, the roads opened. I felt my face blanch with his answer. I only had enough money left for three tickets to Tehran. What about food? If I spend any money on food or anything else, all three of us would not be able to get back home. My employer was a few weeks behind, and with the blockade, there was no hope for a quick cash infusion. *How are we going to survive? Oh, God please help*, I prayed.

"I felt responsible for Ali and Mashdali's survival. Equally important was their need to get back to their families in Tehran, as this chaos could be a lot worse in the capital city, and they needed to protect their loved ones.

"Preoccupied with my thoughts, I walked toward the coffee shop. The moment Hassan *agha*, the owner, saw me, a big smile appeared on his face. He opened his arms wide and said, 'Oh welcome, welcome

Mirza, please come in and sit anywhere you like.' I put my right hand on my heart, tipped my head, and thanked Hassan *agha* for his kindness. At least I would have another meal.

"I sat at a table by the window and looked outside. It seemed as if life was getting back to its normal pulse. A few men were riding old black bicycles in different directions, a few donkeys carrying heavy loads of vegetables were being pulled by their masters, and a few kids were playing games in the street.

"Asghar, the waiter, brought a glass of hot tea with a small dish of sugar cubes. He put a hot tea glass on a saucer and in a slow motion placed them on the table in front of me. 'No charge, it's on us, Mirza,' he said as he put his hand on his heart.

"A few minutes later, Mashdali appeared at the door. I waved him to my table. He reported that the Russians were everywhere, and people were worried. I got closer to Mashdali and asked, whispering, if he had heard of any arrests or unrest. He shook his head. Ali showed up a few moments later and reported no deliveries anywhere. All roads remained closed. People were cut off from their families outside. Russians were controlling the telegraph, radio, and newspaper offices.

"Hassan *agha*, brought a tray of greens, feta cheese, and bread for everyone around the table and asked about any new development. I shared the good news of the halt in the flow of incoming military while wrapping a bite of bread with a chunk of feta cheese covered with basil, mint, and green onion. Hassan *agha* insisted that we stay for dinner. After the customary *tarof*, I accepted. He smiled and ordered Asghar to bring a *ghalyan* for us to smoke tobacco.

"The arrival of the *ghalyan* put a smile on Mashdali's worrisome face. After a few puffs, I offered the hose of the *ghalyan* to Mashdali. He took the hose, got up from behind the table and pulled the *ghalyan* closer to himself. With a big grin plastered on his face, he took something out of his right pocket and was about to put it on the hot charcoals on top of the *ghalyan*, when I held his wrist and stopped him. He complained that he had a difficult day and he needed to relax a bit.

"I looked straight at his eyes with a serious face. 'No opium here. This is a public place. What you do in your private time is your business, but not in public and not when I'm around.'

Mashdali gave me a long stare, then raised his eyebrows and pushed his lips together, obviously irritated with me. But he put the opium back in his pocket.

"We spent several hours at the coffee shop, drinking tea, smoking tobacco, eating dinner, and mostly talking to people who spotted me and wanted to know my opinion about the situation. It was dark when I suggested we leave.

"The moonshine was clear and brilliant. The empty road surrounded by farm lands was adequately illumined. No need for lanterns. The temperature and humidity were pleasant. The air smelled like rice and whatever else the farmers were growing. There were no activities on the road, a clear sign of a road closure. That night belonged to the indigenous creatures: frog choirs, barking dogs, and howling wolves. Soon talking was replaced by singing. Ali had the loudest singing voice among us. Once in a while, Mashdali or I accompanied Ali for a few verses.

"We turned into a small alley behind our unfinished building. I was a few steps behind the other two. 'Stop,' I ordered all of a sudden. I put my index finger on my nose and whispered, 'Ssss, I think I saw a moving shadow up ahead.'

"'Shadow?' Ali wasn't finished with his sentence when a few large men jumped out from the dark and grabbed all of us. After a few moments of scuffling, I felt the cold sensation of a blade on my throat. I stopped resisting, understanding that struggle could be futile. The other two were in the same situation as me.

"'What do you want? We don't have any quarrel with you,' I said.

"The one with a knife on my throat said that they were going to cut our throats ear to ear and take everything we have. Ali was breathing heavily. He was young and stocky. He could put up a good fight. But a miscalculated move could end his life in a moment. I had to calm everyone. Mashdali asked him to calm down and explained that we were just laborers who haven't been paid for weeks.

"'Shut up, old man. Nobody asked you to talk," said the thug who had a knife on Mashadli's throat. Mashdali tried to use his calm, fatherly voice to reason with the thugs. But it didn't work, and only served to agitate them further. I intervened and used my authoritative voice, explaining that I was the boss and if they would release my workers, I would cooperate with them.

"Ha! Once you see one of their headless bodies start to tremble and shake like a beheaded chicken, you will cooperate all right," one of the thugs said. I jerked to release myself in anger and said, 'I said let them go. They are your Muslim brothers and fellow laborers. I will give you whatever you want once they are freed.' The mugger who had his knife on my throat tightened his grip and pressed the knife harder on my skin. I felt a burning sensation on my throat.

"'Wait a minute,' ordered a figure who appeared from shadows and walked slowly toward us. He asked my captor to bring me into the light so he could see my face. The man dragged me into the area where moonlight was more prominent. After a few moments of silence, the stranger ordered my release.

"'What? They have money and food. We are hungry, man!' complained the thug with the knife on my throat.

"'I said let him go. He is a good man, I know him. Let them all go,'

said the man from the shadows. When they loosened their grip on us, I asked their leader how did he know me.

"The man stepped out of shadow, spat on the ground and answered, 'I worked for you in the past. You have always been kind to your workers. Several times you had paid me a little extra at the end of the day. You're a good man. Please forgive us. We are hungry and have not found work for many days.'

"I didn't recognize the guy, but didn't argue with his recollection. I understood that God had heard my earlier prayer. 'I will pray for you. The Russians will leave soon and the city will go back to normal. Just be patient and don't sin, brother,' I said and stepped away from my captor's grip.

"None of us could sleep that night. Mashdali reminded us how the old proverb, *Be kind and charitable in good times and God will return the favor during the difficult time*, saved our life that day. The next morning, despite Ali's sluggishness, we managed to do our morning prayers before sunrise, secured the building, and were on the road by the time the first rays of sun shined on the city of Gorgan.

"We walked in the middle of the empty road carelessly, deeply engaged in conversation, when we were startled by a loud and steady blaring of a truck horn. It was a charcoal truck coming from the nearby forest with its charcoal load. Waving our arms, we stopped the truck and I asked the driver if we could get a ride to the town. The driver agreed and we all hopped in the truck. Curious and excited, I asked the driver if the roads were open. The driver said that after two days of blockade the roads had just opened. We gave the driver the full account of the events in the city. The truck driver dropped us off at the bus station at my request. I rushed to the counter and asked if bus lines were operating. Yes, the roads had opened that early morning and the bus to Tehran was already loading passengers. I used every bit of cash I had left to buy three tickets to Tehran.

"'Brothers, we are going home!' I announced proudly and steered the two pleasantly surprised men forward toward the awaiting bus. I thanked the two for their trust in me. But the place was no longer safe. For all we knew, the whole country could be under siege. In that case, our families needed us and we must be with them. So we jumped on the bus and headed back to Tehran, where our families were anxiously waiting. It was a few days later when we found out that despite Iran's declaration of neutrality in World War II, the Allies had invaded Iran. Soviets from north and British forces from south had taken over our country, exiled our king, and placed his son in power. They used and abused our resources and bullied our young king to obey them unconditionally. Many brave Iranians died defending our country in the months that followed."

With those words he stopped, took a sip of his hot tea and leaned back on his chair indicating the end of the story.

Who *was* this man sitting in front of me? For so many years I resented his choice of occupation as I witnessed many people looking down on us because he was a charcoal retailer. When my brother and I wore nice, laundered clothing, people whispered about how surprising it was to see children of a charcoal man so orderly and clean. When my mother insisted that I go to a private high school with a good track record of college acceptance, people whispered "Why does a son of a charcoal man need to go to a private school?" During my teen years, my sensitivity was at its highest to the judgment of others, and it bothered me that I couldn't get into certain clubs or sports, such as equestrians. These were for teens with well-to-do fathers, connected, rich, or belonging to high-ranking military or government organizations. Unfortunately, I didn't spend that much time with my father when I was growing up as his work hours were long with only Fridays off. I wondered what would happen if I could have spent more time with him when I was young. Our annual one-week vacations at the Caspian Sea were among my fondest memories. It wasn't until my teen years that I recognized we always stayed at cheap motels and not the fancy hotels where my cousins from my mother's side stayed. It bothered me that I couldn't hang out with the cool kids at those fancy resorts, so these vacations became miserable for me.

But the man sitting in front of me that day was a different man, I didn't remember him being so savvy and interesting. My impression of him was changing.

"I didn't know you speak Russian." I said.

"I don't" he replied, grinning. "I just knew a few basic words, as I said earlier, that I picked up from my limited contacts with Russians. I hoped by keeping people calm and busy, the Russians would not harm them."

I pressed my lips together and shook my head in sympathy. It must have been extremely unnerving to live in an era when neighboring countries could easily invade and occupy as they wished. "How could people survive such times?"

My father shrugged. "One day at a time. You are lucky, son. You have grown up in a strong, stable country with a powerful military and experienced politicians to protect us against invasions of foreigners. That's why I appreciate our king so much. Under his shadow, we have safely prospered."

I didn't fully agree with him and decided to risk voicing my opinion. I countered that in modern days, foreign powers don't necessarily need to invade a country via a large military. There are other ways to manipulate, influence, and devastate a country. It was unsettling to know how in the past, Russians, Brits, Americans, and others easily helped themselves to Iran by manipulating or invading whenever they felt like it. I also pointed that we had never studied any of that in our official history books.

He leaned forward and looked into my eyes, "That is even more reason for you to come back here after your finish your studies and do your duty to your country and your people. I told you this story so you could see how vulnerable we are."

He continued on, telling me how the godless Soviets could pour into Iran from the north at any time, or how the ruthless Iraqi leader Saddam Hussein could attack Iran from the southwest and capture our oil wells the moment we were perceived weak. He pressed on that we needed good and educated people to keep the fine balance. He thought my generation was our country's hope for a peaceful future.

"That's my motivation to pay for your study abroad," he explained.

The pressure was on. Now even he wanted me to return and serve the country. At least he was okay with me going abroad for study. But why couldn't I be free to decide what was best for me? I wasn't asked when I would live or where I was to be born. Why was he putting shackles on me? I wanted to choose my own society, nationality, and country. I wanted to build my home where respect was mutual and earned, not forced.

My father never acknowledged the current atmosphere of social unrest. Perhaps he was frightened of the secret police's talons everywhere. He stayed clear of politics and was, on the surface, a supporter of the shah's regime. He always kept his political thoughts to himself. When he sat among the supporters of Islamic revolution, he stayed quiet and respectful of their views. My mother often referred to him as a member of the party of the wind; he would bend toward the direction of the prevailing group.

"Well, that story was fascinating. Thank you for telling me about it. But, we are in the middle of hell, Bajune! Don't you see all these troubles? All this killing, torturing, and mass arrests; and our own soldiers on our own streets shooting our own people? This is not called balance; it's called chaos. I need to get out of this God-forsaken place and find myself first."

My voice had become out of control and loud. The other customers near us were staring at me. Adjusting my chair, I leaned back and took a moment to cool down. Bajune didn't say anything. I reminded myself why I had brought him there. Leaning forward with my elbows on my knees and with a lower voice, I said, "Anyway, I invited you here for something else. I . . . I have good news to share with you."

He lit a new cigarette, sat back on his chair, and looked at me. I felt as if spotlights were over my head. His small and wrinkled face didn't belong to a diminutive man anymore. His incredible story of courage and cleverness had changed that for me. He was a survivor, he had resilience, he had endured so much. I felt insignificant and selfish in my need to tell a man whose fight for survival began at age twelve that his twenty-one-year-old son, whom he had agreed to send abroad for a graduate study, was asking for more.

Perhaps my idea hadn't been a good one—at least not right then.

My eyes moved from him to the tea glass on the table in front of me. I reached for it—maybe just as a delay tactic. The warm sip of tea felt relaxing and bought me a few more moments. I really didn't want to bring up the subject of Neilu, but it needed to be done—just to get it over with.

With the understanding that he had no clue about my personal life, I started from the beginning and told him that I had been dating a girl named Neilu for the past couple of years. I paused and searched for his reaction.

No change in his face, no words. He quietly listened and puffed.

Then I said that we wanted to get married.

His face was hard to read behind the cloud of smoke. He continued his silent listening.

"I want to start the formal process of *khastegary* to ask for her hand. But before breaking the news to Momon, I wanted to ask for your advice. You know how mothers are. Sometimes they get overprotective of their children," I said.

He leaned forward and with a couple of taps on his cigarette, emptied the buildup of ashes into a green glass ashtray on the table.

"Which is it? Do you want to go abroad or get married?" "Both," I replied.

He shook his head and said that he wouldn't pay for two students abroad. My assurance that Neilu's parents would pay for her expenses didn't convince him. I then presented him with a third option of getting engaged in Tehran, and having her join me abroad when she finished her schooling.

He leaned back, looked out the window, and continued smoking his cigarette.

My father had always been a voice of pragmatism tinged with pessimism when it came to my life. His position on the issue and comments suddenly reminded me of our negotiations four years ago concerning my urge to study abroad after high school graduation. I remembered him in a grey-striped, three-piece suit with a dark blue tie, standing in our living room with his cigarette between his right-hand fingers. We were about to leave the house for a large family gathering somewhere when I brought up the subject, and not for the first time.

He exhaled, I watched the swirling, stringy wisps of smoke twist and curl. He patiently explained to me that in his view, there were only two ways for me to go abroad. His face disappeared behind a cloud of smoke as he exhaled again. One was to sign up and complete my tour of duty with the military services, which would set me free as an adult to do whatever I wanted on my own.

The alternative was for him to pay my expenses to study abroad. In that case, he wanted me to get my bachelor's degree in Iran first, and then when I was older and more mature, according to him, I could apply for graduate study abroad.

Serving a compulsory two-year military service with a high school diploma was not the highest priority for an ambitious eighteen-year old senior, like me. I knew I would be treated like a subhuman. I passionately argued against it.

Victory seeped through his all-knowing smile, but like putting salt on a wound, he declared, although the answer seemed obvious, that it had to be my decision.

I hated being cornered by my father into a decision I didn't want to make. My passive-aggressive teenage nature offered a third alternative —joining the Air Force academy to become a fighter pilot. They sent pilot candidates to the U.S. for training.

Knowing very well that I had no desire to serve in any military or other organization that deals with handling weapons or killing other human being, he called my bluff. He claimed that he would not stop me, but my mother would be heartbroken if her son would take on such a dangerous occupation. His reply brought the argument back onto his turf.

It didn't take him too long to add an addendum to his requirements, I clearly remembered. He would only support a degree in medicine, engineering, or business, and not what I wanted, which was music or archeology.

With a sudden move, my father leaned forward and pressed his cigarette butt into the café ashtray several times, which jolted me back to the situation at hand. He stood up. "Look, the wedding subject is your mother's department. I don't dare to get involved. But mixing the two is a prescription for disaster. I won't support it. Choose one or the other."

Gorgan is surrounded by beautiful nature.

12

THE POOR DOG

> 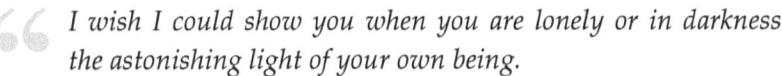 *I wish I could show you when you are lonely or in darkness the astonishing light of your own being.*
>
> — Hafez, Persian Poet (1325-1389)

Her fury raised the hair on the back of my neck, even though she was three-hundred-forty kilometers away in Isfahan.

"Yes, dearest, I understand that my mother was unusually quiet. Perhaps she was in her shy mood," I explained to Neilu from the phone booth on a street in Tehran. A private phone conversation with Neilu was never possible in my house.

She wasn't buying my excuses.

A month prior, on a pleasant nature walk in a well-tended park in the north part of Tehran, Neilu and I decided to spend the rest of our lives together. We had each separately announced our decision to our parents. In our world, engagements were handled in two different ways based on one's social group. Traditional ones were arranged between families first, the second group, the more modern group, the decision would arrive by mutual agreement between the boy and the girl in a non-ceremonial way. Just an intimate conversation. We were part of the second group. As tradition goes, after a private announcement of the decision, the groom's mother and another significant woman, like a sister or aunt, with the groom in tow, would meet with the bride-to-be and her parents. The meeting is called *khastegary*, a significant step toward a formal engagement. Once everyone agrees with the negotiated terms, then a formal engagement party will celebrate the occasion.

Neither Neilu nor I liked or believed in *khastegary*, but it was the tradition and it had to be done, if we wanted our family's support. Neilu was loud and clear over the phone. She countered my argument that *khastegary* was not the right time to be shy, and that my mother knew it well. I could hear her yelling, even with the telephone handset thirty centimeters away from my ear.

I sheepishly agreed with her. We loved each other and wanted to get married. It felt natural to us. However, families typically make a big deal out of *khastegary*. And ours was something of a disaster. My mother had sat uncomfortably quiet during the entire meeting. My desperate small talk during that meeting had no effect in warming up the mood.

Neilu moved the focus of her complaint to my uncle. She thought he was rude and questioned my motive for inviting him into the *khastegary* meeting.

I apologized to Neilu for my uncle's presence at her house instead of my father's. He couldn't make it, and my uncle was the closest older man in my immediate family. Besides, my uncle was not just my mother's sister's husband--he was like an older, more experienced brother to my mother, and his opinion was highly valued in our family. My reason to include him on my team was his life in Europe and his liberal outlook. Neilu's family was a nontraditional one. I thought his foreign exposures and view of life in Europe could convince my mother to give a favorable nod of approval. But instead, he fidgeted in his seat the entire time and never said a word. Everybody understood that he wasn't happy to be there.

"Where was your father? Why wasn't he there?" she screamed.

My wrist watch showed 8:15 p.m., forty-five minutes before the martial law curfew started. The frustrated military responded brutally and often with lethal force to people who disobeyed the martial law. Being aware of the time was crucial. I was twenty minutes driving time away from home.

Some sort of lame excuse spilled out of my mouth about my father's absence. Frankly, I didn't trust my father in this matter. At the time, I thought of my father as an unsophisticated man with no care of any protocols whatsoever. He was unpredictable in social settings. Sensing my mother's hesitation with the idea of our engagement, I asked my aunt and uncle, who had lived in Germany for many years, to accompany my mother to the *khastegary*. That was theoretically my sprinkle of sophistication into an otherwise simple and ordinary flavored family. In our family, we considered my uncle and aunt the most modern ones. My father had made it clear at the end of our meeting in the cafe that he didn't want any part of it.

I dared to politely counter, reminding her that the first meeting in *khastegary* is always understood and considered to be uncomfortable and difficult.

"I don't know. This was my first one. But etiquette indicates civility and respect," she answered.

The chill of the fall night had seeped through the metal and glass frame of the phone booth and was penetrating my body. Time was rushing toward the curfew designation. It was dark. There were no lights other than the streets light and the light in the phone booth. Businesses were closed and the street's uncanny quiet was a tell-tale sign of the coming curfew. This conversation needed to come to a positive conclusion soon.

It had been necessary for me to call Neilu and check on her. I had anticipated her disappointment as she left Tehran the day after the meeting with our parents. We lived in a traditional society, *khastegary* was more of a business meeting than a getting–to-know-each-other meeting. Parents bargain over many issues, how much the groom has to pay the bride, *mehrieh*, what furniture the bride brings into the couple's first house, *jahaz*, and other details of the potential union.

Reminding her of this fact didn't sit well with her.

"No, *you* live in a traditional family. My family couldn't care less," she snapped.

Neilu grew up with her mother and her aunt. Her parents were divorced many years ago. She was given a lot of freedom and was pretty independent. Her mother was at peace to let her live by herself in a city several hundred miles away, travel by herself within the country, wear whatever she wanted, and make her own decisions. Neilu's aunt lived together with Neilu's mother, younger sister and brother without a man's protection or financial support. Basically, they were independent modern women, and I was proud of them for that. But this independence was a deterrent in the eyes of my mother.

I asked if her mother and aunt were also disappointed. She gave me a short and snappy *yes*. It didn't compute for me. I thought they liked me. Knowing the nature of their disappointment was important to me, so I asked her to elaborate. Apparently, I wasn't as much an issue as was my family. After perceiving my family's hesitations, they were questioning the sanity of our relationship.

Something didn't feel right to me. The whole thing was tilting in the wrong direction. I had to do something. To empathize with her, I admitted that it had been hard, especially with her school being in a city several hours away from me and her mother. To shed some positive light into it, I assured her that we would get through it together and life would move on.

Then, I told her about the uncomfortable *khastegary* meeting of my older brother and his wife. Their families' negotiation became a big ordeal, but when the engagement was announced, the storm calmed down, the clouds cleared, and the sun shined for everyone.

She paused a moment and said, "Well, I am not sure if I have the patience for it. It shouldn't be this difficult. It should be a fun and happy event."

This was the opening I was hoping for to promote my original idea of leaving the country as two individuals, not as a married couple. Admiring Western culture's modern point of view in this matter, I reminded her that we wouldn't have to deal with any of these difficult traditions. We both were in agreement that these traditions had their time and place in the history of our society. They were designed to protect the unity of the newly formed family as well as the bride. Since the invasion of Arabs and imposition of Islam, our society had become a male-dominated society, where women were restricted intellectually, socially and physically. It was imperative to have arrangement to protect brides. However, Neilu and I considered each other as equal partners. She was educated, independent, and quite a capable woman. In the U.S. or Europe, we could live together and get married anytime we wanted, without any judgments, prejudices, or families' haggling.

Worried about a reprisal, and before she had a chance to say anything, I switched my position and continued, "Maybe I should venture out on my own and rent an apartment."

She didn't miss a beat on reminding me that I had just gotten out of college and didn't have the income to support myself. That was true, but more importantly, my parents wouldn't go for it and would cut their support. I needed their full support in order to leave the country to study abroad.

I agreed with her, remembering that no one in Iran hires a man who hasn't completed the two-year military service.

After a pause, I perked up. "Come on, Neilu, Let's go to the U.S. and live our lives there without any of these chains."

She changed her tone to a much softer one and reminded me that she had one more year of school left. And how she wanted to finish it before leaving the country. "So, I can't join you right away and—"

"You can't or you won't?" I interrupted.

"I won't! My preference is for us to get married here in this country before you go abroad." She sounded determined.

The stakes for my making a clear exit from Iran were rising. A feud between our two families could put me in a difficult position of choosing between Neilu and my family. On top of everything else, the stress of the squabble between families and the distraction it would bring me could be determinantal for my cause. It would be much easier if she could join me abroad when her studies were over in Isfahan.

With an obvious sadness in her tone, Neilu continued that her mother and aunt thought that my mother was not happy with this union and asked her not to pursue it. The despair in her voice felt like cold water poured on my head.

"Well, my mother is not marrying you and I am not marrying your mother or your aunt. However, if the fanatic Muslims win this revolution, then I can marry all three of you at the same time, as they will make it legal." I smiled with the joy of turning a sour moment to a funny one.

But she wasn't amused. Unfortunately, Neilu's mother and aunt were correct. My parents, mostly my mother, was not happy about my choice of a future wife. In her view, Neilu was too sensitive, high maintenance, and a person with many psychological insecurities. Therefore, she wasn't willing to be instrumental in throwing her son into a fire pit.

I scrambled for a solution, or a compromise of some sort, seeing now that the time before the curfew was dangerously close.

An idea sparked in my mind. My mother never had a chance to get to know Neilu. She only met her once or twice for short moments. I asked Neilu if she would be willing to visit my mother more often to spend quality time with her. To be fair to my mother, she needed a better chance to discover Neilu's inner beauty.

"Think about what you just said. I don't think you meant to say it the way it sounded," she warned me.

I was speechless. I couldn't think of what wrong thing I said.

"Just beautiful inside?" She helped me to realize again how insensitive I was to her feelings.

"Oh sorry, I didn't mean that you are not pretty outside. As a matter of a fact, you are very attractive. But you know, outside beauty is relative, that's why they say, "beauty is in the eyes of the beholder." But the inside beauty is universal. It's the inside beauty that sits on the heart. Everyone likes kindness, thoughtfulness, etc. People appreciate a decent character no matter how the packaging is done."

She chuckled, praised my fast recovery, and asked for my suggestions as to how we could help my mother see Neilu's *inner beauty*. It felt good to hear her in a humorous temperament. It made sense for me to show some cooperation as well.

For this to work, it needed to be a two-way street. Neilu needed to make some effort to learn about my mother as well. In exchange for her efforts, I promised to improve on my effort to learn more about her family. "God knows, I have made my share of mistakes, especially with your mother."

She didn't follow and asked me to be more specific.

Referring to the first lunch I had with her family the previous summer, I reminded her of my unforgivable mistake. During the lunch, everybody was having a good time and enjoying a good meal. I was proud of myself for getting along with everyone and making them laugh. Then, I noticed her mother's stare. When I returned her look, she asked if in my opinion there is any truth to the saying that opposites attract.

Stupid me. I didn't read between the lines. Intoxicated with my success in charming everyone, I replied, "Not necessarily. For example, I have a light complexion, brown hair and light hazel eyes, so according to that saying, I should be attracted to brunettes with dark eyes, and tan features. But I am attracted to blondes, light colored eyes, and light complexions."

Suddenly everyone's faces turned serious, her mother frowned, and the room became deathly quiet. I turned my face and looked at Neilu. At that moment, seeing her jet-black hair and black eyes made me realize what a big mistake I had made in voicing my silly opinion without considering the audience.

"See, stupid comments like that, plus your mother's behavior, convinced my mom that you are not a good fit for me." She was back to her earlier gloomy disposition.

"No, no, I recovered quickly that day by reiterating how much I adore you for who you are as a person, in addition to your physical beauty, and how much I appreciated the beauty of brunette features."

She disagreed with me, and said that there are occasions in which one would never recover from dumb comments like that.

I had to agree with her. She was right and I admitted that it was a life lesson for me. Changing the direction of conversation, and in the spirit of getting to know each other's family better, I asked about her father. Other than he was a military man, her father was an unknown factor me.

"You don't need to worry about him," she snapped.
"Why? Is he dead?"
"He may as well be," she mumbled.
"C'mon Neilu, help me out here. We have to make this work."

She reluctantly acknowledged that he lived in another city with his second wife and a couple of young children. Intrigued by a new addition to my possible in-laws, I insisted on the name of the city, his phone number and address.

"Forget about him for now," she countered. "Without my mother's consent, nothing will happen for us. She needs to feel comfortable with this marriage first. How much time do we have till you leave the country? Where are you in the process?"

I shared the good news of getting my passport and that a few American universities had accepted my application pending the results of the TOEFL or upon graduating from the language school. Due to the postal employees' strikes that had crippled my activities, I had decided to bypass the TOEFL results and go straight to a language school in Los Angeles and then to graduate school. I estimated my departure in less than three months.

She asked if I could arrange for her to meet with my mother again. But, she warned me, before the meeting, I needed to work on my mother's attitude toward Neilu and her family.

Before I got a chance to reply, with the same breath, she added, "I'm still upset about your family's behavior. Plus, I'm not really happy about your marrying me and then leaving the country right after. Perhaps you should delay that." After a short pause, perhaps for taking a breath, she ordered me not to purchase my airline tickets without talking to her first.

My charm, humor, and negotiation skills were not producing the result I wanted. She was not happy. My heart felt heavy. We could not resolve any of those issues this way. We had to end the phone conversation soon, and I told her so.

First she thought I didn't bring enough coins for the public phone. After reminding her of the imposed martial law, she sarcastically said, "Oh yes, I guess President Carter lost his influence on our government. Our king is back in command of the situation."

It felt important for me to counter that sarcasm with a response. Perhaps the Iranian dictator was accepting a higher rate of civilian casualties as part of the cost of a solution.

She quickly replied, "Or the military generals have won the argument. Some say that Carter's administration policy in pressing the Iranian government to improve its human rights condition has backfired. I'm not sure if our people are ready to handle democracy yet."

"That's hog wash! Oppression, bullying, torture, and deception will never work in the modern world. It will only make things worse." "It has worked before!" she exclaimed.

Imposing martial law had ironically opened the doors to a much more effective way for the public to express their opposition. Rooftops were becoming the place to be during the curfew. Every night after dark, people gathered where the military couldn't see or reach them and chanted *Allah-O-Akbar*. I explained to her the incredible sensation of witnessing that phenomena. "Imagine listening to a choir of several thousand members expanding several kilometers in every direction while sitting in the middle of them."

"So what? Who cares about a few people saying some Arabic words on their rooftops at night?"

Her response struck me as harsh—even blasphemous. *Allah-O-Akbar*, was not just some Arabic words. It means "God is Great." I explained that this phrase reverberating over thousands of voices of unseen people put fear in the soldiers' minds that God is with the rebellion. It had become a powerful symbol of resistance during the Iranian uprising in 1978. The long and echoing wave of *Allah-O-Akbar* resonating throughout the large metropolitan city of Tehran had a significant psychological effect on both parties. It connected and strengthened the uprising, while it weakened the hearts of the security forces. The haunting echo of this powerful phrase was spreading all over the city, night after night. It was psychological warfare.

She changed the subject and questioned the wisdom of using a public phone booth in such a dangerous time.

To answer her question, I had to walk a fine line of explaining my parents' viewpoint without making a mockery of them to her. My parents considered our home telephone as an emergency communication device. Even on important calls, we were ordered to keep it below three minutes. Our phone was not a socializing instrument to them. At that time, the technology was unable to alert people of other callers. What if a family member was in need of urgent help? However, I didn't share with her how much I despised my mother's eavesdropping to every one of my phone conversations.

Calming her required more time, which I didn't have. My ticking watch reminded me of that.

"I have to go! It's 8:40. Martial law curfew begins at nine and I am twenty minutes away from home!"

We said quick farewells. I hung up the phone and jumped in the car as soon as I physically could. The radio was on. Shortly after I began driving, the music was interrupted, and a stern voice announced that martial law would be enforced at 2100. The announcer gave a firm warning that the military will enforce the law, and that soldiers were authorized to use lethal force when necessary.

With the trigger-happy soldiers, a small mistake could be fatal. I had to be very careful. My heart was racing and my mind rehearsing the possible encounter with security forces. I drove as fast as I could. The streets were empty; the city looked like a ghost town. It was eerie to be the only car in a dark night on a well-lit, three-lane boulevard.

My speed must have been around a hundred twenty kilometers per hour, when suddenly out of nowhere, about a hundred meters ahead, a dog appeared on the side of the road. It was a white, midsized mutt of about ten kilos. It seemed to be contemplating crossing the road.

"Oh no, please stay where you are. Don't move for a few seconds," I said out loud.

The dog turned its head toward my direction. As precaution, I drove in the middle lane. The mutt stepped on the road and walked briskly to cross. A quick glimpse at the clock showed 8:52, only eight minutes before the curfew, and I was about ten minutes away from home. Any slowdown would increase my chances of being caught by the security forces.

"Okay, run doggy, run! If you run fast you will make it," I shouted.

The road was wide with no traffic. I could easily avoid hitting it if the dog would move forward with the same speed or even if it would stop where it was.

I honked my horn several times hoping to alert the dog of my direction and speed. The dog passed the first lane and moved forward at the same pace.

My car traveling at over a hundred twenty KPH was rapidly getting closer to the dog. To help the dog see me and figure out what to do, I switched to the first lane on my right while maintaining my speed and direction as I kept honking.

Fifteen meters away from the dog, it passed the middle lane.

Five meters away, the dog suddenly stopped.

My yelling in the car ordering the dog to continue had no effect.

The beast changed its mind and decided to turn back.

All my shouting was useless, the dog couldn't hear me. I was in the far-right lane, with the sidewalk lined with trees to my right. At that speed, things happen fast.

A moment later, while screaming, I heard a hit, felt a big bump under the front of my car, and a fraction of a moment later a bump on my rear. Holding the steering wheel tight, I glanced in my rearview mirror. A large cloud of dust appeared in the back. It was impossible to see if the poor dog survived.

Mentally, I was exhausted. My unproductive conversation with Neilu made me feel as if I had been hit by a car. Just like the poor dog. The dog, hmm. Was it possible that the universe or karma was giving me a message? That a massive metal box traveling at the speed of hundred twenty KPH hit me because I altered my course?

Confusion had settled in my mind like a dense fog. I made it home at exactly 21:00. Shaken up from the incident, I met my anxious parents standing outside of our house door looking for me.

"Where have you been child? Don't you know about the curfew? We thought you were arrested!" My mother's monologue showed how upset she was. Seeing my upset face did not help the situation. Her eyebrows were tied in a knot and her big brown eyes were full of questions and concerns.

"I am okay, let's go inside. I will tell you all about my evening."

13

NAKED TRUTH

 I closed my mouth and spoke to you in a hundred silent ways.

— Rumi

I often thought of Neilu as an undiscovered island, an uncharted place where no one knows what lies beyond its shoreline. It's rising ridges were surrounded by cold, mysterious water, where its army of waves consistently pounding the fragile sand.

She carried an aura of mystery from the first day she appeared in my life. An indefinable, unexplored, thrilling sensation overcame me when I saw her, and I had to explore the possibilities. Thus, I pursued her.

Two years into our relationship, on a Wednesday afternoon in mid fall 1978, I was sitting in my car waiting for her bus to arrive. She had called me the day before. That was our routine. Whenever she returned to Tehran for a family visit, I would pick her up and then we would spend a few hours at the park. She budgeted one third of her time for me, and the rest was spent with her family.

Having parked on the busy street that fronted the terminal, I kept my eyes glued to the entrance gate so as not to miss her arrival. She usually traveled light, only toting a small carry-on bag. She was truly a minimalist in every aspect of her life. Her room at the university's dormitory had no colors. The walls were white and naked, a simple metal-framed bed, more like a cot, was on the left with a thin, dark green blanket as a cover. On the edge of the only window in the room she had placed one small plant wrapped with aluminum foil. The plant appeared healthy. The room's nakedness emitted a transitory sense of the occupant.

A chill ran up my back the first time I saw her dorm room. It was telling me stories of loneliness and distrust. I was drawn to the plant right away. It was the only bright color and living thing in that otherwise cold, empty room. I was intrigued by the amount of attention the plant was getting. The foil wrapping around the pot was meticulous, and a spray water bottle sat near it. I remember putting my finger in the pot when she wasn't looking. The soil was moist.

Why just one small plant?

I didn't ask her the question. Perhaps it was her maternal instinct, summoned to at least care for one small living thing. Or, perhaps, she was testing the plant to see if it would also betray her.

The air in the room, the objects in the room, however limited, belonged to her. I felt close to her in that room. My arms were eager to hug her and hold her tight. My mind wanted to tell her that she could trust me and stay close to me without fearing that I would betray her trust. I wanted to give her the gift of love.

A glance at my watch worried me. Her bus was late.

She didn't have many needs. Her worldly possessions consisted of only a few items. She appeared satisfied. From her small potted plant to her friendships, she was particularly selective. People in her inner circle would receive a good deal of attention. For example, if you were her friend, she would look at your eyes, and if you deserved it, she would grace you with her smile. That genuine smile was a rare treat, not available for everybody.

My gaze was fixed at the bus terminal. The cassette player was playing music in the background. I had an unsettling feeling in my stomach.

My mind took off to the very first time I was formally introduced to her two summers prior. It was at a prestigious, nationwide student art competition camp near the endlessly tantalizing Caspian Sea.

My objective was to travel to the camp and compete in the classical guitar contest. Traveling to the Caspian Sea on a train was an adventure by itself. The uncomfortable ride with old cars from the forties made the two-hundred-kilometer journey last much longer than one would anticipate. But the rough ride was well compensated by the beauty of the scenery over the height of the imposing Alborz Mountain range. We went over several bridges, over deep drops, and many sites of green forests, rivers and streams that appeared and disappeared as the train made its way on to the north of Iran where the largest lake in the world, the Caspian Sea, is located.

Once we arrived, a bus took us from the train station to the camp. My college buddies and I arrived at the camp in the afternoon with hoarse voices from loud singing during the trip. A fresh, gentle sea breeze welcomed us as we stepped out of the bus.

The camp was a sprawling compound consisting of many dormitory buildings, a large dining hall fit to serve several hundred hungry students, a good-sized amphitheater, a large sandy private beach and many other smaller special buildings for workshops and other purposes.

After settling down in our rooms, we were called to a general meeting in the cafeteria, a large circular structure with no walls at the center of the camp. When I arrived, about fifty students had already gathered. The camp director with a booming voice went over the schedule and the rules. He finished after thirty minutes and dismissed everyone. In search of any high school friends, I scanned the crowd. As the crowd thinned out, my eyes froze on one person. I moved closer to get a better look.

Yes, it was him. Farhad. What a surprise! Curious to the reason for his presence in that camp, I approached him cautiously. He nonchalantly acknowledged me and asked if I had just arrived.

My mind raced to find a justification for his presence there.

Confused, I desperately looked for reasons other than competing in the same classical guitar competition where I was participating. He was a student at the military academy. What was he doing there? And for what purpose? Perhaps he was there to compete in drawing. Music was what he was best at. Drawing was his second best artistic talent. His presence was unsettling. I needed answers to my many questions, so I unleashed them, one after the other.

"No. I'm here for the same reason you are here!" He replied as if it was no big deal.

He then looked deeply into my eyes, perhaps searching for any elements of fear. I stared back, as the word 'betrayal' was presenting itself.

Now, it became clear to me why he had acted peculiar during his short visit to Tehran two months prior. He had asked if I was competing in the guitar contest at the camp. Usually he didn't care, but that day, he insisted on going over every one of my pieces, claiming he was there to help prepare me for the competition. He failed to mention that he was going to compete with me in that contest.

Without wasting a moment, I commented sarcastically on how funny it was that he didn't mention his plans to compete to me two months ago.

"This is life, my friend. You never know what is coming!" he replied staring into my eyes.

My face felt unusually warm. I could hear my heart pounding loud and fast. I tightened my right fist and moved my face closer to his face, "What is this? Machiavelli? Or is it another one of your experiments on tolerance? Oh no, wait a minute, I got it. It's a bet between you and your new college buddies to see what it takes for me to punch you."

"Look, it's water under the bridge. Don't worry about it. You're a good guitarist, so you'll do just fine. Let me introduce you to some of my friends. We will hang out together," he said.

It took me a lot of restraint not to punch him. I didn't want to hang out with him or his friends. I walked away.

It was time for me to reassess my work. He was a formidable competitor with an unfair advantage over me. In his visit to Tehran, he had learned all about my techniques, good and bad.

After an hour of practice, I went for a walk on the beach. The smell of the sea, the view of the endless horizon, and the sound of the steady rhythm of waves eased my mind. The view of a group of busy little Caspian Sea birds relentlessly running after the waves to catch food made me smile.

The dinner bell rang after sunset. Avoiding Farhad, I joined my college friends for dinner.

The next morning, an empty table in the corner of the cafeteria looked perfect for my breakfast in solitude. My second bite wasn't yet swallowed when Farhad, unexpectedly, plunged himself right in front of me and said, "You need me."

"Like a plague," I answered while keeping my head down and continuing to eat.

He accused me of being too shy and added a comment about the camp being an open season for hunting. He asked me to let him to introduce me to a few cute girls.

Without looking at him, I reminded him of his difficulty talking to a girl without turning red, and mocked his newly claimed ability to meet and become friends with girls. I was not happy with him. His behavior agitated me.

"I have changed. I am a magnet now. They follow me everywhere," he answered and snatched a piece of bread from my tray.

Reacting to his aggravating behavior, I jumped to smack him. But my body froze in its tracks when at that precise moment, I saw a brunette girl with a wide smile, tap him on the back and ask if she could join him. She didn't give me even a smidgen of a glimpse. She totally ignored me, as if I wasn't sitting there.

He looked at me with an all-knowing smile plastered on his face, pointed to the girl and said, "This is Neilu."

There were butterflies in my stomach when she acknowledged my existence with a quick look. I introduced myself and shook her hand. She sat next to Farhad, teasing and laughing with him. Thirty seconds later, another girl came and sat on the other side of Farhad getting cozy with him. I was stunned!

After breakfast, we all departed and reported to our respective competition areas. Although this had been the first time I was introduced to Neilu, I had a strong feeling that I had seen her somewhere else before.

On the afternoon of the second day of the camp, while sitting on a pile of sand on the beach, I watched Neilu and Farhad, horsing around. She was strong, fast on her feet, and well grounded. In some instances, she actually threw the larger and heavier Farhad on the ground. Her moves reminded me of someone with martial-arts training. Suddenly I remembered. She was the arrogant girl from the officers' sports club.

During my high school years, I was a member of an exclusive athletic club for military officers and their family members. My uncle, who was a full colonel in the army, had arranged for my membership there. I had seen her walking around on the club's ground in a Taekwondo uniform with a green belt. I recalled her demeanor of being overconfident and unapproachable.

Her arrogance, in particular, was carved into my memory when one afternoon, her younger brother barged into my space, interrupting my tennis practice against the wall. Despite my objection, the kid took over my space and started hitting balls on the practice wall next to me. The interruption, and especially his rudeness, annoyed me. Surprised by his insolence, I looked around to see if he was with any older sibling or parents. Neilu was a few steps behind him. She snobbishly joined her brother, ignoring me and the fact that they interrupted my practice.

"Excuse me! I am practicing here!" I protested.

"You don't own this court," Neilu said arrogantly as she and her brother continued hitting their tennis balls against the practice wall.

Astonished by her impolite and condescending behavior, I said, "Can't you wait until I am finished?"

She ignored me and continued hitting balls without looking at me.

My anger over her rude manners added a twist to my strange attraction to her. I was fascinated by her self-confidence. That summer, every time I saw her, a mixture of disgust, appeal, and curiosity pushed me to a challenge. Was she really as solid as she led people to believe? Would she go out on a date with me?

My few attempts to start a conversation with her failed miserably that summer. My curiosity remained unfulfilled. Years had gone by since then, and I had forgotten about her until that morning at the camp breakfast table.

Sitting on the pile of sand, observing her play with Farhad, helped me to remember.

Is she still the same arrogant, self-absorbed girl that I was fascinated with a few years back? Would I have a chance with her?

She took a break from playing with Farhad and plunked down on the pile of sand next to me. I snuck a quick look at her. Since her eyes were shut, I allowed myself a long look, and studied her body contour. Her slim, fit body was shapely with a pair of long legs, a well-defined waist, a relatively small chest, a long neck, and then her face. Her face was an example of well-proportioned elegance and balance, and held a hint of a smile, as if she knew I was watching her.

"You should try it," she said it without opening her eyes.

Nervous, I looked away and said, "Excuse me?"

"Lie on your back, close your eyes, and relax. It's magical," she answered.

Following her advice, I lay down on the sand and closed my eyes. It was relaxing. After a moment, I summoned some courage and asked if she had studied Taekwondo martial arts.

She confirmed and added that she had a brown belt. And immediately asked, "How did you know?"

I half opened my eyes and found her on her elbows staring at me. Without answering her question, I asked if she was a member of the officers' sport club in Tehran a few years ago.

"Yes!" A big smile appeared on her face with that answer. She looked at me as an explanation was due.

Watching her martial art moves on Farhad, I revealed, made me realize that I had seen her in the officer's club before and how I thought of her as a snob.

She laughed and repentantly said, "Probably well deserved."

Her smile and her look with those big black eyes shook my heart. Like an amateur boxer, who after long years of practicing finally gets his chance to face his most sought-after opponent, I felt exuberant. I had a feeling that I was going to get to know her much better. "But man is not made for defeat," a quote from Hemingway's *The Old Man and the Sea* bounced in my head as I gazed out over the water.

Excited with my entry to a challenging relationship with Neilu, my affection for her grew daily. Her simplicity impressed me. Contrary to many people I knew, possession of worldly materials seemed unimportant to her. Her mind seemed sharp and clear on what she wanted. We continued to see and write to each other after the camp and I realized that my fondness of her was more than just a friendship. I had fallen in love.

A loud and obnoxious bus horn brought me back to the time at hand. It was her bus announcing its long-awaited arrival. Excited to see her, I rushed out of the car and walked straight to the bus.

When she stepped down from the bus, I greeted her and took her small luggage, waiting to hug until we were out of the public eye. She suggested that we go to *Aria-Meher* Park for a little while before I took her home.

The park was one of the newer parks named after one of the many titles of the Shah, the king of Iran. *Aria-Meher* meant the one who's loved by Arians, as some believe that most Iranians are Arians. The park was vast and its open-design landscape with many ponds, water fountains, and large well-groomed grassy areas was a good place to have some quiet time. As we arrived, the clouds rushed away, and much-welcomed rays of sunshine touched our skin. The sun's warmth and bright emissions were pleasant relief on a cold autumn day.

We held hands as we strolled along a path. Her unusually quiet demeanor concerned me. My guess was that the business of our wedding was taking a toll on her. Hence, I inquired about her thoughts, and if the question about getting married in Iran or abroad was bothering her.

She nodded in agreement.

My view on the subject had recently become clearer. Getting married in Iran was not the right thing to do for us. Going through all the stress and rigmarole of getting married in Tehran, and then bearing a long separation right after it. It didn't seem wise to me. My hope was that she would understand my thinking.

Endless arguments with my family, and stress over her family's needs over our union, had been added to the anxiety of my day-to-day ambiguity of life and uncertainty of my future. I had started questioning the soundness of the decision to marry. I was aware of the social complexity of weddings in Iran, but as an outsider. This was the first time I had actually felt the burden of its enormous weight on myself and all the people involved.

"Then, don't go to America!" she said—nearly shouting. "Or at least stay here till I finish college. That's all. Real simple."

One more year of postponement? That is, if there were no more interruptions, no more school shut downs, or the total collapse of the government. I had a gut feeling that it wouldn't work. In addition, the threat of the draft was dangerously close and real. When I explained all that to her, she dismissed my worries and claimed that I was paranoid.

Her hands were on her knees when I pulled her left hand close to my face and placed a gentle kiss on it. Again, I reminded her, the continuous waves of social unrest were a strong indication of the country's heading toward a full-blown revolution. Nobody could accurately predict what changes would occur after the regime change.

My thoughts strongly leaned toward preparing for the worst.

She looked away. "All of my family and friends are here. It's much better to get married here where everyone can attend."

My gaze moved to the open landscape in front of us as my stomach churned with anxiety. This conversation was not going well. Far away, through the smog and polluted Tehran air, at the end of the open space stood the Alborz Mountains, tall and imposing. Their enormity and powerful presence often were used by us, the Tehranians, as a symbol of courage and determination. The metaphor helped us to weather the troubles ahead. My inner voice was loud and clear, "A mountain is strong and resolute in its course and so should I be."

There was another veiled reason for my hesitation to marry her then and there. Uncertain of her reaction, I never spoke of it before as it required courage. Thus, defaulting to my previous position, I reiterated once again my argument with a new twist. Our nuptials in Iran would be followed by a physical separation shortly thereafter, either my leaving for the United States, or my forced enlistment in the military. We would be unable to see or touch each other for a long time; we would be a separated married couple. Wasn't that the opposite of what marriage was about?

Neilu took her hand away from my grip and snapped back, "Then, apply for graduate school here. There are many masters and doctorate programs here in Iran. By extending your studying, you'll delay the draft. Wait until I finish, and then we'll go abroad together."

She was one year behind me because of multiple shut downs of her university due to strikes and conflicts with the security forces. No one could predict when she would graduate from college for certain. It could easily extend beyond one year.

"I have just one more year—"

I interrupted her. "That is *if* the teachers or students don't go on strike and *if* the government doesn't shut down the university for the entire year." I was getting frustrated. We had had this conversation many times before.

All my life, I had been told that my first duty was to be subservient to God, second to my country, third to my community, fourth to my family, and very last, to my dreams. Who was I My dream of liberty was being threatened again. It was at risk of being shattered to pieces because of my love and desire for this girl. Both were imperative to my future. It was unlikely for me to have both at the same time. I felt cornered and forced to sacrifice one of them. A flood of other thoughts rushed my mind: Farhad's comment about my study abroad, *it's a cop-out*; Hassan's proposal to stay and hold a strong position within the local militia, or perhaps the one to sacrifice was the one of pursuing self-liberty. Perhaps favoring my life partner was the right choice.

All my life, I had been told that my first duty was to be subservient to God, second to my country, third to my community, fourth to my family, and very last, to my dreams. Who was I to contradict that? Challenging a tradition rooted in my culture for millennia required courage.

Neilu insisted I postponed my dream of going abroad and stay with her. Farhad, my old friend, thought I was selfish and decadent. My acquaintance from the old neighborhood, in a nutshell, put my departure as a sort of security issue for my family. And my father was indifferent.

My head was throbbing. I hated to be restricted like this.

She was silent.

Once again, I resorted to her understanding of my long endeavor in planning, dreaming, and waiting and waiting for years to move abroad. Of course, for a twenty-one-year-old, five years is much more than just quarter of his life. For me, it was closer to half of my conscious life as I believe my self-awareness as a person, started around age nine or ten.

I begged her to reflect on what she was asking me to do—calling it all just as the final moments of my long wait was about to come to pass. With the political situation rapidly depleting, I could get stuck there forever! Would I ever forgive myself for not following my dream?

She remained silent.

My mind was racing. Staying was not a good decision for me. Any day our borders could shut down for a long time. Softly, but resolute, I broke the silence. "I have to follow my dreams."

She looked down on the ground. Sadness was strong in her silence.

I took her hands again, but they felt cold and heavy. "Why don't you join me now? Transfer your units and finish your study in the U.S."

"That would put me behind even more. I want to get my degree from the University of Isfahan where I started. I want to finish one stage of life before entering another," she insisted.

My attempt to clarify that a bachelor's degree from a college in the U.S. is still an internationally accepted degree with the only difference being the name and location of school, didn't work. I expanded that life sometimes changes the game. Our priorities and objectives also change. A bit of flexibility to adjust our plan when necessary is not such a bad thing . . .

"How come your logic doesn't apply to yourself?" Neilu cut me off and pulled her hands away.

She noticed my puzzled face and clarified further. Basically, she took my logic and turned it around. She referred to our decision on getting married as destiny's attempt to change the game. Therefore, according to my own logic again, my priorities and objectives should have changed to her, and our life together. This, she resolved, should have had a higher value than my immediate trip abroad.

That wasn't bad enough. She advised me that it wouldn't be the end of the world if I changed my plan and postponed my trip. America and Europe would still be around, and their universities would continue accepting foreign students. She added, "Let's get married here and stay till I finish school, and then we'll go abroad together."

Our communication was not effective. I shook my head. We were not connecting.

"Yes, how does it feel to be on the other side of the table? Why can't *you* be more flexible?" she continued, clearly annoyed.

It was time for me to switch my argument to the one with more perils. In my view, the political turmoil was much more serious than what she thought. The regime could change completely, and borders could shut down, in which case, we would get stuck in Iran, indefinitely. Heck, for all I knew, the country could even get into a war within a few months. Iranians were always conscious of the possibility of invasion from neighboring countries. In that case, I would be definitely drafted, regardless of my excuse, and who knew if I would return to my family alive?

She turned her head and looked at me, her eyes opened wide. "A war? Your imagination is going wild. What war? You are making this up in your paranoia."

Did I need to remind her of our nation's colorful history? Or was she so focused on driving home her point that she ignored the harsh reality of our time? Surely, she couldn't be so naïve not to see the signs or hear the murmur of change. My desire to educate her took over, and I went over how one could easily find many examples of countries in history whose militaries, during a revolution, became distracted and divided, and their neighboring countries took the opportunity to invade. Saddam Hussein in Iraq, our arch enemy in the southwest, and the Soviet Union in the north, in its search for an easy access to the international waters of the Persian Gulf, were ready to pounce. With the military so distracted, I placed a high probability on one or both, would invade Iran soon.

Agitated, or perhaps even irritated by my long monologue, Neilu sat up straight and with animated arms said, "First of all, you're paranoid. Second, if that happens, you are supposed to stay here and defend your country! What kind of a man are you?"

Oh, she was hitting below the belt. Once again, patriotism was used as an anchor to stop me. Of course, we all are interested in protecting and fighting for what is dear to us. However, I found it provoking when others, and now Neilu, tried to intimidate me to adhere to her set of values. My very survival as an adult in an autocratic society would be in jeopardy, I was certain. I felt I would explode if I didn't speak my mind.

"A society that bullies you on every corner as a norm is not for me. I've waited a long time to experience this phenomenal thing called freedom of expression, to be able to read whatever I want without persecution, to write whatever I want without fear of losing my life, to wear whatever I want without getting spit on, to believe in whatever I want without getting hung by the executioner. The desire of being treated as a human is becoming like oxygen that I no longer can survive without. I'm afraid I'll perish if I stay much longer," I proclaimed.

"Good grief, what a long-winded answer," she teased. "Then let's get married here in this county and then you go. I will join you whenever I'm done here." She was focused and knew what she wanted. If she couldn't keep me in Iran, then the next position to fall back on was to tie the nuptial knot before I leave the country.

My logical approach was dissipating. Our challenging future had been occupying my thoughts quite a bit on those days. There was a troubling scenario looming in her proposal. My indirect references to point out the problem were not working. In her relentless pursuit of the subject, I had to bring this lingering, unstated issue up in a more direct fashion. There were no other ways around it. I took a deep breath. "It's not wise."

"Why?" She turned her face toward me and looked straight at me. Her eyes were wide open and her brows were arching upward. Her face reflected a determined yet somewhat frustrated person.

My imagination had taken me to America many times. I had flown over the multiple continents in my mind and pondered multitudes of maps. The physical distance was far. But in Neilu's pragmatic mind, a girl who had never stepped outside of Iran, the phrase *oceans apart* perhaps didn't have that much bearing. She was all about being practical. This time, I took a more direct approach and emphasized the strong possibilities of long periods of physical separation. The best scenario was one year. The worst, many years. Uncomfortably, I added, "During the time that we're physically separated, we won't be able to see each other or touch each other. Communication will be difficult, and we may grow apart—"

"What are you talking about?" she interrupted.

Looking down on the ground, I shuffled my feet on the gravel. She was asking me to spell it out. A grim possibility of reality, the way I saw it. My worries were the cost of misinterpretation. What if she takes it the wrong way? I hesitated, but she kept staring at me, demanding an explanation.

Reaching for her hand, which she let me hold, I looked up, "If we get married here and I leave soon after, there is a possibility that we each will change during the long wait. I have never been in such a situation before, so I don't know how I may change." I had read a number of articles about it. I was convinced that people do change during long periods of separations. I paused, looked her in eyes. "You may change too. Our world is so fragile that it may crumble any moment and transform to a totally unimaginable new world. Our experiences dealing with these new worlds may deeply impact us. We each may become a different person. What if I lose my strength after a long period of wait and fall in love with someone else? Then, for you, a married woman, life here would become difficult. If we get married now then dissolve our marriage later, you will be marked as a divorced woman. In this country, most people don't look favorably on a divorced woman. The situation would become a lot worse if the country falls into the hands of religious fanatics. I know this is the worst case scenario, but it may happen and it won't be fair to you."

Her eyebrows dropped, she took her eyes away from me. A deep sorrow moved across her face. She pulled her hands away from me and looked down on the ground, rubbing her temples. A dreadful silence took over. A few moments later she raised her head and stared at the swans gently floating on the pond near us.

Respecting her need to process her thoughts, I remained quiet.

A few ducks played on the other corner of the pond. The scene was serene. Only the giggles of a few children playing could be heard in the distance. It was too quiet.

After a few minutes, she turned her head away from me, wiped her tears, and without looking at me said, "I don't want you in my life anymore. Not your kind of a man."

Her words hit me like a lightning bolt. She was offended. Many questions in reaction to her comment spilled out of my mouth. Questions such as: what *kind* of a man? can you elaborate further?

She stood up. "We are finished. Take me home."

Bewildered, I stayed seated on the bench. I looked up at her and begged her not to be hasty. I tried to be honest and transparent about my thoughts. This was not a small decision in our lives. We needed to examine every possibility. "Life is not a fairy tale!" I cried.

She walked toward the parking lot in brisk, determined steps. I followed her, begging her to reconsider. When she reached my car, she stood next to it, facing away from me, waiting for me to unlock the passenger door. Reluctant and confused, I unlocked and opened the car door for her. Despite my many attempts, she did not talk in the car. I knew her well enough to understand that her silence wasn't a game. She was hurt.

Once we arrived at her house, she quickly got out of the car and took her small suitcase. All I could say was, "I'll call you later!"

When she heard that, she bent down, looked at me through the lowered passenger side window of the car and said, "No. I don't want to see you ever again. Do not call."

Numbed, I sat in the car and watched her walk into her house. After she disappeared inside, I waited a few more minutes, but I'm not sure why. Perhaps I hoped she would come out and talk to me. Dazed in a fog of confusion, like a zombie I drove away. A flood of questions rushed into my mind as I slowly put distance between us.

Did I blow it? Was I too honest? What did I say that deserved such a radical reaction? Could I take any of it back? Would she take my calls? "A spoken word, like a lost opportunity doesn't come back." Who said that? I think this was Cary Grant's line in a movie. What was that movie's name . . .

After a few days of many unsuccessful attempts to contact her, a heavy lump of reality lodged itself in my heart. The burden of potential loss was overpowering. Her image was my companion every moment during those days. Every time the phone rang, I jumped to answer it, thinking, hoping that it was her returning my numerous calls. Everywhere I looked, a reflection of her was in the background.

The possibility of losing her permanently became unbearable.

My unstoppable tears were making the passing of days unbearable. I begged in vain to her mother, her sister, or whoever answered her house phone, to let me talk to her. She never called back. Every time I called, their answer was the same, "Don't call again, she doesn't want to talk to you anymore."

It was time to question my motives and re-examine my purposes.

So I did it, over and over.

What is it with this new world that I seek so intensely?

Why is the pull so strong that I'm giving up my love for just the sight of it?

Is this new world worthy of the trade?

How far must the sacrifices go?

Maybe, it was a hope that was pulling me like a strong magnet, a hope of a promise.

A promise of the possibilities for who I could become.

Could I truly become who I wanted to be in the new land?

Would I have the chance to explore my independent self without fear?

Or perhaps it was the assurance of tolerance that was so attractive to me.

Tolerating me as who I am.

Or maybe, it was the endorphins of hope, the excitement of losing fear--the fear of living on eggshells all the time.

Fear of spending every moment of my existence maneuvering the tangled web of social, religious, and malicious laws that I had never nor would I ever have a chance to influence.

Maybe it was the dream of respect.

Not the phony façade of respect, but a real respect that I and others would give to each other based on trust. Not just my trust, but the trust that others would have in me and my challenge to be worthy of their trust.

Imagine experiencing that world!

Neilu was a creature of habits. She always used the same buss company, and always returned to Isfahan on the last day of the week, Friday. The temptation was irresistible. I had to go, for one last chance.

That Friday afternoon was cloudy, windy, and dark. Her bus was parked on the street facing south, loading passengers. To see every passenger, I parked my car across the street facing north. My eyes searched for her, longing to see a glimpse of her. But there was no sign of her. I waited and carefully scanned every car and everyone near the bus station.

Suddenly, there she was. My eyes found her in the passenger line, waiting to get on the bus. In one rush of a moment, I reached for my car's door handle to open it and run to meet her. Our bodies were less than twenty meters away from each other. I could defy the busy traffic and be next to her in less than a minute.

Then my hand froze on the door handle. My respect for her wish stopped me. The girl I loved, the ever-poised and yet sensitive Neilu got on the bus. A few short moments later, the bus departed.

A drop of rain hit my windshield, and then another one. As the bus pulled away, I saw that she was sitting by the window facing my side of the street. She looked composed, as always.

A teardrop ran down my face, and then another one. Soon I found myself weeping uncontrollably. My right hand was clutching a crumpled piece of paper. I opened it to reveal the poem I had written for her.

Do you remember our first touch?
The first kiss?
Do you remember the first time your heart pounded loud?

> *So loud,*
> *as it was breaking free from its cage.*
> *Do you remember our first laughter together?*
> *When you floated on heavenly clouds of romance?*
> *Did you feel the trembling?*
> *The one that takes over your body, in harmony with tears.*
> *The one that makes heavens sad for you, rain for you,*
> *reaches for your heart, and embraces you in a cold, sympathetic, heavy fog.*
> *Have you felt your heart crushing under the weight?*
> *Have you ever said good-bye?*

One more time, I crumpled it and threw it on the passenger seat. It would never reach her hands.

It was raining hard. I started the car and followed the bus. Could I get another glimpse of her face?

My windshield wipers were working hard fighting off the rain. The low visibility made it hard to see. I maneuvered around the traffic like a menace to catch up with the bus.

I could see it up ahead. My heartbeat increased rapidly, and I sped forward. The streets were wet and slippery, but I didn't care. I swerved and zig-zagged, trying to get closer to the bus. A solid red traffic light stopped my insanity. A rush of vehicles, excited to see the green light, flooded the intersection. I pounded the steering wheel with my fist and shouted. The bus merged into the traffic and disappeared in the mist of heavy rain.

Dark clouds had occupied Tehran's sky that day. Typically, I dislike cloudy days, but that day, clouds were my friends, weeping along with me at the sorrow of my lost love.

Neilu was gone.

14

CASPIAN SEA

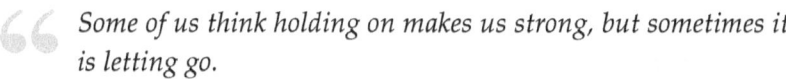 *Some of us think holding on makes us strong, but sometimes it is letting go.*

— Herman Hesse, German-born Swiss Poet, novelist
(1877-1966)

"Is this the best of times or the worst of times? I can't decide," said my troubled friend Davud, paraphrasing Charles Dickens.

"I don't know, maybe it's both, bitter and sweet." I philosophized along with him while sitting on a bench overlooking a large pond, eating tasteless hamburgers we bought from the stand in the park. A hundred meters in front of us, a few swans elegantly swam.

Davud and his girlfriend, Fariba, had just broken up and he wasn't taking it well. My hope was to cheer him up, and perhaps in the process, I would help myself deal with my own separation from Neilu. More importantly, I wanted to ensure that our romantic setbacks didn't slow our primary objective: to leave Iran before it was too late. I reminded Davud how close we were to our exit day, and that the excitement of starting a new life in a new world is the "sweet" part our current situation. An added bonus was that he no longer had to suffer through a long-distance romance. Traveling light was a blessing.

He disagreed when I finished describing the "bitter" part, which was the misery he had to suffer until he could forget her. He emphasized life without his gentle Fariba could never be sweet, and that he would never forget her.

He perked up when I shifted the argument to his mother. He was looking forward to a life away from that woman. Slapping me on my back, with a loud and humorous voice, he declared he couldn't tolerate her one more day.

Delighted with my ability to change Davud's mood, I took a hefty bite of my sandwich and nodded.

He went on about his dreams of a life far away from his domineering mother, how she was never satisfied; nothing was good enough for her. Then after a bite of his sandwich, his monologue changed course back to Fariba. To him, she was the opposite of his mother—quiet, soft spoken with a lot of love for others. He could envision her gentle hazel eyes smiling at him while he stroked her wavy red hair.

Davud had managed to switch back to his depressing mood. He fixed his eyes on some distant horizon. In a quiet, low voice he asked, "Aren't you sad that Neilu dumped you?"

He had quite a way with words when it came to me. *Dump*? First, his choice of words offended me. However, a few moments later, reality hit me. Yes, she did dump me. I became more disappointed than sad. The first week was the most difficult one. But, over days, I learned how to cope with it. Once in a while, a big wave of sadness tumbled over me.

He looked totally drained, as a person with no energy. I stopped talking about myself and looked at him. His neck tilted to the left and his eyes gazed at no particular place. It had a whirlpool effect on me, sucked my energy, and took my vigor to a dark and desperate place where I didn't want to go.

Apparently, sucked into his own depression, he didn't hear a word of what I said. After a moment, with the same low and quiet voice, he asked my opinion as to why his Fariba left him.

"Snap out of it, man!" I exclaimed.

This wasn't the first time he had experienced the end of a romantic relationship. He had gone down this road several times before. I reminded him of that—and that we had to stay focused on our goal. Our acceptance paperwork from American schools were due to arrive any day.

Davud kept his pitiful posture, mumbled that perhaps he should go to Mashhad and beg her to marry him.

The poor guy was bewitched. The city of Mashhad was over eight hundred kilometers away. Her parents were conservative Muslims, and they would never accept him. Even if they did, in my opinion, he would be miserable there. I became angry with his gloom. In a scolding voice, I went over how it would play out if he did it.

Yes, my words might have been painful for him to hear, but it was time for action. I had to do something to bring him to his senses. Abruptly, I punched him on his arm and proposed a trip north to the Caspian Sea for a few days. The city of Bandar Pahlavi came to mind. Their lagoons were legendary, and I had never been there. Fresh sea air and change of scenery sometimes does wonders on a depressed mind.

He remained silent. Then a few moments later he muttered, "Bandar Pahlavi?"

"Yes!" my excitement jumped out of me. It would be our first adventure together without anybody else around. We both badly needed it. In addition, this trip could be a good mini-test to see how we could get along in our travels. After all, we were about to embark on a journey together to a new world with a different language, different culture, and totally different set of rules.

He didn't respond to my injected dose of reality and continued his sad stare at the two swans floating away from us on the pond. The serene atmosphere of the park, being large enough to muffle the sound of traffic, lent itself to an environment easy to unwind and ponder about things.

He turned his head and paid better attention when I noted that this might be the last time we could go to the Caspian Sea. After a few more moments of silence, he agreed, with a warning that during the trip, he would most likely talk a lot about his love, Fariba.

My jubilance brought me to my feet. As I was getting up, he returned my punch with a much stronger one on my left shoulder.

The old Davud was back.

Early the next morning, despite the surprised look on the faces of my parents, I packed my bag and left Tehran for the shores of the Caspian Sea and Bandar Pahlavi, an old port city about two-hundred sixty kilometers north of Tehran.

We took Davud's car and selected a scenic, yet unsafe, mountain road called *Chaloos*. The road goes through the Alborz Mountain range with its deep valleys and lush rain forest called *Jangale Mazondaran*. Driving on the *Chaloos* road was considered risky due to its poor condition, lack of safety, narrowness, sharp hairpin turns, and deep drop-offs.

It felt good to go out of town without any parents, siblings, or girlfriends in tow, just two buddies. I actually thought that we were two dissimilar friends who, by coincidence, became similar in many ways.

My curiosity of knowing if he and I would get along was tantalizing.

As usual, his neck tilted to the left and his gaze was fixed on the horizon as he drove. His mind was somewhere else and his body was on autopilot. The first fifty kilometers of road was a straight freeway.

We drove along in silence for the first few kilometers.

Ten minutes into the trip he mumbled, "I miss her."

Unbelievable, I thought. We had just started! I had to change his mood. Shuffling through a box of cassette tapes, I found a Simon & Garfunkel tape, my favorite. I swiftly inserted it in the cassette player.

Music immediately occupied the space in the car. We both silently listened to the music for a while. It was during "The Sound of Silence" that I saw a few teardrops run down from the corner of his eyes.

Gazing at the road ahead, he softly spoke about his own tale. He explained that his story was a story of a man who was chasing a phantom for many years. He thought finding the one whom he could trust enough to drop his walls was like chasing a unicorn--a phantom, so he gave up. He compromised and settled with easier, physical relationships. The more friends he got, the lonelier he felt. He had a good job, many friends, and a steady girlfriend, but deep down, he was lonely. Then one day, when he wasn't looking anymore, he saw a shadow pass by him. Out of despair, he chased the shadow. To his disbelief, the shadow belonged to a unicorn--an elusive, dream-like companion that he could trust. So he did what he always wanted to do with his unicorn. He dropped all the walls and freely danced with his newly found cohort. His courtship immersed him deeper and deeper into the hope that he had finally found his soul mate. Just about that time, the shadow faded away and the unicorn disappeared. Now, he was left baffled, wondering if any of it was real.

Touched by his words, I searched for a response, something profound that could soothe him, but not give him false hope. Unable to come up with any words of my own, I quoted Merton, "The man who fears to be alone will never be anything but lonely, no matter how much he may surround himself with people." In my opinion, Fariba was a temporary bandage for a permanent wound. He was heartbroken, but she was not the right answer and I told him so.

A long silence followed that conversation. We let the music fill the air. When the tape ended, I immediately rushed to eject it. He snapped and scolded me on being harsh with his newly installed state-of-the-art cassette player equipment.

His short temper worried me, I had never traveled with him alone before. My fingers gently touched the buttons of the tape player. They were soft and rubbery. Compliments for his new tape player did not generate a response; changing the mood needed more substance.

At that point, the only thought that came to my mind to share with him was about my first exposure to car players. I must have been nine or ten years old when my older brother bought his first cool car. It was a white German Opel coupe, with a beautiful, smooth, aerodynamic body. The first time he allowed me to sit in the front passenger seat, I noticed a big gizmo hanging out underneath the dashboard in front of my knees. I asked him what it was. He explained that the unit was a car turntable! I couldn't believe my eyes! A record player that could play records as we drove. My brother took a red 45 RPM vinyl from his Beatle collection and inserted it in the player.

"Those units are gone now. This cassette player is the new fad." Davud smiled and pointed to his new cassette player.

Happy about getting him off his sad mood, I inserted a popular tune called "Popcorn" by the band Hot Butter and blasted the volume. We moved our bodies to the loud, rhythmic music and forgot all about the troubles of the world for those three minutes.

Fifteen minutes later, we entered the city of Karadj, about fifty kilometers west of Tehran. Since the next town was several hours ahead, Davud stopped in front of a grocery store to get ingredients for our picnic lunch. We decided to take our lunch farther down the road in the woods by a stream. He was excited about it and told me how much he loved camping, and that camping gear would be the first thing he would buy in America.

From the grocery store we bought feta cheese, tomatoes, basil, a few Persian cucumbers and a couple of bottles of Canada Dry. After the grocery store, we went to a bakery and bought *lavash* bread.

Leaving the city of Karadj, the road curved around mountains and valleys. After about half an hour driving on the winding road, we welcomed the view of a large body of water a few hundred meters down at the bottom of the drop to our right. Moments later, the scenic Karadj dam and Lake Karadj, surrounded by tall mountains appeared.

Not too long after that, Davud pointed to the road ahead with disappointment. There was a traffic jam on the narrow, two-lane highway. Shortly thereafter, we came to a complete halt. Davud pulled the emergency brake lever up with his right hand and got out of the car. He walked to the cars ahead of us and asked if anyone knew what was happening.

Suddenly, to the left of us, on the mountainside about three hundred meters up, a cloud of dark smoke appeared along with a loud boom. I jumped out of the car for a better view. It sounded like an explosion.

Someone said that a team of Green Beret commandos were having war game exercises. The roads were closed until the exercises were over. We surveyed the mountains around us on the left side of the road. Over a large boulder, I spotted a few of the soldiers using ropes, dropping down the rocks rapidly from where the black smoke was coming.

Davud pointed to the water and shouted, "Oh, look down on the water, they are firing machine guns. It looks like a real war!"

The cracking sound of automatic firearms, booms of explosions, maneuverings of fast boats, all played like an action movie. The commandos' combat exercises were a fresh and welcomed change to our boring daily life. The trip was off to a great start.

Thirty minutes later the exercises ended, and the road re-opened. We continued our trek north. The road became narrower and more winding with deep drop-offs and no guard rails. The rusted carcasses of three cars on the downslope was a reminder of how dangerous that road could become.

The scenery reminded me of a few years prior. I wasn't more than a few months older than eighteen when my father, on our return from our annual family summer vacation, pulled our 1958 VW to the side of the road and asked me to drive. My parents, my younger brother, and a cousin were on board. My driving license wasn't more than a week old then. I was excited about the challenge and the fact that my father trusted me with everyone's lives. But it soon turned frightening as a dense fog covered the road, so much that I could only see one meter ahead. No guard rail, faded lines on the road, and incoming traffic on a narrow road with a drop of two hundred meters or more next to me!

I shared that memory with Davud. With his usual crude humor, he asked, "Did you wet your pants?"

"I was very close to it after seeing big trucks and busses on sharp turns coming so close to my face."

Inside, I was smiling. Davud's mind was far away from his romantic troubles. Apparently, the beauty of nature, the challenges of the road, or perhaps just the plain fun of a road trip distracted Davud from his melancholy. He was becoming his upbeat self again.

We decided to take advantage of the beautiful nature around us and hike into the forest for a few minutes. For city dwellers like us, this was a quite an adventure. It didn't take long for Davud to find an opening on the side of the road.

He parked his car. We got out, stretched, and inhaled the fresh air blended with the scent of the forest, the musky smell of damp earth, wood, and soggy fallen leaves. The lively tapestry of fall was on full display, delivering a feast of colors to our eyes.

We found and followed a narrow trail. The calls of birds mixed with the sound of a rushing river at the basin of the gorge and mingled with the unique scent of rain on the tree bark, took my mind off all the worries of life.

We hiked for thirty minutes. Majestic oak, beech, yew and chestnut trees surrounded by berry and other bushes added to the delightful sensation of being cuddled by Mother Nature.

Davud took a deep breath and declared, "Ahhhhh, the first thing I'll do when I get to the U.S is buying camping gear, and then I'll go embrace nature."

"Won't it be dangerous with all the wild animals?"

With a serious and all-knowing face, Davud recalled his conversation with a few people who lived in the U.S. and camped regularly. According to them, camping was a popular activity. The U.S government had thousands of camp sites. There were trails, maps, and many books available. America, apparently, was a haven for camping enthusiasts.

My knowledge of camping was limited. I asked him if he knew of any organized camp sites in Iran.

Davud responded, "Are you kidding me? In this country, if you want to go camping in the wilderness, you are on your own. There's not much help or support available. Heck, you can't even find any half-decent camping gear here."

"But, we do have thousands of beautiful sites prefect for camping." Davud shook his head and answered that most were wild.

We talked and fantasized about the fun we would have camping in the U.S. hiking another half an hour before returning to the car.

After another hour of driving, Davud declared his hunger and wanted to stop for lunch. Despite my objection, he found a small pullout in the road and parked car.

His unilateral decision typically would not sit well with me. However, I let it go. This trip was also for me to learn how to compromise and get along with him.

In spite of my disapproval, the location was perfect. We took the lunch sack and walked toward the river. The resonating sound of rushing water bouncing off huge boulders filled the atmosphere. The melancholy masterwork of nature's fall colors in multiple shades of yellow, orange, red, brown and so on created a three-dimensional drapery of color and texture. The fact that we were walking right in the midst of it was surreal. And the contrast between our trivial human size and nature's giants, such as huge boulders and tall trees, produced a unique feeling of solitude for me.

We found a combination of tree stumps and large rocks near the river that served as chairs. Our simple lunch purchased at the grocery store was a perfect meal for the untouched nature surrounding us. For the first fifteen minutes, nature's intimidating presence silenced us.

We absorbed every bit of it.

Davud, looking up at the mountain adjacent to the river, praised the beauty of the indigenous natural elements.

"Including wild animals," I inserted. "Bears, panthers, foxes and others. Have you heard about the woman who was abducted by a bear in this area a few years ago?" Davud shook his head.

"As the story goes, a bear abducted a woman, took her to its cave, fed her for many weeks and licked her feet continually."

Davud interrupted me. "Why? Was it because she walked on a beehive?" Then he chuckled.

"I suppose the bear did it so she wouldn't escape. But she did, and survived the ordeal," I explained. "Also, my father said that in his youth, when he was assistant driver for a charcoal truck, he saw a panther passing right in front of them not too far from here," I continued.

He nodded his head while quietly observing the surrounding beauty. I couldn't help feeling spooked a bit. We were at a total disadvantage if attacked by any of the wild animals.

Back in the car I felt safer but didn't admit any of my fear to Davud. Our journey continued north.

The welcome sign of our destination city, Bandar Pahlavi, received a loud and harmonious cheer from both of us. Unlike during its crowded summer season, we found the city a cool, mystical, and quiet fishing town—just the right place to heal our broken hearts.

The town was surrounded with lagoons and marshlands. When we rolled down the windows, the salty aroma of the sea with a hint of fish and the serene view of the lagoons immediately comforted us.

Finding reasonably priced lodging was not difficult during the low season. We located a nice hotel that fit our budget when we passed the first traffic square. After settling into our room, we went out to discover the city. As a major port city in northern Iran, Bandar Pahlavi was encircled by openness, clean air, and friendly people.

In our walk toward the beach, we came across a large, wrought iron gate with a sign on top of it that read "Polish Cemetery" in English.

It was only a few weeks prior, that I had read an article about the history of the Polish army in Iran during WWII. Stalin, the then leader of the Soviet Union, had allowed an army to be created from thousands of Polish prisoners he had held in Russia. That army, on its way to the Italian front, entered Iran and stayed in Bandar Pahlavi for a while. Then they moved to Tehran and eventually joined the rest of the Polish troops fighting against the Italians and Germans. They also had thousands of civilians with them, many of whom were blonde Polish girls with blue eyes who stayed in Iran and married Iranian men. After sharing the history with Davud, I suggested we enter the cemetery and visit such a unique historic site, but he was anxious to get to the sea.

A few minutes later, the Caspian Sea, with all its might, welcomed us to its shores.

Silently, we observed the salty mist rolling off the water, deeply breathing the fresh sea air, and losing ourselves in the vastness of the Caspian. The view was splendid. Waves pounded the shore relentlessly. Gulls, ducks, and some geese were busy searching for food. And over the horizon large flocks of birds were continuing their migration south.

"God, I love her so much!" Davud screamed suddenly.

"Oh, man! You ought to let it go! She is gone! She ended the relationship with you and went to Mashad. Period." My anger at his continuous whining was getting the best of me. Did he have to ruin the mood?

"I can follow her to Mashad," he continued.

I begged him to get her out of his mind and focus on the future.

"I love her. For her, I will become a conservative Muslim. How can I exist without her?"

I had to be more direct, "How can an alcohol-drinking, pork eating, music-loving free man like you put the heavy yoke of conservative Islam on his shoulders, and carry the heavy chains of Islamic laws and culture every day, every hour, and every minute of his life? It will kill you, man. It will kill you!"

Davud was not a religious person at all. Religion was as foreign to him as the Chinese language. Chasing the flock of birds deep into the horizon with his eyes, he said, "I tried so hard to understand her. I did everything possible to accommodate her needs."

I was in agreement with him on that particular point. His gentle behavior was on the border of unreal when he was with her. He was extremely loving and passionate toward her. "I think you were intoxicated with her love. You are not naturally a gentle guy," I continued.

"Apparently, my devotion to her wasn't enough."

"Perhaps she wanted something you don't have," I offered.

Davud turned to me with his eyebrows tangled and tight. "Like what?"

"As much as I hate to say it, you can't blame yourself." I continued with my analysis of recent changes to our society and the psyches of our people. The heat of the revolution had influenced many people's minds and lives. New breeds of thoughts and beliefs were popping up everywhere. People on the fence had changed the most. Many of them had either become conservative Muslims or communists. Even some were mixing the odd combination of Marxism and Islam together, two conflicting viewpoints.

I concluded, "So, it's not so strange that she is turning more toward Muslim conservatism. She grew up as one. Our new social and political climate is very fertile for those tendencies. The time is hot for flight or fight. You and I have chosen the flight part, and she has decided to fight."

"So, what is it that she wants that I don't have?" Davud asked again.

Briefly, I pointed to the reality of an empty spot in their relationship.

With a concerned look he asked, "What was missing?"

His working harder for the answer, I thought, would give him a deeper understanding of his situation and with it, hopefully, he would have a more enduring resolution. Instead of telling him what he wanted to know, I kept asking questions. "What is the common theme of this revolution?"

Davud turned his head toward the sea again, shook his head and shrugged his shoulders.

"It's the demand on personal sacrifice for the good of the larger mass. People everywhere are re-evaluating their priorities in life. Like many others, she wants to stay here and fight for a better world. Shaping her future, the future of her country and possibly the world. To her understanding, I suppose, the right way of doing it is to go back to her conservative roots. So, my guess is that now, she thinks a conservative Muslim man who lives in Mashad is the right person for her."

"Then, I will become that guy," Davud replied immediately.

I pounded the small pile of sand near me with my fist. "No! You can't! You're missing the point!"

"I love her so much that I can endure anything." He was hanging on to that idea like a child to a big colorful, delicious lollipop. I had to explain why the lollipop was toxic for him.

"You loved the Fariba who was in Tehran with you as a student, hundreds of kilometers away from her environment. To you, she was this western-looking, tan-skinned redhead with a perfect body. An angel who fit flawlessly into your world. But in reality, she is from a different world."

Davud shrugged his shoulders again, I took it to mean he didn't understand what world I referred to.

"A world opposite of what you are accustomed to. I know your love for her is very strong. But, if you enter her world, you would be like a fish trying to live on land. You will flip and flop and then die."

Davud moaned, "The air feels so heavy without her. I'm not sure I can survive. Why don't we both scratch our plans for going abroad, and follow the loves of our lives and marry them?"

This was not good. An alarm went off in my mind. My buddy, my comrade, is backing out. Together, we have gone through so many obstacles to facilitate our dreams of studying abroad. He had just joined the group of people who have petitioned me to scrap my plan, my dream, and stay in that quagmire of complexity.

Keeping his feet on the ground of reality was one way to bring him back to his senses, but it would drag the conversation out much longer than I could stand. Instead, I decided to be more blunt and go much deeper by opening the wounds and remind him of the pain.

"Living in a world that operates on fundamentals that you despise with every fiber of your existence is like breathing a deadly poisonous air, in which you cannot survive."

He shook his head and looked down on the sand.

I continued, "Passive-aggressive behaviors, bullying, intimidation, oppression, harsh unkind judgments, and continuous, never-ending preaching are the norms in her world. Going abroad for us is much more than just going to another country to earn a degree--"

Davud interrupted. "If you are insinuating that I like girls and parties, I am not in that mood now."

Disappointed in Davud, I shook my head and explained that going abroad was a matter of life and death for us. Life without liberty was the worst shape of death. It was a real hell in its true meaning.

"Hell is hell no matter how you slice it. We don't have a fake hell and a real hell. I don't believe in hell anyway," Davud complained.

His silly comebacks were signaling me that he was turning around.

However, he didn't want to give me the satisfaction of it so soon. Since his knowledge of religions was poor, and we were talking about hell, I thought it was appropriate to turn the heat up and give him a dose of hellish description of the inferno he was considering getting into.

"Okay, but humor me for a second," I continued. "Imaging dying of excruciating pain, but the suffering doesn't stop with death. Instead, you come back to life and die again. The cycle continues and stakes become higher and higher each time. Pretty soon you become a zombie who doesn't feel pain but lives a soul-less, purposeless existence."

"All that will happen if I stay here with Fariba?" Davud asked.

He knew it well, but to secure the point, I felt it was necessary to explain what we were facing. In our autocratic system, the course of a life was determined by a set of rules put in place by a few ruling individuals, with no value given to or respect for individual rights.

"Well, I highly doubt this situation will change in our lifetime, and, my friend, life with those conditions is not worth having."

Davud sighed. "For Fariba, I will adapt."

"Yes, there are many people who adapt to the difficult conditions and learn to live their lives in shackles. Not me, and not you. Freedom is like fresh air to us. Without it we cannot survive."

He argued back that it was highly unlikely we would end up with another oppressive regime. In his view, people were sacrificing their lives to shaping the future and bringing democracy to Iran, not another dictatorship.

He was still trending on Fariba. None of my tactics worked. Time to change the approach. I had to break him out of it. Perhaps instead of telling him, I should lead him. Let him come to his own conclusion.

"Open up your eyes, and tell me what you see," I asked.

He played along and replied, "The Caspian Sea."

"Okay, what is abundant in the Caspian Sea?"

"Water. It's the largest lake in the world," he replied.

"Yes, but I mean economically. What does the Caspian Sea have that is unique to the world?"

"Best caviar in the world!"

"That's right. This country is blessed with unbelievable natural resources, such as huge oil reservoirs, uranium, copper, etc." I continued telling him what he already knew, such as Iran is strategically located in a significant place in the world. Iran also can easily close the Hormuz pass in the Persian Gulf and starve the world of petroleum. World powers would not allow one country to control all that, of course. But as the old Chinese proverb goes, m*uddy waters make it easy to catch fish*; I concluded that stability was not in the future of this country. Many powers were coveting Iran's natural resources and its location. Then I asked, "Aside from all that, what group is leading the revolution so far?"

"Muslims," Davud answered.

"Yes, and their leaders are the clergy groups, who have been suppressed for many decades. History has taught us that after any revolution, the victorious oppressed go after revenge and dominance. Usually in that situation, the first two victims are democracy and individual rights. Living in a society that lacks freedom is hell no matter what doctrine or political system is in place. If you are burning in hell, does it matter what fuels the flame?" Davud shook his head. A silent no.

"That's right, my friend. Fire is fire and you are burning."

Davud looked at me and then he turned his face toward the sea again. "Your situation is similar to mine. Neilu dumped you recently, right?"

I nodded.

"Don't you want to stay and be with her? You loved her, man." I looked away and sighed.

Davud then brought up the amusing circumstance that we both started dating the two girls at the same time, and they both left us at the same time. With a grin on his face he continued, "Wouldn't that be something if we both stay here, grovel to them to take us back, and have a double wedding! What do you say? It would be fun."

I smacked him in the head and said, "Did you hear anything I said?"

Davud reacted and raised his clenched fist to my face.

His threat didn't faze me. I looked down and said, "Seriously, don't take this issue lightly. It's not easy, but, personally I will leave as soon as I get a chance. With or without you."

We watched the sunset in silence. After a while, I asked him if he had received his acceptance letter from the English school in L.A. He nodded yes. Mine hadn't arrived. Nevertheless, I reiterated, as soon as mine arrived, we needed to set up an appointment at the American embassy to apply for our student visa.

Davud stretched his arms, yawned and said, "Let's get up early and go fishing tomorrow."

"Fishing? We don't have any gear."

He grabbed the back of my neck, squeezed, and shook it as he got up. "Don't worry, I will take care of it. All we need is line and safety pins."

Releasing myself from his hold, I asked what he was going to do with the safety pins, but he didn't answer.

We strolled through the town in search of dinner. Not too far from the beach, the strong aroma of barbecued lamb liver tickled my nose. Looking for the source, I found a *Jigari*, a street vendor selling barbecued lamb liver, about five meters to our left. The man stood next to his small grill where strips of liver on skinny metal skewers were smoking away on top of it. Next, he, sprinkled salt, and then fanned the charcoals. While fanning his grill, he belted out a melodious chant, calling passersby to sample his tasty barbecued lamb livers.

We looked at each other. No words needed to be said. It was perfect. The vendor expertly put four cooked skewers in a large piece of Persian flat bread, *sangak*, and pulled the skewers out. Smiles appeared on both of our faces. That was exactly how we wanted our barbecued liver, with the juice soaked on the bread.

Traveling the winding mountainous road through the forest worked as a filter. It separated the duplicity and complexity of living in a jungle of concrete buildings among millions of people and cars from the simplicity of life in a small town surrounded by nature. The slow pace, the modest shy smiles of locals and the clean sea air washed away our compiled anxiety. It amazed me how quickly we felt our human roots once immersed in nature.

After dinner, we bought a couple of line pulleys, went back to the hotel, and set the alarm clock for six a.m.

The next morning, the quacking of a few nearby ducks woke me before the alarm went off. It was at the break of dawn, and the refreshing scent of the sea permeated the air. Davud was sound sleep.

The dawn in that quiet, small town drew me out of the hotel room. Outside a light fog had enveloped the city. The chilly air smelled like fish. A few vendors were opening their shops, city janitors were sweeping the streets, and there was already a line at the baker's shop. Some fishermen had returned from the sea, preparing their catch of the day for market. The pace of life was slow and authentic.

On my walk, I bought fresh flat bread, feta cheese, and milk. Davud was still in bed, sound sleep when I returned and the alarm was sounding loudly.

"Get up you lazy bum. It's time to go. I've already got breakfast. Get up!" I yelled while shaking him.

Over his multiple protests, I rushed him out the door. Outside, he stretched and yawned, made a comment about the strong scent of the sea, and shouted a warning to the fish in the lagoons, threatening them of our arrival. We drove on a dirt road that took us into the woods. I was curious to see how he was going to make fishing poles out of just a few meters of line and safety pins.

We founded a secluded spot on the edge of water. Davud parked the car, got out, asked me to wait there and disappeared in the woods. A few minutes later he returned with two sturdy tree branches. He handed me one and instructed me to strip the leaves and insert it into a line pulley. Once he cleared the leaves off his branch, he took a safety pin and tied the end of the line to it.

"Now all I need is bait. For that we will use worms," he declared.

"Worms? Where do you get worms and how are you going to hook the worm to the safety pin, so it won't slip away?"

He bent down and quickly searched for worms by digging into the damp earth. He found one and demonstrated, by zig zagging the pin through the worm's body. It looked disgusting to me and I wasn't shy to declare it.

Davud gloated, "That is how it is done my friend. If you don't have the stomach for it, you can sit there like a cissy and watch the master."

I followed what he did exactly. Within a few minutes, our socks and shoes were off, our pants rolled up, and we stood knee deep in the water, joyfully casting our lines.

We spent several hours in the serene nature of the lagoon, away from cars, traffic, and any other distractions of the civilized world. The quiet of the surrounding, broken only once in a while by calls of birds or the jumping of frogs into the water, was soothing to our wounded souls.

No talk was necessary during our fishing expedition. I felt closer to him as silence cast its magic. Once again, I thought of Farhad and his saying, "Close friends don't need verbal communication to connect." I don't know how Davud felt, but I assumed we both realized that going through the exit plan, we would be facing many emotional and physical struggles that required each other's close support.

No fish ever bit our bait and we headed back to Tehran after lunch.

During the long drive home, I asked Davud to share more tales of his nightly adventures from the Sheraton hotel's basement where he worked as the room services manager for the night shift.

Davud with his big, fuzzy blond hair and his round, puffy fishlike eyes enlarged by thick glasses, could deliver funny jokes very effectively. Just looking at his face during a joke would make me laugh. He particularly, enjoyed telling stories about his waiter Jamsheed, who was from the same city we had just visited, Bandar Pahlavi.

He prefaced the talk with a folk myth about men from the Caspian Sea region. The joke was about their lack of interest in sex.

"Not Jamsheed," he paused, smiled and continued. "The first evening that I started the night shift supervisory job, right at the beginning of the shift, Jamsheed complained about a backache. I told him, 'Jamsheed, if you have a bad back, I'll have to dismiss you. The job here requires carrying heavy trays of food to the guest rooms.' He excitedly answered, 'No, no, boss, please don't dismiss me. It is actually my wife.' His answer shocked me. 'What has your wife got to do with your back problem?' I asked. 'Sir, she demands me to perform the marital ritual as soon as I get home from work. Every day, seven days a week, with no break,' he complained." Davud laughed aloud.

After a few chuckles I asked, "Well, did you ask him why she is so unreasonably demanding?"

"Yes, I did. He said that his wife suspected him of having an affair at work. She thought that the best test of his innocence would be how he performed in bed with her." Keeping his eyes on the road, Davud continued. "I didn't get a straight answer from him when I asked if he was guilty of her suspicion. But, I noticed, some of Jamsheed's deliveries were taking an unusually long time. After a few warnings, I threatened him with dismissal if the delays continued.

"'Oh boss, no, please, don't dismiss me,' he pleaded. 'I have a family to feed and I'm just an innocent server.'

"Warning him that I didn't have the manpower to cover for his irregular behavior, I asked for his input on how to solve this puzzle. With his thick, northerner's accent he said, 'Just don't send me to any calls from female guests.' I shouldn't have asked for him to explain it, but I did. He sat on a chair and continued, 'Well, boss, I am very weak when it comes to foreign women. When I deliver the food, some of them demand additional services, and I can't refuse.' He looked down and shook his head. 'I am so weak when it comes to women, boss, especially the flight attendants. Oh, God. They are the worst.' He was in tears admitting his problem."

"So, what did you do?" I asked.

"I couldn't do much about it. I was short staffed, and some of the women guests were specifically asking for him. But when we were swamped, I would take some of his calls. The ones that were women, of course," Davud answered.

"Was his claim true? Did you have the same experience?"

Davud turned his face toward me with sparkles in his eyes and a big smile plastered on his chubby face. We both laughed. His story was like a delicious dessert after a satisfying dinner. We were reset.

The trip helped me cope with my emotions and I learned how to compartmentalize my feelings. In that sense, the short break was a success. We were able to put our failed romantic lives behind us and direct our focus to the tasks at hand: staying alive, overcoming the barriers in our way, and doing everything possible to speed the exit from Iran.

However, a small nagging voice in back of my head troubled me. What if I received a call from Neilu just a few days before my departure?

The Polish cemetery in Bandar Pahlavi (Anzali now)

A lagoon in Bandar Pahlavi.

15

ROZEH

> *No State shall deprive any person of life, liberty, or property, without due process of law; nor deny to any person within its jurisdiction the equal protection of the laws.*
>
> — AMENDMENT XIV, 1868, THE UNITED STATES BILL OF RIGHTS

Every third Tuesday of the month, it was our family's tradition to host a religious gathering called *rozeh*. The tradition was so old that most relatives and friends knew the date and time. There was no need for formal invitations or reminders. It entailed lunch for a few close friends of my grandmother and my mom, and dinner for closer relatives such as my uncles and aunts. In the afternoon, about four o'clock, several clergymen, one after another, would appear in their traditional attire—a thin dark brown or black robe, a long white shirt over dark pants, a white turban, and some would sport a green scarf around their necks. Their job was to preach to a crowd of about fifty— mostly women covered in *chadors*. The afternoon audience was generally conservative Muslims who saw value in spending a few hours listing to the same clergies reciting and chanting the exact same things in any and every *rozeh*. I suppose the entertaining values of *rozeh*, in addition to the belief that God would look upon them more favorably, was the attraction. For me, it was the most boring day of the month.

On this particular Tuesday, winter had started. Cold air had moved in with no signs of snowfall. My mother, while frantically dusting the living room, reminded me of it being a *rozeh* day (which of course, I knew all too well). In my opinion, it was a big waste of money and effort, especially when there were no Islamic rules obligating people to do it. However, sharing these thoughts about *rozeh* with my mother proved to be a mistake.

She stopped dusting, turned toward me, put her left hand on her waist and replied, "It is our religious duty and family tradition. By having *rozeh*, we feed people, we employ people, we educate people, and make them feel closer to God. In addition, many of our family and friends come to *rozeh*, and we enjoy each other's company. God rewards people who help others. As Muslims, we are obligated to help others. If you read your Quran, you will see how many times it has encouraged people to help others."

She made it sound like it was a great economic and social event. I argued back, "Paying a few jack-ass fake mullahs to come and sing from the top of their lungs about some religious fables, which everybody has heard a million times, doesn't help the economy."

She waved her arm to swish me away from her, prayed to God for my forgiveness, and ordered me to wash my sinful mouth before God hit me with lightning. Just about then, the doorbell rang.

I got up and opened the front door. It was Fatimah *khanoum*, a helper whom my mother hired every time she had a big event at our place. Fatimah slid her slim, old, and slightly bent body through the opening of the door, and almost immediately wrapped her *chador* around her fragile body and disappeared into the hallway to help my mother.

Fatimah *khanoum* always started cleaning from the back rooms and worked her way into the living room. She wouldn't let her *chador* go, as there was a man in the house. Me. In spite of her frailty, she expertly swept the carpet and moved the furniture to clean the underneath.

Still sprawled on the couch, I thought about my mother's argument on contributing to the local economy. Maybe she was onto something. We hired about five clerics for every *rozeh*. We also hired one or two helpers, bought groceries for an elaborate lunch and dinner, and fed thirty to fifty people. If a million Iranian families spent as much as we did on their *rozeh* every month, we were talking about a good size economic activity. I could've written my college dissertation on the economic impact of *rozeh*!

My mother's agitated voice, asking me for the second time to go to the store made me jump off the couch and brought me back to the time at hand. Picking up the basket and the cash, I asked if she was going to invite at least one decent mullah, or was it going to be the same theatrical bunch we had every month.

She walked toward me and asked for an explanation of my rude words.

With the basket hanging on my arm and cash in my hand, I elaborated, "Well, these cheap clerics you hire are entertaining all right, but they don't have any substance. Why not get at least one or two more educated preachers, from the more learned *rohanions*, so people actually learn something."

She countered that her choice of clerics was less expensive, and people loved them. To prove her point, she used the father and son team, who recited verses together as a duo, as an example. Their performance was so dramatic that many people cried every single time.

This had become an enjoyable conversation for me. Acknowledging her method of measuring success for each preacher by the number of women crying, I challenged her to consider if she would be willing to help the attendees learn something. Without waiting for her response, I again proposed to hire preachers from the *rohanion* group, who were educated, versus cheap street mullahs.

She lost her patience. Declaring she did not wish to spend all day arguing with me, she asked if I had any particular mullah to nominate. My uncle Akbar was close to the conservative Muslim groups that were leading the uprising, and he regularly hired highly educated preachers with graduate degrees and doctorates. Those preachers were referred to as *rohanion*, a polite term for preachers who were well respected among elite Muslim groups. My suggestion was to use a few of his preachers. They were less theatrical in attire and showmanship, and higher quality in content and depth of subject.

She shook her head. "Some of those *rohanion* preachers are dangerous. They talk about political stuff. We don't want trouble."

Her reply stopped me on the doorstep of the kitchen. I retorted, "I have news for you, the way current events are turning, I wouldn't be surprised if this turmoil turned into a revolution and we end up with an Islamic regime. When that happens, all these political preachers that you don't like will be running the country. Then, you'll be glad that you hired a few of them when you could."

"It will never happen!" I could sense the agitation in her voice. She continued, "Even if it happens, the *rohanion* crowd may run the country, but who will run the streets?" My mother jerked her head, signaling me to hustle.

Once again, I was impressed by my mother's insight. Her intuition was correct, in my opinion. Often with a revolution comes anarchy. In the absence of a government, who would protect the streets, houses, and families? Thugs, or perhaps people like Hassan *laboo*, my friend from the old neighborhood. The cheap clerics were very close to those people. They would run the politics of the streets. Hassan had warned me about it.

On my way to the store, I reflected on the many *rozeh*s in my past. We had hosted over a hundred of them, but I had participated in hundreds more. I was hoping this would become the last one I had to endure, but then chuckled when I thought of the most joyous memory. I was thirteen years old...

It was the third Tuesday of an early summer month. As always, we had *rozeh*. Bored with the day, I was flopped on the couch observing my mother and her helper re-arranging the furniture and preparing for the event. A brilliant idea came to my mind on how to turn a boring day into a fun day.

In the bedroom in the back of the house, I had a shoebox full of electronic gadgets hidden under my bed. I picked out several small speakers without enclosures and a few meters of wire.

The walls of our "L" shaped room in front of the house were lined with cushions for women to rest their backs on while seated on the carpeted floor that was padded with layers of soft blankets. The center of the room was left vacant for helpers to serve water, tea, or pastries to the attendees. Using long thin wires, I connected the speakers together and carefully placed them underneath the cushions in the women's room.

The bedroom in the back was my control room. I hid the wires underneath cushions and then extended them under the carpet in the hallway that led to the bedroom at the end. I connected the speaker wires to my cassette tape player in the bedroom.

At 3:00 p.m. women trickled in and sat in the "L" shaped room on the floor, drinking hot tea and gossiping. In my estimation, there were about thirty-five women present when the first preacher arrived. He immediately started his work with a few verses from the Quran and then launched into reciting the typical dramatic storytelling. A few women wept. The second cleric arrived a few moments before the first one finished. He started immediately after the first one left and was a great hit. He managed to get the ladies to howl loudly. The third one was noticeably late. The break gave the ladies the opportunity to dry their tears and chat. That was my cue to execute my plan.

A tape of the Beatles' music was already loaded in the tape player. I turned the volume knob to zero and played the tape. Gradually and very carefully I turned the volume up on the forbidden music.

With every turn of the volume knob, I rushed to our living room adjacent to the "L" shaped room to check the sound level and the reaction of the ladies to the music. Volume level one did not create any reaction. The room went to an abnormal silence with level two. At level three, the women, content with the pleasure of chit chatting and spiritually fulfilled with religious drama, noticed the sound of the illicit evil.

First, they asked each other about the noise. Then, they started looking for the source. Once they all concurred that the noise coming from the floor was music, they became furious and called my mother.

The call of *Astaghforellah*, God forgive us, was coming from every corner of the room.

Spying on them from our living room was exhilarating and fun. I ran to the bedroom at the end of the hallway to explode in laughter every few minutes.

"Naji *khanoum*! Naji *khanoum*!" They shouted my mother's name frantically. My mother was in the kitchen getting tea glasses ready to serve. In my control room, I was rolling on the floor with laughter. My mother stopped pouring tea and rushed into the "L" room to see what had caused the hysteria.

"What is this horrible sound?" asked one of the more vocal women.

My mother gasped in horror. The volume was loud enough that the rock and roll music could clearly be heard.

"Where is it coming from? Naji *khanoum*, can you please stop it immediately! Music is forbidden, you know!" several women demanded.

My poor mother's face turned red. She didn't even search the room. Instead she rushed straight to the back bedroom looking for the devil behind all this. She knew very well who was the source of this wickedness and where to find him. She caught me in the bedroom laughing hysterically.

"Cut this off, NOW!" she shouted.

I wasn't expected to be caught that fast.

"They have cried enough, Momon. Now it's time for them to dance," I replied defiantly, knowing well that dancing is considered an even a bigger taboo, a big insult.

My mother's face was as red as a cooked beet. She lifted her right arm with a shoe in her hand, aiming at my head. I pressed the stop button at once, preventing her from throwing the shoe at me.

"Your father will hear about this, you rascal!" said my mother angrily, pointing her index finger at me before she left the room. The rest of her afternoon was consumed with apologizing to people and begging them to forgive her.

I couldn't wait to tell my friends about my "scientific experiment."

• • •

On my return from the store, I saw that all my grandmother's friends and two other ladies my mother's age were at our home visiting. That meant a great meal was about to be served for lunch.

My thoughts circled around the realization that this could be my very last *rozeh*. Putting the groceries on the table in the kitchen I shared my thought with my mother.

"Don't talk like that," she replied while adding saffron to a large platter of white, long-grained, fluffy rice.

"No, I'm serious! Once abroad, I may never come back."

"Nonsense. Of course, you will come back. Don't count your chickens before they hatch. You don't even have all your paperwork completed yet."

She was right. The country was becoming more volatile by the day. The situation was so fragile that it could change rapidly. Strikes could paralyze the country or even cause a complete government shutdown at any time. Any of several regional ethnic tribes could use the opportunity of a weakened central government to declare independence.

Her words reminded me how easily my world could collapse. I had to stay focused and use every opportunity to push for my imminent exit. I couldn't do much about it that day, so I let the elaborate lunch my mother had prepared ease my mind. Multiple entrees, hors d'oeuvres and other amenities were on full display. We all sat on the floor, cross legged, around a long rectangular white sheet, *sofreh*, that worked like a table cloth. All food items, dishes and utensils were placed on the *sofreh*.

The fragrance of steamed basmati rice mixed with aroma of cooked greens and lemons had taken over the whole house. I imagined everyone else was as eager as I was for the taste of the actual food. The main entree was my favorite, *ghormeh-sabzi*, a stew of kidney beans, black lime and turmeric-seasoned lamb cooked with sautéed parsley, leek, and cilantro and seasoned with dried fenugreek leaves. My mother always placed the fluffy basmati rice, *chelo*, that was served with *ghormeh-sabzi* in a large, oval platter. She arranged the rice to an ecstatically pleasing mountain shape and on the peak she sprinkled the yellow saffron fluffy rice.

The second entrée was *baghali-polo*, which I called 'the green rice.'

The dish was made with basmati rice, mixed with lima beans, dill, lamb, and of course, the yellow saffron rice sprinkled on top.

After lunch, my mother and her helper rolled blankets and sheets on to the floor of our living room, which was covered with a large thick Persian rug, so the elders could take a one-hour nap. At three o'clock in the afternoon, the clerics showed up, one after the other, and recited their verses for the audience who were already sitting along the walls of our "L" shaped room. As usual, their theatrics brought many to tears.

My older uncle and his family arrived around six-thirty. His oldest son, my cousin Khatam, who was only five hours older than me, showed up as well. This was a rarity; he seldom came to our *rozehs*. We had a lot of fun growing up together. Khatam's arrival brightened my day.

With a chuckle, I recounted the dramatic duo's performance for my cousin. He looked puzzled. A humorous tale of a team of father and son preachers who put on an entertaining show followed. Giving him a better image of the performance, I described it similar to *ta'ziyeh* with the added value of a lot of tears.

Ta'ziyeh is a popular religious theater, mostly telling the story of martyred Shiite Muslim saints.

Khatam, a know-it-all and a pragmatic type, educated me that *rozeh* became popular since Reza Shah, the king at the time, forbade *ta'ziyeh*, in the late 1920s. He pointed out the two were related. Without waiting for my comment, he asked if I was serious about going abroad.

"Of course, I'm serious," I replied, and then explained in more detail how my departure was depending on if and when everything worked out. At that time, I had conditional acceptance from a few universities. They needed to receive my passing score on the English exam, TOEFL. Because of the postal employee's strike, my test results had not arrived yet. Everything was delayed or lost. Further, I explained that I had also applied to an English school in Los Angeles, just in a case my TOEFL results were confirmed lost.

Khatam had a light complexion, a pair of hazel eyes, light brown hair and a large head. I always thought that it was because of his large head that he was such a good student. He explained that his graduation has been delayed a year due to the student and faculty strikes. He studied engineering in one of the top technical universities. He and I enrolled in college in the same year and yet, just like Neilu and thousands of other students, he still had another year to complete his bachelor's degree, if lucky.

He looked me in the eyes and asked if I would return home.

"Who knows? The future is unwritten. I don't know if I can even get out."

"Well, don't forget me," he said.

"Are you kidding, I'll never forget you. You're the only person who taught me how to run down the hill without killing myself," I answered.

He didn't remember the event.

We were nine or ten years old. I reminded him that it was during my visit at his summer house in the village.

He shook his head. He still couldn't remember.

The helper brought hot tea in slim-waisted tea glasses on a tray for everyone. I picked one. The dark red color of the tea was radiating through the transparent glass. I picked up two lumps of sugar and continued telling him how stubborn and arrogant I was at the time. We had climbed up a hill and I challenged him to a race down to the bottom. He warned me not to run down the hill unless I knew how to do it correctly. But, I was mister know-it-all and had to show off.

Despite his warning, I ran down the hill as fast as I could.

He nodded his head and said that he finally remembered. His arm went to pick up his hot tea glass, a saucer, and then he meticulously placed a lump of sugar in his mouth and continued the story for me. "And a moment later you rolled down the hill like a big potato, all the way to the bottom." We both laughed loudly.

Nodding my head up and down vigorously, laughingly I continued. "Yet still, I beat you! I remember it vividly. I got to the bottom of the hill first. But my entire body was covered in blood." He confirmed the reminisces while sipping his tea.

"Nevertheless, I stood up and humbly listened to your instructions on how to properly run down the hill," I claimed.

"No, brother, you were crying and screaming. My brother and I had to carry you all the way home. Then, my mother applied Mercurochrome all over your body to disinfect it," he corrected me.

"Yes, it was so ugly. My entire body was red from the Mercurochrome and covered with ugly bandage dressings. Was I grounded?" I asked.

"Yes, my mother forbade you to go outside. We had to play in the house for several days. It was after you were healed that I took you to the same hill and showed you the right way of running down. So now, you certainly know how to out run soldiers when it comes to fighting them in the hills," he said.

His last sentenced shocked me. He was a shy, quiet nerd. Had he joined the dissidents? Could I trust him?

If his last comment was an invitation to talk about the uprising, I didn't buy into it and continued evoking memories of that summer. I reiterated the enormous amount of fun I had in his house in the village, even when grounded. Stuck in the room that was facing the yard, and thanks to my injuries, we had decided to catch flies, hold them with their wings, tie a long thread to one of their legs and let them fly.

He laughed and nodded.

"It was so beautiful to see fifteen flies flying around in the room, each with a long, colored thread tied to their legs. The threads were gracefully following the flies in the air," I described.

About 7:30 p.m. my younger uncle, my father's third and youngest brother, arrived. All the men in the room stood up and greeted my uncle with the customary two kisses, one on each cheek. He was a full colonel with the police force in charge of undercover detectives. The police force was a national security organization and used the same ranking designations as the other armed forces.

He lived in the city of Karaj, about one hour west of Tehran. It was a rare occurrence to see him attending our monthly *rozeh*s. He was a likable, humorous man, a bit shorter than his other brothers, had dark black eyes, and unlike my father and other uncles, he had a full head of well-groomed hair.

As usual, it didn't take long for the conversation to turn to politics. He told us about the tremendous amount of psychological pressure the security forces were enduring. Daily, they had to examine their loyalty and act upon it. Many were abandoning their posts and joining the dissidents.

Most of our regular *rozeh* guests left by eight o'clock that night. Close family members stayed for dinner, which was served around nine. Right before the dinner, my uncle with the police force signaled me over to a corner. He took his hot tea and sat on a chair. He patted the chair next to him, signaling me to sit there. Following his cues, I sat next to him. Like my other uncle who was a full colonel in the air force, this one was also sympathetic toward the conservative Muslims line of uprising.

"It's time that you learn how to handle a weapon," he whispered. "The way things are going, you may need to use it soon."

Confused by his approach, I explained my intention of going abroad for graduate study, which I was certain he knew.

He took his revolver out of his holster and emptied all the bullets. "Don't be naïve. The country's infrastructure is crumbling faster than you think. Your trip may not happen so soon. Let me show you how to handle a gun."

He had my full attention when he shoved his gun near my face.

"This is how you aim," my uncle continued. "There are two sights on a gun. A front sight and a rear sight. To aim the revolver, place the front blade on the target, and then place the front blade in between the "V" of the back sights. Breathe normally and squeeze the trigger at the natural pause between the end of your exhalation and the begin-ning of your next inhalation." And then *click,* he pulled the trigger. My exuberance hiked beyond what I had ever experienced before.

He handed the revolver to me.

That first touch was unforgettable. The cold mass of metal felt heavier than what I imagined. It smelled of a mild mixture of grease and gun powder. Realizing that only a small number of people were allowed to hold a handgun in Iran, I felt privileged.

Watching people using handguns in the movies, I had romanticized this moment throughout all my life. Rolling the bullet chamber, closing it, aiming the gun, and pulling the trigger. I knew about the front sight and the rear sight and how to aim. I learned that by playing target practice with the BB guns. During the summer when school was out, we had multiple vendors walk the streets shouting and enticing all the boys of the neighborhood to come out and pay for a few rounds of target practicing. They carried an "A" fame target board and one or two BB guns that shot sharp little darts.

As I handled the gun, close family women joined the men in the living room. Since *rozeh* had officially ended and there were no strangers in the house, some women took off their scarf or *chador*. My uncle's wife, Mehrahn *khanoum*, who was helping my mother, came by and collected our emptied tea glasses. She had removed her scarf.

Revolver in my hand, I glanced at her and smiled.

Mehrahn *khanoum* returned my smile and said, "Learning how to defend our cause and fight for our freedom, hah? Good for you!"

Suddenly a chill came over me. The story of Hussein, her nephew, flashed in my head. Graciously, I returned the gun to my uncle and went to the balcony for fresh air.

My uncle's wife's family members were beautiful people both inside and outside—gracious, kind, thoughtful, and smart. However, a good number of her young nephews and nieces were involved with a revolutionary guerrilla group called *Mojahedin–e-Khalqh Organization* (MKO). The group was one of the two main underground guerrilla groups that were actively striking political targets, assassinating government officials and foreign dignitaries. They brought fear into the core of the current regime. The MKO's political and social aspirations were rooted in Islam with socialist tendencies.

Only in the past two years, with my new political awareness, had I realized the irony of my family's situation. My uncle, a high-ranking police officer had a wife whose relatives were members of underground political assassins and freedom fighters, the very people that his organization hunted on a daily basis. The fascinating part was that they all mingled with each other in the religious gatherings such as *rozehs* and other family occasions, hugging and kissing each other's cheeks as if the outside world were a different universe. That is, until a warrant was issued for them, and they went underground, no longer appearing at any family gatherings or activities.

While I had held the gun in my hand, the heavy, cold piece of metal that could so easily end the life of many people, didn't give me the sensation I thought it would. Instead, it felt that I had touched something dirty. Pain, not a physical pain, but more like the emotional pain of a burden overwhelmed me. I was embarrassed for my juvenile enthusiasm affecting my senses when I held the gun.

The air on the balcony was chilly. The cold winter had begun its tease of snowfall.

I stood there with my arms rested on the railing, gazing into the darkness of the yard. The comments of my uncle and his wife confused me. Do they know something that I don't? Do they really think I'm naive to desire to improve myself? Will I have enough time to exit? But most troubling was that I couldn't shake off the thought of Hussein.

He was a smart engineering student who joined the military right after college as part of the mandatory two-year military service. He quickly moved up in the ranks and joined the Special Forces commando units. However, after completing his service, he joined MKO, the underground freedom fighters. A few years later, he was captured by SAVAK, the secret police.

It was getting even colder on the balcony.

Khatam came out to join me with a coat in hand. "Here, put this on if you're going to stay out for a while. You don't want to miss your chance of going abroad by getting a bad case of pneumonia."

Thanking him, I asked if he remembered Nasser, Mehrahn *khanoum's* nephew.

He nodded.

My next question was if he had ever seen him in any of the family gatherings.

"No," he replied, "but, he is a hero at my college. He graduated from there, and his photos are posted on many walls, with his quotes from the famous trial."

His arrest and trial were big news, as he was one of MKO's most effective operators.

Khatam gazed out into the dark yard but didn't say anything more for a while. Then he bent over the metal railing of the balcony and rested his arms on top of it. He asked if they put Nasser on TV. Usually when the regime captured members of underground freedom fighters, they tortured them first, then the bargaining would begin. If the prisoner agreed to a public admission of the crime, and the humiliation of fake sorrow, then the government might reduce the sentence from execution to life imprisonment. The TV appearances were very theatrical. Usually, the prisoner wept and begged for forgiveness.

But this was not the case with Nasser. He never repented. He was a resolute man. The interrogators' inability to break him forced the agents to get his family involved. First his parents, then his aunts, uncles, and other members of his extended family were asked to convince him to plead for forgiveness. None were able to convince him. Nasser was defiant. He really believed in his cause. The case went to trial. His show began in the courtroom, not on the TV.

Nasser's story had occupied my mind to the point of obsession when I was a freshman in college. I collected every report and article that was written about him. His trial opened my eyes to the underground opposition movement. It was during that time that I recognized the regime's propaganda was just shallow images of what they wanted simpletons to believe. The reality was different. The deeper I searched, the more I realized the importance of my study abroad, and my longing to experience the outside world.

Khatam shifted on his feet and asked if I could tell him more about Nasser and his trial.

Recalling a short story I had written about Nasser and his trial, I asked Khatam if he would be interested in me reading it to him.

He nodded.

Excited about having an audience for my story, I ran downstairs to my room in the basement and picked up my short story journal. Once upstairs, I read only the closing segment of the trial part for him. As this cherished journal has remained with me, I can share what I read to him on that cold night on the balcony of our house:

Nasser sat emotionless in the front row of the court room. His comrades, ushered one by one by guards, sat next to him. When the three judges entered the room, everybody stood except Nasser and his comrades. The security officer elbowed him and ordered him to stand up. But Nasser remained seated. The three judges sat. Silence took over the room.

The judge in the middle opened the file on top of the pile of papers, looked up and called Nasser's name. He didn't reply. The guards pulled Nasser up, his hands were cuffed in front of him and he had shackles on his feet. He stood up reluctantly. Then, a moment later, he changed to a firm and purposeful disposition, as he seemed to remember something.

The judge said, "The charges against you are of heinous crimes against the imperial majesty of Iran. That includes taking many lives. Do you repent, or have you anything to say in your defense?"

Facing the judge, in a stern voice Nasser responded, "This court has no legitimacy. You are simply a representative of a criminal dictatorial regime. Your court has sentenced many heroes to death. You, personally, have signed execution orders for many brave souls, passionate for their country, democracy and their people. I do not recognize this court. If I'm released, I will continue my fight for a free and democratic Iran. You can be assured, the first thing I will do is to execute you in the same way you did my brothers and sisters, riddling your body with bullets."

A few days later, one early spring morning, in Evin's prison-yard, when the first chirpings of the birds were heard, when dew's most magnificent work on leaves was about to go on display, the peaceful dawn was vulgarly interrupted.

The firing squad rifles peppered Nasser's body with bullets.

After I stopped reading, silence, like a blanket of thick fog, permeated the air for a few moments. Breathing had become harder. Gently, I closed my journal and turned around. Mehrahn *khanoum*, Nasser's aunt, was standing behind the sliding glass door in the room connected to the balcony, listening. A few tears were running down her cheeks. She then disappeared into the darkness of the room.

Khatam put his arm around my shoulder. "It's getting cold here. Let's go inside." He opened the sliding door to the room, and as I walked in, he whispered, "Nasser's cause is a good reason to pick up arms."

16

AN OLD FLAME

> *The sphere upon which mortals come and go,*
> *Has no end nor beginning that we know;*
> *And none there is to tell us in plain truth:*
> *Whence do we come and whither do we go.*
>
> — Omar Khayam, Persian poet, (1048–1131)
> English translation by Ahmad Saidi

"Hey *goombey* boy," said Rahim khan, my mother's cousin, who, along with his twenty-one-year-old daughter, Mahtaab, was sitting in our parlor, visiting. "I've heard you're going abroad. What country?"

"America," I answered with great restraint so as not to let my reply reflect my repulsion of him calling me *goombey* boy. Apparently, during one of his visits when I was learning how to speak, I dragged a rather large beach ball from underneath my bed and ran toward him yelling excitedly, "*Goombey, goombey!*" It is not a word with any meaning, and no one knows how I came up with that silly name for the ball.

But ever since then, he had called me the *"goombey* boy or Vahid *goombeyee"* and repeated the same story over and over every time he saw me. The tale had long ago lost its charm.

He continued to grill me with questions, inquiring about my field of study and so on. It was only polite to sit and visit with him, as my parents expected that. My mother was in the kitchen preparing the hot tea. I reached for an orange from the brimming fruit platter on the coffee table in front of us. Why not, I thought. I had to sit there for at least another five minutes, so I may as well enjoy an orange. And Mahtaab, as attractive as ever, was ignoring me, which was fine. I was over her.

"Management?" his exclamation disrupted my thoughts. "What happened to archeology? A few years ago, you were adamant that archeology was the only major you wanted to study."

That was a good opportunity for me to vent about my father's push for me to study management or engineering. Since my mother was still in the kitchen, I found it liberating to freely explain how repressed I was in choosing my field of graduate work.

The conversation was a bitter reminder of the price I had to pay for my independence--studying the least interesting subject, management, in exchange for the financial support required to launch my new life in a new world.

"So, what was all that fascination with archeology?" he prodded.

I swallowed a section of orange. "I don't know, maybe our several thousand years of civilization." I knew I was being facetious. Maybe bordering on rude. And I was caught, as my mother had entered the room and had begun serving hot tea on a silver platter. Her worried expression prompted me to control my response and keep a more polite composure. I changed my tone, explaining that my curiosity about who we were, and what we were, was still strong. But I admitted that it was time for me to be pragmatic. I was unlikely to make a good living with a degree in archeology.

He moved to pick an orange from the platter, but his large belly made the attempt very difficult for him. Nevertheless, he managed while probing me further. "You still haven't told me what got you interested in archeology. I don't buy your first explanation. What is the real reason?"

"Actually, my first spark into the world of archeology was ignited by my mother's story," I replied.

He paused his peeling of the orange when he heard me, and then looked up. He was curious to which story that was.

"The one about the house she grew up—"

My mother jumped in. "Well, I can see that your love of endless talk is about to drag Rahim khan in its whirlpool. Don't you have something important to do, Vahid?"

Elated by my mother's help in getting me out of that conversation, I excused myself. I needed to leave the house and go to the Iran America Society to finalize my paperwork for study abroad.

Mahtaab, suddenly energized, interjected herself into our conversation and asked if she could tag along, claiming that she had never been there.

Surprised by her request, after a short pause, I stuttered using an excuse of grabbing my jacket, to leave the room immediately. I didn't know what else to say. Mahtaab, my second cousin, was my age. Her straight, waist-long brown hair and dark brown, almond-shaped eyes had always attracted me. In Iran, marriage between cousins is acceptable and sometimes even encouraged. She happened to be the first girl that I fell in love with, the first girl I expressed my love to, and the very first girl who returned my affections with the bitter taste of rejection. "This is crazy! Don't talk to me on the way to school ever again!" were her exact words after I confessed my crush on her during my tenth grade year. Those words devastated me for months at age sixteen. I had been mad about her. Her round face, her voluptuous lips, her hair, her dark gleaming brown eyes, her soft laughter, and even her duck like walk drove me crazy. It was hard to admit I still felt the sting of that experience.

Later, I found out that she had been in love with a boy two years her senior. It is ironic how destiny works sometimes. That boy went to a college in England. A year later, after she graduated from high school, she went to England to surprise him. Instead, she caught him having an affair with a British girl. Perhaps it was their story that spooked me about my situation with Neilu. Mahtaab and this boy loved each other, or so it seemed to me. I saw them together once, and the mutual fondness was apparent from their behavior and looks. But I also saw that being young and apart are two elements detrimental to a lasting romance. Heartbroken, she broke up with him, but stayed in London for two years, attempting to get into a college there with no success. She had recently returned home.

On the way to my room, I carried a few tea glasses and dishes to the kitchen to help my mother. Coming out of kitchen, Mahtaab blocked me in the hallway. She stood only five centimeters from my face and begged me to take her with me, because she couldn't stand her father. She added, "I also want to see if the folks at the society can help me go to America."

My tongue was frozen. I bypassed her without saying anything. She followed me. Being alone with her in the car for forty minutes didn't sound appealing to me. I used the first excuse that came to my mind to deter her. Something like, I was meeting my friends there and I couldn't take her back home.

"Oh, don't worry. You don't have to take me back home. I will take a taxi or call one of my friends for a ride. Please take me out of here. If I leave by myself, it'll be rude to your mother and my dad," she pleaded.

The encounter was strange. I had never seen her persistent like this before. Was she trying to get close to me? After all these years?

She came closer and this time with a softer voice said, "I am also curious to hear about the story that your mother so cleverly stopped you from telling."

Her breath smelled of spicy-sweet cardamom, a spice that my mother had added to the hot tea she served. Her eyes, her lips were so close to mine. My heart palpitated so wildly, I could feel heat in my earlobes. While it is common in Iran to get very close to someone when speaking, especially among friends and relatives, I felt nervous given our history. My mind was racing.

What she said gave me an idea, an excuse to put some space between us. I asked her to wait there in the hallway and rushed down to my room in the basement.

On my desk lay the journal of my short stories. I picked it up and went back upstairs. She was waiting for my return in the hallway. I handed her the journal and lay down my mandate. She was to read a story from that journal out loud while I was driving.

"What story? Is it the same one you told me about—the boy and girl—when we were sixteen? You have written it down?" Horror was visible on her face.

She was referring to a concocted story I had told her to confess my love to her when we were sophomores in high school. It was the first time she had ever mentioned that miserable day. The worst day of my young, sixteen-year-old life. It took me a couple of seconds to collect my thoughts and respond. "No, I want you to read the story my mother told me about her childhood. This is the one that got me interested in archeology. I turned it into a short story. I want to hear it when someone else reads it out loud. Also, your opinion matters to me."

Her audible sigh showed her relief. Her face lit up as she extended her hand to seal the deal.

Mahtaab sat in the car, put my journal on her lap, turned to me with a smirk on her face, and asked if I knew about the affection her father and my mother had toward each other when they were young.

Of course, I knew that. It was my aunt who told me about it. It was Mahtaab's grandfather, my mother's uncle, who forbade her father to ask for my mother's hand. The ordeal was devastating to my mother. After that, my mother's parents forced her to marry her dreadful first husband to avoid further trouble.

"Sometimes things work for the best, even though at the time, we don't like it. You and I wouldn't be here, if they had gotten married," she replied.

She was right. To end any further conversation with Mahtaab, I asked her to start reading. She still made me uncomfortable.

She looked at me, seemed to reflect for a moment, and then opened the journal.

"Naji and the mystery of the dig," she loudly announced the title.

The story was about an eight-year old Persian girl named Naji, my mother, who woke up to an unusual sound on an early summer morning in 1942. Three strangers were digging in her courtyard. She was bothered by the commotion. The summer season had just begun, and she had hoped to sleep in. Nevertheless, the strangeness of the scene and her unquenchable curiosity motivated her to investigate.

Later, she found out that the strangers were digging a new septic hole for their outhouse. Naji's sixth sense warned her that something suspicious was down beneath the yard. Frequently, adults in her life had warned her about different terrifying creatures. She was horrified that *Loo Loo*, a monster type that appeared in many forms, was underground and might become upset by the dig.

Her determination to get close to the dig and experience the abyss herself grew more intense as the dig was getting deeper. Toward the end of the day, all three diggers one by one disappeared into the deep hole. There were no responses from any of them. Her father's face showed signs of deep concern. Everyone was edgy. Her mother was praying and even her grandmother joined the prayers.

Finally, after a long wait, they heard from the diggers and pulled them up one by one. The diggers told the most exciting and unexpected tale of what happened to them. They claimed discovering a dark tunnel at the end of the dig, leading to a large open area similar to a market, with remnants of an ancient city. A city underneath!

Naji, relieved by the absence of monsters, and motivated by her intuition about the existence of a mystery underground, joined the workers and her brother in begging her father to allow a more in-depth exploration of the city underneath. However, her father had a different plan. He assured everyone that the tale was nothing more than hallucinations and the effect of underground gasses. To everyone's disbelief, he ordered the diggers to seal the dig for the use of the new outhouse.

Mahtaab stopped reading. A few moments of silence followed the end of the story. My patience ran out and I asked, "Well?"

"I like it!" she replied with genuine enthusiasm. "But what happened after that day? Did anyone ever excavate the site later?"

That had been my question as well. My research indicated that no one ever reopened the dig after it was sealed and used for the outhouse. However, the story began my intrigue with the world of archeology.

Looking at the road ahead, I revealed to her how much I would miss being close to the cradle of civilization if and when I leave Iran. Not having the certainty of knowing if I would ever have the opportunity to examine the great and ancient Persian sites and relics was painful to me. I could hear the somber note in my voice as I spoke to my cousin.

"Then don't go. Stay here and devote yourself to digging up the past. Do what you love. Discover the magic of ancient Persia." She made it sound so simple.

But for me, it wasn't that simple.

She paused for a moment and then swiftly turned to me and asked if we were there yet.

While parking the car, I answered, "Yes, we are. The building is to your left. So, what do you think of my writing?"

She opened the car door, and on her way out said, "It's okay." And left.

She walked to a payphone nearby and dialed a number. *Strange*, I thought, and proceeded into the building.

Fifteen minutes later, she still had not entered the offices of the Iran America Society. Curious as to her whereabouts, I peeked outside from a window. She was standing at the curb. A moment later, a car stopped. My further attempt to recognize the driver by changing my position was fruitless. However, I did notice that the driver was a young man and he wasn't her brother. She got in the car and it disappeared into Tehran's heavy traffic. I can't say I was sorry to see her go, but it felt like she had jilted me once again.

Mahtaab's words, "Do what you love," echoed inside my head. A strange urge came over me and my whole body tingled. What if I do stay? What if I change the course of my life and explore the world of archeology and the history of the ancient world?

Would that make me happy?

17

BOOKS

 *To change masters is not to be free.*

— Jose Marti Perez, Cuban poet (1853-1895)

Cold winter winds had crept to and settled upon Tehran, pushing the indecisive fall weather out of the way. However, autumn wasn't the only departed party. The atmosphere of farewell was found everywhere at the end of 1978. Many people were leaving the country, and with them large sums of money exited Iranian banks. The surge of students going abroad was at its peak along with families horrified of the imminent regime change and its effect on their lives.

A great exodus had begun.

My paperwork had been completed, and I had my acceptance from a language school in Los Angeles. It was a temporary setback from my original goal of going straight to graduate school. Davud and I had taken two TOEFL exams and never received any of the results. Foreign mail had to go to the translation department. Someone would have had to translate the foreign words into Farsi and send the mail back to the distribution section. With all the strikes and disgruntlement going around, we were not surprised that our mail from the United States never got to us. Nevertheless, we both were excited and ready to proceed to the next step, the visa process.

We made appointments at the American embassy in Tehran to apply for the student visas. Our plan was to buy tickets for the first flight out of Tehran as soon as we had the visa stamp on our passports. With the substantial number of people leaving Iran, finding airline tickets had become increasingly difficult. However, we had no choice but to wait for the American embassy's visa before reserving our tickets. Many visa applicants were denied. Therefore, the looming dark whisper of possibly not receiving our visas was lurking in the back of our minds.

Strange and mixed feelings of sadness and joy had come over me. The possibility of not seeing my friends ever again depressed me. On the other hand, getting closer to the reality of so many years spent dreaming and planning was exciting. Drama wasn't my intention, my plan was to continue my graduate education and obtain a doctorate either in the U.S. or France. One of my law professors, who had a degree from the Sorbonne, had persuaded me to continue my education by applying there, after completion of my master's degree. After that, who knew? My intention was to stay in a country where the dignity of individuals was respected as one of its core values.

In my farewell mood and preparation for my departure, I started a long process of saying good-byes to my friends and extended family members. Some were not easy, and I procrastinated the inevitable.

The most difficult one was with my friend Firoozeh.

It was another cloudy and cold day when I finally called her. My mood was melancholy, matching the sky. Cloudy days made me somber and lethargic, and I disliked them. The phone's receiver felt much heavier than usual. Reluctantly and slowly, I dialed the number. The thought of not seeing her for a long time, or perhaps forever, rested heavy in my heart.

She answered the phone on the third ring.

My stomach dropped when I heard her soft voice. I mustered some enthusiasm and asked her if she would like to join me to shop for books to take abroad. She agreed. Firoozeh's voice was calm with a hint of an accent. I could never determine if her slight accent was because of her spending a couple of years in the U.S or due to a small speech problem she may have had when she was a child.

Her voice echoed in my head after I hung up the phone. I leaned on the wall behind me and closed my eyes. I would miss that voice.

Why was my heart beating so fast?

At that point in time, I had already been abandoned by my two closest friends—Farhad, who had disappeared into the fog of life with his now-pregnant girlfriend—and Neilu, who had not called me as I'd hoped. That chapter was closed. Firoozeh had always been a kind and loyal companion. I could say she was now my closest friend that I had to leave behind.

Across from the Tehran University's main gate, near where she lived, was a bustling book market with many bookstores next to each other. She liked books, and I figured shopping for books would be a good distraction to soften a sad farewell.

An early afternoon rain had created the odd smell of fresh earth mixed with the scent of wet asphalt. It almost felt like fall season was trying to return one more time before giving in to the winter. But it was too late; the winter had arrived and destiny was already written.

Firoozeh lived on the fourth floor of an upscale apartment building thirty minutes north of me. Her voice greeted me over the intercom, and a few minutes later the elevator door opened and there she was.

Her image, her persona, her subtle, charming smile felt like a long awaited sea breeze. She was short and had a light complexion. Her beautiful blue eyes were magnified by a pair of thick glasses. Her honey blonde hair was styled into a pony tail, and as usual she was wearing an oversized coat, such that her fingers were hidden inside the long coat sleeves. I appreciated her gentle, peaceful demeanor and her easy-going attitude. With Firoozeh, there were no unreasonable expectations; there was no pressure, no complaints, no negative talk, and no gossiping. She never demanded anything, yet it seemed she always knew what she wanted and how to get it.

Looking up into my eyes, she greeted me with a smile. I had the urge to embrace her, letting her friendship and positive vibes vibrate every cell of my body. But I couldn't. Cultural barriers, religious codes, and conservative upbringing disallowed me. All the yokes that I hoped would disappear soon. So I simply smiled back.

"This is a first!" she exclaimed, still smiling.

My puzzled expression revealed my obliviousness to her claim.

As we walked, she elaborated, "Shopping! We've never gone shopping together before," she replied.

She was right. I had never asked her to run errands with me. Usually we would go to classical music concerts, ballets, operas, film festivals, museums, or play music together.

She was curious about the occasion.

Her innocent face, her pure and unpolluted smile, and the thought of missing her selfless friendship, put me in a gloomy mood. God!

How could I tell her?

"What happened? Did I say something wrong?" she asked, reading my face.

"No, no, I just want to buy and take a few books with me to the U.S., and I thought you could help me select the right ones since you've been there. Plus, I enjoy our talks and time together." I just couldn't bring myself to tell her that this was the last time we would see each other.

She acknowledged a mutual delight in our mingling and quickly asked what kind of books I was looking to buy.

A good dictionary was the best company one could have when traveling abroad. That was my firm belief. Going abroad for graduate study required the best and most comprehensive Farsi to English and English to Farsi set of dictionaries. The ones I had were not comprehensive enough for graduate work. Reference books were next on the list.

With a serious face, she acknowledged and approved my effort to not taking graduate school in America lightly. She immediately launched into the type of books I should take.

"Poetry, I love poetry. Take some of Nima Youshige's work. He is the father of Persian modern poetry. And take books that are the essence of our culture, literature, philosophy, music and so on."

We always had a good time together. She was an intelligent person, an avid reader, and a highly competent musician. One of my fondest memories with her was when we played a Schubert piece called *Ständchen in D 957*. She played the piano part and I played the vocal part on my classical guitar. Her spirit, her personality, and her whole essence were as pretty as Chopin's nocturnes played well on an excellent piano. She was simple in appearance but deep in intelligence. I enjoyed our platonic friendship.

She had studied for two years of high school in the U.S and in the back of my mind, I was worried and curious about homesickness. I asked her if she had ever felt homesick during her stay in America.

And if she did, how would she describe it?

She pondered for little while and then said, "You'll see a lot of people, but they all are strangers. You'll hear a lot of words, but from a different language. The food you eat will have a different taste. Nothing that you'll come in contact with will be from a familiar place. You get homesick when you crave like crazy for even a small taste or a sound from your homeland."

Her poetic expression was touching. I didn't think it would happen to me. I liked all those strange things, so I thought I would be in heaven. Perhaps different people react differently.

Having said that, an amusing story about my older brother's recent visit to America came to my mind. He and his very pregnant wife had recently returned home from a long vacation in the U.S. His wife delivered a boy two weeks after their return. "Can you believe that?" I asked.

Puzzled, she looked at me and asked, "What's the problem?"

"We're talking about only two weeks! If they would have stayed there, my new nephew would be an American citizen!"

"Maybe she didn't want her son to be an American citizen. Perhaps she wanted to make sure her son was born in Iran."

That was the exact answer my sister-in-law gave when I asked her the question. She wanted her son to be born in Iran.

We entered a small bookstore. The fragrances of paper and ink dominated the air--a pleasant, welcoming atmosphere to remind us we had entered into a world of thoughts. Books were stacked all the way to the ceiling. I bought two enormous and complete dictionaries.

One was Farsi to English and the other English to Farsi.

Firoozeh was a freshman in the University of Tehran for about four months at that point. The University of Tehran was a difficult school to get into and it was rapidly becoming a hot bed of Muslim conservatives. Student confrontations with security forces were an almost daily occurrence. She was a music major. A difficult place to study music. I asked how she liked being a university student in such a potent environment.

"I like the intellectual intensity. They are really serious. Professors are demanding, and I love all the dialogues," she replied.

Political turmoil had always been tough on Iranian universities. I reminded her, like other major universities in Iran, her school would shut down whenever there was a major student protest, and that would certainly create long delays in earning her degree.

She didn't mind. She loved the dynamics of her university. With the new political openness, many in-depth and open dialogues that were impossible a few years prior, or even a few months, erstwhile were blossoming everywhere. She was ecstatic about the intellectual atmosphere there.

The pre-revolutionary atmosphere was engulfing most, if not all, higher education institutions in Iran. Although my graduation from college was as recent as six months prior, I felt out of touch. Curious to her view, I asked her to elaborate further.

"Oh, you know, these days nobody can get away from political discussions. So there are a lot of deep political conversations and other topics such as economics, art, religion, contemporary history..."

"Okay, I got it," I interrupted. "Just don't get too involved with the political stuff. Strange things are still happening to the activists."

My over-protective personality took over. In addition to the regime's watch dogs snooping everywhere, my experience in Isfahan with the bikers had made me hyper-sensitive. Her views were liberal with a hint of socialism, and rooted in music and art. Conservative Muslim students, conversely, were rooted in tradition and were rigid, religious, and superstitious. I just didn't want anyone to harm her.

"No, no, the political climate has changed!" she answered. "The kidnapping of students, torture, beatings, mass arrests, and imprisonments by the regime are all basically gone. Nowadays, with the turmoil comes more freedom. Solidarity among people is amazing."

"That's not how I remember college," I answered.

"Yes, but as I said, things have changed."

Reminding her that I had not been out of college for more than six months didn't help.

She smiled and said, "But doesn't it feel like five years of changes? Nowadays, things change at a much faster pace. Each month is about a year of changes compared to the previous years. Come and see for yourself. There is a gathering in the music department tomorrow night."

I didn't respond right away. I needed to think about it. My mindset was in a departure mode. The last thing I wanted was to get arrested because of some political scrimmages on campus. As we walked out of the bookstore, she turned backward and looked at me with a smile that hinted of a challenge to me. I took the bait.

"Hmm, so what will be the topic? The impact of atonal music on the democratic society?" I felt remorse immediately about that comment. It had a mocking tone, which I didn't intend.

"Actually," she ignored my tone and explained, "we are all going to listen to the recently smuggled audio tape of Ayatollah Khomeini's speech in France."

It was ironic and humorous. I chuckled reflexively. The music students were going to listen to Ayatollah Khomeini, the exiled religious opposition leader, whose opinion of music was that it should be banned as it dulls the mind. His argument was that music involves pleasure and ecstasy, like drugs.

She replied, "Yes! What's wrong with that? He is currently the most popular opposition leader."

My immediate response was to inform Firoozeh that he was among the most conservative of the Shiite Muslim leaders. He believed music was evil and dance was a satanic byproduct of music. I maintained that if he came to power, art in general, and music and dance, more specifically, would be among the first victims of his regime.

Firoozeh shook her head. She refused to believe the "dark image" I described, would ever happen to Iran. Nevertheless, she claimed, many students, regardless of their political views, believed in his leadership and that he was going to navigate the Iranian nation out of Pahlavi's oppressive regime. She was on a roll. Without a pause, she sustained that with so many secular intellectuals in every aspect of Iranian society, it would be hard to imagine a world in which they all were silenced.

Playing devil's advocate was one of my strengths. No one knew what the future would bring. She could be right, but somehow, my gut feeling was worried about a different scenario. Her romantic view of the future was heartwarming. It also reminded me of a similar gathering she invited me to at her cousin's college four weeks prior.

Recollecting that event, with a smile, I asked her if she remembered.

"Yes, and I also remember that you left early that night. What happened?"

My stomach gurgled, reminding me of the time. A sandwich shop was nearby and next to it another bookstore. I asked if she wouldn't mind going to the bookstore for my last two books and then to the sandwich shop for dinner where I would describe what happened that night.

With her nod of approval, we went to the bookstore adjacent to the restaurant. She helped me with purchasing two books about Persian literature. After that, we went to the sandwich shop and ordered our food.

Her cousin was a freshman at Azad University, a private college with low admission standards and high tuition. My impression of Azad University's students wasn't too complimentary. I considered them a group of wild party goers with a state of mind far away from anything serious, including politics.

While explaining my thoughts, I pulled out a chair for her to sit.

"Okay, you are wrong!" she replied, "I think you're underestimating the impact of the recent social changes on the students and ordinary people. *Everybody* is interested in what's happening to the country. Everywhere you go, you find people discussing government policies, international affairs, reforms, revolution. Even the taxi drivers don't leave you alone!"

She was right. I was just concerned about leaving her in the chaotic world that was shaping rapidly in Iran and wanted to help her, as a friend, to have a balanced point of view. Realizing I should not have judged, I apologized. During social chaos or a revolution, everything goes into hyper mode. Frankly, it was a positive change when everyone becomes aware and pays attention to who governs them. The seductive realization that people's opinion could matter in shaping the future *was* intoxicating.

Without further delay, I launched into describing what happened that night at her cousin's college.

"The room had been packed with young college students. Honestly, I was surprised to see so many upper-middle-class kids in the room, sitting on the floor, which they typically consider a lower class act, listening to a small cassette tape player in the center of the room. You were sitting on the floor near the center, listening intensely to the scratchy sound coming off of the tape player--"

Firoozeh interrupted me. "Yeah, I remember you tapped my shoulder and squeezed yourself next to me on the ground. But you didn't stay that long. Did something go wrong?"

"The poor quality of the tape coupled with the unusual dialect of the speaker made it difficult for me to understand the spoken words. Add a crowded room to the mix, and that made me antsy."

"The cassette tapes are smuggled into the country," she explained, "and are copied many times over, so the quality is not the greatest."

This wasn't anything new. Ayatollah Khomeini's communication with his followers via cassette tapes had been an effective outreach system despite all the prohibition and regimes' crackdowns. His movement was experienced in effectively smuggling cassette tapes.

They had been doing it since his exile from the country in 1963.

"Nowadays, his speeches are played in thousands of small and large mosques, universities, and other gatherings throughout the country," she continued.

Nodding my head in acceptance, I swallowed my bite of food and continued the story.

"The room was too stuffy for me that night, so I got up, left the room for fresh air and stood by the door. Standing there had two advantages: enjoying the cooler air while still facing the inside of the room, and listening.

"Two students were speaking softly behind me. It was hard for me to ignore them; I took a step back and adjusted my position to hear them better. One of them spoke in a voice barely above whisper, complaining that people were listing to that mullah, referring to Khomeini. I turned around to look at him. He was short and clean shaven and had a raspy voice. The other one demanded him to show respect for the man, as he was *the* Ayatollah Khomeini! The short one smirked and claimed that Ayatollah Khomeini was not his real name, and that his real name was Ruhollah Mustafavi—"

Firoozeh cut me off again. "But *ayatollah* is a title and not a name. It's given to a Shiite cleric when he reaches the highest rank! Didn't he know that?"

I shrugged. "I'm sure he was referring to the name Khomeini."

"Well that's easy, when a cleric reaches the *ayatollah* level, it is tradition that he adopts the name of his place of birth. Khomeini means from the city of Khomein," she continued.

Her enthusiasm was refreshing and brought a smile to my face. She asked me to continue the story.

"The clean-shaved guy said that it bothered him to see more and more people were listening to this uneducated mullah, referring to Ayatollah Khomeini. The other guy's tone changed. He became more serious and warned the clean shaved one again to have respect for Khomeini. He continued on explaining how difficult and long it was to achieve the rank of ayatollah, the highest rank in Islamic studies.

Just because it was not a typical Western education process, it didn't mean that it was inferior or to be taken lightly. Then he explained about the several books Ayatollah Khomeini had written.

"The other student cut him off. He got agitated and protested that he once again had gone off the track. He said, 'Who cares if he has written some religious books! Some people are acting like he is our revolutionary leader and are even considering making him the head of our country once we win this revolution.' Then he launched into speech about how a head of country impacts the destiny of that country. He said something about how the head of a country will be involved with every aspect of the country's affairs, such as economy, politics, military, health, finance, education, social, and many more complicated issues that are national and international. And then he posed an interesting question to the other guy. He asked, 'How can a cleric, a mullah, or even an ayatollah who all his life has studied religion, understand all these complicated modern issues? Let alone, to make crucial decisions and lead a nation!'

"I turned around and took another look at them. They were standing outside by the wall smoking cigarettes. A dim light from a lamp post nearby was the only illumination source. Shadows and darkness made it hard for me to see their faces clearly, but I could figure out the other one was also a skinny guy, but he had some sort of a bushy black beard.

"The bearded one shook his head and responded, 'Islam is an all-encompassing religion. It covers all aspects of life.' He elaborated further that Ayatollah Khomeini's teachings were clear in that subject matter. Islam does not divide the secular from religious. Islamic rules cover all the affairs of a nation, including the secular domains such as economy, politics, finance and so on."

"Well, it's dangerous to allow a religious figure to lead a revolution and run the country after that. From history, we learned that every time a religion governs a nation, the first victims have always been human rights and freedom as a whole!" I nodded in agreement with her.

"Going back to the two men, the clean shaved one did not agree with the other one's opinion and warned, if people were not careful, they would end up replacing the dictatorship of a king with a theocracy by clergy. He then said something like theocracy was worse than a dictatorship. He justified his view, that a dictator does not govern what goes on inside our mind! However, a government empowered by divine mandate, imposes its rules outside *and* inside of our mind. He claimed that he had read a few of Khomeini's books, and in his books, Ayatollah Khomeini tells us what to do behind the door and walls of our own bathroom. He then changed his tone to a softer one and concluded that people should go for the ideologue who promotes freedom of individual rights, and who allows the democratic process govern our country.

"The bearded guy wasn't giving up. He shook his head and replied, 'But my friend, Ayatollah Khomeini was the only one who stood up strong against the might of the Shah's government.'

"I suspected he was referring to the early '60s when Ayatollah Khomeini warned the Iranian people against the most humiliating agreement the king of Iran signed with the U.S. The agreement was about the 'capitulation' law or as some people called it then, 'status-of-forces agreement.' The agreement granted immunity from Iranian laws to American military personnel and their family members. No matter what crime Americans committed in Iran, the Iranian government had no authority to prosecute or even investigate the issue!

Khomeini called it the document of the enslavement of Iran.

"The cleaned shaved one admitted that those were good points about Ayatollah Khomeini, and even said that he respected him for his courage and ambition. But quickly, he went back to his previous position. Citing historical references, he claimed that history repeatedly had shown ideologues do not make good heads of governments. He insisted that people should install democracy, where everyone participates. He hoped in the future, government would be by the people for the people.

"The bearded student replied, 'Brother, Ayatollah Khomeini knows what is best for Islam and for us. We must trust in his judgment.' The other guy shook his head and said, 'God have mercy on us if any radical group takes over the government after we rid ourselves of this regime. All of our hard work and sacrifices will be in vain.'

"The bearded student, who I assumed belonged to a conservative Muslim group, threw his cigarette butt on the ground and stepped on it. As he exhaled the last puff he said, 'We need to stay focused on toppling this regime and not dwell too much on what happens after that.'

"At this moment, a third person emerged from the dark and put his arms on the shoulders of both men. 'Common friends,"' he said, 'remember, democracy is a matter of faith, a faith in the soul of man and faith in human rights.'

"Intrigued by the wisdom of the third voice, I turned my head to see the person. He was a slim, narrow faced man with an ample nose. He wore a beret. 'Oh, Doctor Alimoodi,' one of them exclaimed. 'Now, who said that? Is it one of your own famous quotes?'

"'No my friend, I can't claim that one. It's a quote from President Truman,' Doctor Alimoodi replied. The bearded one didn't know who President Truman was. Doctor Alimoodi didn't bother to explain it. He then guided the two students back into the room to hear Ayatollah Khomeini. As they walked away, the clean shaved one said, 'You know. Doctor, the problem with these conservative Muslims is that they don't believe in human rights, let alone to have faith in it.' Then he went on telling how the Muslim's fundamental belief is that humans are subservient to God and their destiny is to fulfill the will of Allah. He continued his monologue saying that for Shiite Muslims, the ayatollahs are supposedly ordained by the great divine to be the only interpreter of God's instructions and intentions on earth until their twelfth imam appears to rule on earth. He felt this was the complete opposite of individualism and respect for human rights.

"Dr. Alimoodi cut him off. 'Farzan, my friend, then we can refer them to what the prophet Isa Massih (Jesus) said on how serving people is serving God. But for now, let's set aside all these philosophies and listen to the tape in peace.' He gently pushed him into the room."

Firoozeh finished her drink, tilted her head, and said that she couldn't understand my point by telling her the story.

"My point on retelling that conversation was based on a new observation I recently made. I believe we are witnessing the birth of a new collusion. Some sort of social evolution at the ground level. Traditionally, Muslims and secular fractions wouldn't tolerate each other. But, they were talking about unity. This was like asking oil and vinegar to mix!"

"So what? Firoozeh argued back. "Strange political mixes typically happen during any major transition."

But this was not a political compromise coming from the top. This was happening at the grass-roots level. These were individuals learning to put their differences aside and join forces to eradicate a common enemy.

She reiterated, whatever this was, it was happening all over the country and it was energizing. She was truly excited about it, as she thought it was unifying and enhanced solidarity among people. She stopped talking for a moment, turned to me and seemed to be going to say something else, but changed her mind. I noticed it and asked her to say whatever it was. She hesitated a bit and then said, "Maybe you should stay! Who knows, our society may experience something fantastic and unique, like utopia. I'd hate to see you miss it."

She looked down after she said that. It was a shock to me to hear it. Now, even Firoozeh wanted me to scrap my plan and stay. It took me a few moments to collect my thoughts. Whatever this society turned into, utopia or not, unique or not, I had a dream to ride. I had to be true to myself first. It was hard to toss out a plan after so many years of fantasizing about it. Her views were noble and too rosy for my taste. Sheepishly, I excused myself from being a part of that bright future she pictured to me.

She nodded her understanding. "Anyway," she said, "Khomeini's voice is like a beacon that is leading ships—secular or non-secular—in a foggy night to shore."

I swallowed my last bite. "Fine, as long as these ships don't get stuck in an eternal darkness."

Watching her talking passionately about her unique experiences with various revolutionary student activities was amusing to me. I never knew this side of her before. We usually talked about music, poetry and literature. A short burst of thought occurred to me that perhaps she suggested my stay for a different purpose. But quickly I dismissed the thought.

Absorbing every second of our moments together, I tried to memorize the look of her eyes, mouth, the smooth white skin of her face, and her perfectly shaped white teeth. I didn't have a photo of her, and based on my upbringing, it wasn't appropriate to ask for one. The physical distance between us would be enormous and therefore make visits almost impossible. Even telephone calls would be expensive, assuming that Iran would stay intact after this political quagmire, and that communication lines stayed open. The only affordable and somewhat reliable means left would be via letters and postal services.

My thoughts were consumed with how much I would miss her, and if I would be able to remember her face two years from now. With her, I have always felt relaxed and true. There was never a need for any pretense. She listened to me with empathy and never judged me. Her words were like music to me and her movements were part of this unforgettable delight of a demeanor that left a lifelong impression in my mind.

A quick look at my watch showed how time was unfairly running fast. It was getting late. Security forces were more nervous around the universities and especially the one we were nearby, Tehran University.

But before we rushed back to her house, I had to tell her the truth.

I could no longer delay this.

Still sitting, I looked at my plastic cup and turned it around a few times. With my eyes on the cup I said, "Look, my paperwork is almost done and I'm expecting to leave Tehran very soon. That is, if my student visa is granted and this country doesn't fall into a civil war before I leave." I looked up at her, her kind eyes had a comforting expression, as if she knew and that everything will be okay. I continued, "So, probably, I won't able to see you again before my flight."

She played with her plastic cup. "I kind of figured it out. I'm happy for you, Vahid." She looked at her cup, smiled and continued. "It's unlikely for this country to have a civil war. I see a bright future. But when you settle in L.A., write to me." Then she looked at her watch and said, "Let's go."

When we left the restaurant, the sky was dark, it was windy, and the air was chilly. Naturally, I picked up my pace. We were deeply engaged in conversation and I didn't notice that my fast pace made her scuttle to catch up with me. A gentle pull on my left sleeve brought my attention to the matter. She was holding the tip of my coat sleeve as part of her attempt to stay up with me. First, I thought it was cute, then, my heart raced when I wondered if this was her way of suggesting holding hands? Oh God, these last few minutes are important to her too. But should I?

My brain was working overtime. We had kept our relationship platonic so far. She was among the friends that I enjoyed most. I didn't dare to think of her romantically. Our friendship was too beautiful to jeopardize it with romance.

In my culture, the way I understood it, holding hands would send a romantic interest signal. It would not be fair to her to open up that window, starting a romance at that point. I was about to leave the country. Emotionally, I really wanted to hold her hand and feel her warmth. Whatever that sentiment was, I didn't understand it. It was strong but nothing that I couldn't control. The timing was off. My future was unknown. Holding hands would confuse both of us and had the potential for trouble.

We approached her building. The lobby door was locked for security. She turned around and faced me but her eyes were on the ground. An overwhelming desire of hugging and kissing her good-bye took over me. But I had to control my urge.

"Well," I said, trying to smile, "This is it. Let's write to each other, okay?" I kept my tone light, hoping to cover up my burning desire.

She glanced at me and replied, "Okay." And then she looked down again.

Her look melted my heart. My knees started to tremble, and my heart was jumping out of its rib cage. A voice in my head was screaming, "Don't do it. Don't give her false hope. The future is uncertain. This relationship doesn't have a chance. Long distance romance is a fallacy."

My shyness, my conservative upbringing, and the bad timing were the brute forces preventing me from doing what felt natural. So, I just simply said, "Good-bye."

She looked me in the eyes, smiled and said, "*Beh-omid-e didar*, with a hope of seeing you again." She turned around, unlocked the door and vanished inside.

On my way home, my thoughts were circling around the notion that if there ever was a reason for me to stay, Firoozeh would be the one.

Would I ever see her again?

18

THE CURRENCY

 *The price of freedom is eternal vigilance.*

— THOMAS JEFFERSON, THIRD PRESIDENT OF THE UNITED STATES OF AMERICA

Swoosh! My face barely missed the back of a truck as I weaved through Tehran's heavy traffic on the rear seat of my cousin's motorcycle. Hadi was two years older than me and shorter than the average young men his age, but an expert on maneuvering through Tehran's traffic jams on his Honda motorcycle.

Hadi and I had met in a café to say good-bye and he was giving me a ride home. I switched my grip between Hadi's waist to the chrome handles on the side of the back seat of his bike.

"Watch out, you jerk," a taxi driver yelled at Hadi as he cut him off.

From behind him I shouted, "Can you stay and visit when you drop me off at my home?" My voice had to fight against the traffic noise and the wind noise.

He turned his neck to the side and yelled that he couldn't. He had to help his mother prepare a welcoming party for his cousin who was released from prison a day before. It became easier to speak when he stopped for a red traffic light. His cousin had just completed a ten-year prison sentence.

The cousin he referred to was not from my side of the family. Several cousins from his mother's side were involved with one of underground political rebel groups called MKO.

The light turned green and we were off again. *Swoosh*! Another near miss with a car. Riding behind a small motorcycle, zig-zagging through heavy traffic with no helmet or any other protection was not uncommon, and it wasn't fun. Every time I had done it, the question of making it to the end of the ride in one piece lingered in my mind during the ride.

I shouted, "Take Kakh Street, it's less crowded."

He nodded his head and turned his bike toward it. Tall, luscious trees and quiet streets were two significant characteristics of the upscale neighborhood of Kakh Street. In Farsi, *kakh* means palace. Clear views of several royal palaces from a large royal compound which had been turned into museums and parks, were added visual benefit of this route. Once we entered Kakh Street, the beauty and quiet of the area made the ride much more tolerable. Then ….

BOOM!

An explosion rocked the street. The bike swerved radically, but Hadi controlled it well and stopped. "What was that?"

"It sounded like an explosion! Back there," I pointed my finger to a building about a block away from us. A house was on fire. Flames were pushing out from the blown-out windows of a one-story building surrounded by large trees.

A moment later, the front door of the house burst open and a heavy-set man ran out screaming. His clothing was on fire. He ran in short circles screaming something in a high-pitched voice.

"Let's go help him!" I shouted.

My cousin didn't move. "What's hanging off of his head?" he asked.

It looked like his left ear was torn off and dangling from his head by just a thin strip of burning skin. "Come on! Move! Let's go help," I shouted again.

The man tried to jump in the *jube* outside of the house so the flow of water in the *jube* would extinguish the fire, but it was too narrow for his large body. He rolled on the ground and put his arms in the *jube*, frantically throwing cold water on himself.

Hadi shook his head and said that it would be better if we didn't get involved. That man could've been making explosives. He assumed SAVAK agents were going to swarm there soon. In that case, they would close the area and would take everybody within the two blocks of the incident to interrogate. He thought, given the hyper-agitated mode of the social condition, it could take weeks before we could get out of jail.

Still sitting on the back of his bike, I urged him to ride and find a public phone to call an ambulance. By then a few neighbors were out and running to help.

BOOM!

A second explosion from the same house rocked the neighborhood again. A neighbor who was running toward the burning man flew backward by the force of the explosion and was thrown to the ground a few yards away. He lay still on the ground.

My cousin started up the bike. "Let's get out of here before the police show up. The neighbors will call the fire department."

I had to agree or be left behind. The house was fully engulfed in fire when we left. What was going on with Hadi? His behavior seemed unlike him. Was he also active with the rebel group? Or was it his connection with his rebel cousins that deterred him from getting involved with the man on fire?

We were both quiet the rest of ride. A few minutes later he dropped me off at my house, then disappeared into the smoggy, busy streets of Tehran.

My mother was busy dusting when I entered the house. She beamed when she saw me and said that I just missed a call from the Iran-America Society. I passed her silently and went straight to wash my face in an attempt to calm my tense nerves.

My mother followed me to the bathroom. She apparently noticed that I didn't look or behave normally. According to her, my face was as pale as the plaster on the wall, and that worried her. She asked if anything was wrong.

I waved her off, signaling I needed a few moments to collect myself. But that didn't work, and she asked again. I blew up and told her that I had just witnessed a violent explosion of a house and begged her to leave me alone for a moment.

She ignored my request and asked if the house was in our neighborhood. The only way I could get her to leave me alone was to give her the exact location and change the subject to something totally different. It worked, she sighed, slowed down, and gave me the telephone message left for me.

My paperwork was approved! The next step was to purchase a plane ticket and notify the Iran-America Society of my departure date, which couldn't come soon enough for me.

I had to call Davud.

My mother carried on with her usual monologue, praying for the people who got hurt and she left me alone.

The two explosions and witnessing a burning man's desperate attempt to survive had given me a case of sensory overload. The images appeared in my mind in slow motion over and over again. I had to sit and process what just happened. If Hadi hadn't hesitated, and if we had run toward the burning man, the second explosion could have killed or at least injured us. I shook my head when I thought how ironic it would be to die or lie in a hospital bed on the same day I received the green light to purchase a ticket out of Iran.

Still dizzy with the recent experience, I turned the rotary dial of the phone. It rang three times and then, "Hello?" A female voice answered. Suddenly, a chilled sweat covered my back. I slammed the handset down and disconnected.

Neilu? What was I doing dialing her? And, she answered! She is home. Oh, God, it was odd to hear her voice. My hands were shaking, my face felt hot, like I was on fire, and my heart palpitated as if it were ripping out of my ribcage. A voice inside me was yelling to call her back, call her back, talk to her.

In my mind, I raced to her house and pictured myself sitting in the car staring at her front door, craving to knock on the door and ask many questions. It was only when my wet eyes counseled me, I realized that it was time to leave.

A few minutes went by before I could collect myself.

My right arm reached the dialer on the phone, and this time, I paid attention to what I dialed.

Davud's mother answered the phone, as usual. After answering her multiple questions, she handed the phone to Davud. According to Davud, that's how she snooped on her kid's affairs. I shared the good news with him. He had just received a call from the society as well.

The government had recently lowered the maximum amount we could take abroad to $3000 per person. The flood of exodus had impacted the treasury, and this was their attempt in slowing down the flight of money out of the country.

Bank employees were on strike without any indication of the end date. Naturally, no bank could function without manpower. We needed a bank to convert currency from *toman*, Iranian currency, to the dollar. Travel checks were a safer way to carry cash across borders and they were only sold by the banks. Going to a strange land for the first time without cash was considered extremely risky by our families. We had no established address, no bank account in the U.S., and the language school in Los Angeles expected tuition in cash in advance. We also needed to find a travel agency to purchase our airline tickets.

It was time for action. We agreed that I would tackle the currency problem, and that Davud would find us a travel agency that could get us out as soon as possible.

My ultimate source of information about contacts who could facilitate my need for obtaining American currency was in the kitchen, my mother. She had a good knowledge of people we knew who could open various doors for us. In a society where favoritism plays a major role, who you know makes a vast difference in the speed of progress.

She asked me to sit down and have lunch with her. The lunch was *ahbgoosht*, my favorite.

The hearty aroma of the lamb and potato stew was inviting and hard to refuse. She diligently arranged a table setting in front of me and poured the soup portion of *ahbgoosht* into a bowl. She sat next to me with a gentle smile on her face and attended to my tale of challenges ahead. She listened attentively as I described our team approach and my dilemma of solving the currency problem. I needed someone with contacts within the banking industry.

My mother advised that my uncle Akbar was the only one who could help. As the head of the air force logistics procurement, he had connections everywhere and could help with my bank problem. He was the same uncle who hired educated clergies in his monthly *rozeh* gatherings. She ordered me to call him right away.

My uncle Akbar was a reserved and quiet man. I had never seen him volunteering to help others with their problems. "Will he help? He's usually…"

She interrupted me with a frown. "Yes, of course he will help. You are his nephew!" After a pause she continued, "He had better help! Your father sacrificed a lot to help him with the means for a decent education and the life he has now. He owes that to your father."

It took several phone calls to locate him. Uncle Akbar was on the side of conservative Muslims, with many loyal and influential friends. He was brief and to the point in his talk with me. After asking a few questions, he promised to make a few phone calls and get back to me.

An hour later, Davud reported back with the address of a reliable travel agency, who agreed to meet us the next day. Worrying about the possibilities of a million things that could go wrong, I asked Davud for assurance that the travel agency was trustworthy. We just didn't have time to play silly games or get tangled up with some scam. The social chaos, coupled with a quickly deteriorating government, had created a fertile atmosphere for scammers and con artists.

He assured me that it came highly recommended by a reliable source, and then he quizzed me about solutions to the currency predicament. My wish was to return the favor to him with a solid lead on banking, but all I could say was that it was in the works.

He was worried, no one in his camp of friends and relatives had come up with a solution. We discussed a plan B, to take *toman* with us and exchange it once we were in Los Angeles. We both understood having dollars in our pockets would be much easier during our transit.

Once our phone conversation ended, a strange feeling took over me. The last few weeks, my focus had been on saying my farewells to friends and relatives, but I'd not given any thought about my personal belongings. Realizing anything I left behind could stay out of my life forever gave me a shiver; I'd never been this close to parting with life the way I knew it.

Standing in my room in the basement, the challenge was how to sort my belongings. Journals, photo albums, books, paintings, sheet music, stamps collections, my favorite audio cassette tapes and records, they were all there. Each had a piece of my life connected to it. How does one choose what part of their memories should stay behind?

Later that night, a phone call from Uncle Akbar churned my stomach. He spoke softly with short and purposeful sentences. "Write down this instruction. The bank I refer to you will raise its security bars half open between 10:00 to 10:30 tomorrow morning. But the doors will remain locked. Knock on the door and give them your name. They will help you. Don't be late!"

He gave me the name and the address of the bank. I immediately called Davud.

The next day, Davud and I drove to the bank. It was as my uncle described. The metal security curtain was half opened but the door was locked. We parked the car on the street in front of the bank and knocked on the bank door. A man came to the door and asked my name and what I needed. After I said who I was, he checked a list, unlocked the door, raised the iron curtain higher, looked to left and right and said, "Get in."

Inside the bank was quiet. Only two employees were working. Most of the lights were off. The semi-dark, empty space felt eerie. The man who let us inside asked for our money. Each one of us quickly exchanged Iranian *toman* for three thousand US dollars in cash and travelers checks and left the bank. The creaky sound of the metal curtain being lowered and then the cranking sound of the bank door being shut and locked behind our backs signified the seriousness of the bankers' strike. They didn't want anyone to know that some people can still get banking done. People who had contacts.

Once in the car, we felt safe to talk about the experience. It felt good to breathe easier. We talked about how spooky it was and the excitement we both felt, as if we were part of a spy movie.

Next was the trip to the travel agency to buy our airplane tickets.

"Yesterday, I saw a house explode." The words just blurted out from my mouth. I had no idea why I shared that information with Davud.

"What?"

"Yes, you heard me. It was in Kakh Street. The house burned rapidly, and a guy ran out in flames, screaming, with his ears falling off."

"God! Did you help?"

"No, that's the sad part. I was riding on the back of my cousin's motorcycle and he was afraid of what SAVAK would do to us."

Davud didn't say anything in reply. We all knew what the secret police would do to its suspects. A few moments of silence took over. Part of me felt sad that I couldn't help a fellow human. In contrast, another part of me was happy that I wasn't lying in a hospital bed or dead or being tangled with police.

I broke the silence. "What are we becoming?"

Davud shifted in his seat, griped the steering wheel tighter and changed the topic with the news of a strong rumor about the airport employees' upcoming strike. It would shut down the airport.

"So what if we buy these tickets, and a day later the airport shuts down?"

"This travel agency is highly recommended by a trusted friend. They are in the know. If there is a strike, they won't sell us tickets," Davud answered.

None of us wanted to get stuck. We were so close. After all this work, it would be terrible to get left behind. Frustration over the new potential threats to our plan made me forget how I felt about the house fire.

Subconsciously, we felt better by trying to analyze the events that might trigger the strike. It gave us a false sense of control. We thought the strike would be a response to the shah's removal of the civilian prime minister, and appointment of a military man, General Azhari, as prime minister. The general's first order of business would be to declare stricter martial laws and establish tougher curfews.

Davud tilted his head to the side as usual and hypothesized that perhaps the potential strike was the work of the regime to slow down the exodus. Many rich people were leaving the country and taking their wealth with them.

My opinion was that the silly flip-flop of prime ministers was dumb. People knew that prime ministers, and the rest of the government, were puppets of the shah, the king of Iran. The exodus was because of people's fear of prosecution if his regime toppled.

Our only concern was the Tehran airport. We concluded that the airport employees' strike wouldn't impact the government. The airport was shared with the air force, therefore, in the case of a strike, the air force personnel would assist the government's flights. The strike would impact only the ordinary people, like us. It would make our lives more complicated.

"What if the air force personnel also strike?" Davud asked. "I have heard another rumor that air force support personnel loyal to the opposition, may also join the strike."

I shook my head. "That may seriously impact our plan."

There were other ways to get out of the country, such as taking the train to Turkey and flying to the USA from Turkey. Or taking a bus to Pakistan and flying from Karachi. But they were all much more difficult. We decided to create good vibes by staying positive.

The travel agency was not difficult to find. It was located in the upscale part of the town and was packed with clients. We were recommended to speak with the managing partner, Mariam. She was with a client and asked us to wait for her. Some of the customers were sitting on the edge of their chairs, and some shook their heads as they talked to their companions. Typically, buying tickets to travel outside the country is a happy occasion and is considered a pleasurable thing to do. But not that day. After about ten minutes she called us to her desk.

After the introduction and some polite small talk, I went right to the point and asked if she would be able to help us with the first flight out to Los Angeles.

"You and everyone else here!" Mariam replied widening her large round eyes and starting her search on a large computer terminal with a noisy keyboard. After a few loud clicks on the keyboard, she bit her lower lip and glanced at us out of the corner of her eyes. Several more clicks on the keyboard and she stopped. A slight grin appeared on her face. After a few phone calls, she turned toward us and said, "The earliest flight with two seats is on Swissair with multiple stops. It leaves in three days, this Sunday."

The stops were Damascus, Geneva, with a brief time to change planes to New York, then another change of plane with arrival in Los Angeles estimated to be a few hours past midnight local time. Total travel time was going to be twenty-two hours.

Davud and I looked at each other. Sunday was the second day of the week. Fridays and the second half of Thursdays were weekends, and everything shuts down. This would leave us very little time.

"We will take it," Davud jumped in. We were ready.

It would be nice to sit next to each other during such a long journey. I couldn't resist to ask for such a possibility.

She smiled, nodded, and worked her magic. After a few phone calls and a few key strokes on her computer, she gave us our tickets and an itinerary that after twenty-two hours would put us in Los Angeles on January 15, 1979.

She was a perfect person to ask about the potential personnel strike at the airport. However, she frowned when I asked, and after a short pause she disclosed that it was serious and a real threat. It was supposed to happen soon.

Our flight was in three days. What were the chances of it happening that soon? Davud was tense. His voice cracked when he asked the question.

She patiently accommodated us and explained that there were many people leaving the country and no one wanted a strike. There was an enormous amount of pressure on the airport personnel to delay their strike. Many family members of influential people were among the traveling crowd, which was a positive force in our favor.

The ticket cost was substantial. Would we get a refund if the flight was cancelled? The thought of losing the money created more stress. Missing the chance to fly out would pose a grave setback. Losing the ticket cost on top of it would add additional strain. Cash was extremely valuable. No one trusted a rosy picture of the near future.

Squirming in my seat, as politely as possible, I posed the question. The tickets were rather expensive and a refund in the case of flight cancelation due to the strike would be helpful.

Mariam raised her brows and pondered the question. She explained that depending upon the circumstances and how we would miss the flight, we could get a partial refund. However, she immediately added, "But don't start worrying about it. Stay positive and, *inshallah*, everything will be fine."

Davud recognized that we had taken too much of her time with her agency being so full of people. He agreed and elbowed me to get going. Hustling out of our seats, we both bowed our head in gratitude and thanked her.

"Bon voyage," Mariam said with a smile.

Tehran in 70s

19

SINS AND DECEPTIONS

> *Be like the sun for grace and mercy. Be like the night to cover others' faults. Be like running water for generosity. Be like death for rage and anger. Be like the Earth for modesty. Appear as you are. Be as you appear.*
>
> — Rumi

Oh, my God!

My head reticently turned away in an attempt not to stare. It was hard for me to believe the view in front of me. Her long, fit, and bare legs were fully extended as she bent over the desk in front of her, flirting with the clerk sitting there. The lack of fabric on her short tennis skirt didn't leave anything to my imagination.

"Hey, she likes you!" my cousin Kahmron whispered in my ear. He was standing next me in the line to reserve a court. I was his guest at the exclusive, elite tennis club he belonged to on the north side of Tehran, where mostly affluent people resided. He had invited me to the club for the first time as a departing gift.

Responding to his comment, I assured him that the girl in front of us was flirting with the man sitting behind the small wooden reservation desk.

"No, you idiot, look how she turns her head and smiles at you."

He was right, she did turn her head a few times and smiled at me. And every time, her micro tennis skirt went up higher. Her almost nonexistent white underwear matched her tennis outfit. My eyes immediately dropped on the ground and a warm flush covered my face.

Kahmron mumbled in my ear something about his father's BMW and the girls. He cursed himself for not bringing it, otherwise, he claimed, we could pick her and her friend up and have some fun.

His obnoxious comments annoyed me. He was immature for his twenty years. Maybe his short stature compelled him to have a big mouth. I reminded him that we drove there in my car, which was a brand new Peikan, made in Iran.

Kahmron had grown up on the north side of Tehran. He went to the school for upper-echelon kids and his family considered themselves elite. He ridiculed my car as it was too simple for girls in that neighborhood. We lived in a society with defined, and yet unwritten, social codes for multiple sects.

The girl shifted her weight and wiggled a bit, and that made the view even more suggestive.

Speechless, I secretly wished that moment would freeze so I could stand there forever. My face burned with all the blood rushing to my head. I felt ashamed for looking at her. Turning my head upward to look at trees and then down at the gravel were short-lived remedies, however. My eyes were seduced by her charming body language, and it was like being compelled by a magnetic force, they always returned to her legs.

It wasn't that I had not seen short skirts before. It was the 70s and miniskirts were high fashion and abundant wherever the upper middle class and upper crust socialized in Iran. My shock was in how comfortable this girl was with her sexuality in public. My mind became hostage to her Eros.

"Next!" announced the clerk behind the desk. My cousin moved up and showed his membership card. The man behind the desk assigned us a court. The sexy girl in front of us moved away from the desk and walked toward her assigned court. On her way, she turned and looked at me again and giggled with her friend.

I was stunned and stood motionless as a log. I didn't know how to respond to her. Girls on my side of the city did not act like this. My cousin pushed me away from the desk toward court number three.

On our way, we saw many more girls wearing micro tennis outfits.

The lush green campus of the tennis club was a botanical wonder, but my twenty-one-year-old libido was more absorbed with the abundance of beautiful girls in skimpy tennis outfits. On the other hand, my conscience, like the annoying cry of a fussy child, interrupted my desire, reminding me of the consequences of such thoughts. Nevertheless, dozens of questions bombarded my mind. What did these girls want? What was I supposed to do? How should I react? What constituted appropriate behavior in such a setting? It bothered me that my cousin ridiculed my new car. Did he do it because my car was made in Iran and not an exotic foreign make like his father's? Feeling bolder than usual, I asked him that question.

"You don't get it, do you?" he answered. "This is the Royal Tennis Club. These girls were probably dropped off here by their drivers in their limos. They don't go to bed with boys with lower social status, only equal or higher." After a very short pause and a chuckle he added, "Unless one is extraordinarily handsome, which you are not."

The tennis ball hit me at that moment as I stood motionless in disbelief. The fact that he suggested these girls actually have sex before they were married stunned me. To be sure I heard it correctly, I repeated what was said and added "Here in this country?" for emphasis.

"Yes, stop being so naive. What country are you from?" My cousin served the ball.

That was a good question. I wondered that myself. It was only a few weeks ago that my father had invited me to go along with him to a wedding in the slums of Tehran. It was the wedding of one of his laborers' daughters who lived in the south of Tehran, where the poor and underprivileged lived. There were more than seventy people packed in a small, one-bedroom house with a small yard. Men were not allowed to see women without cover, so men and women were separated by a large curtain in the middle of the yard. The spirit of jubilance was everywhere. The abundance of simple food, humor, and laughter had left no space for hunger, gloom, and complaints. There was no alcohol or drugs to make them feel good. Their happiness and joy were derivatives of the occasion. In that part of the town, a simple smile to a woman would cost a broken bone. A touch or a peek of any exposed part of a woman's body would end in murder. The contrast with the prestigious tennis club boggled my mind.

"So... have you?" I asked my cousin as we were playing.

"What? Cat got your tongue? Say it. Finish the sentence," he taunted as he tossed the ball to my side of the court.

I just couldn't verbalize it. It was too awkward for me. Even though it was only the two of us in a large tennis court surrounded by bushes and trees.

He tortured me further by raising his voice. "What? Are you too shy to say SEX?"

Sweating with nervousness, I looked around to see if anyone had heard him. No one was around, but I asked him to lower his voice and be more discrete.

He was agitated at my evasive referencing. With the same obnoxious and loud tone, he explained how freely boys and girls fornicate for fun. He was educating me about life in the northern part of Tehran, where the elite lived.

My uncle, his father, was a relatively wealthy full colonel in the army who had deep ties with the Iranian intelligence apparatus, SAVAK. Somehow, the fact that my uncle worked for SAVAK never entered my conscience as an evil thing. It was, perhaps, compartmentalized in my mind to a more docile role, such as a liaison between military intelligence and SAVAK. His children, my cousins, were members of many exclusive Royal Clubs, such as Equine Royal Club, Polo Royal Club, Tennis Royal Club, etc.

His arrogant response reminded me of the deep division between the affluent and the underprivileged in the country, hence the unrest. I reminded him that what he and his kind consider *fun* is judged as sin by the majority of people in the country. "Doesn't that bother you?" I asked.

He dismissed my assumption and explained that it is only considered sin by lower class folks and some zealous religious people. He further pointed to a double standard and a deep hypocrisy hidden within the Shia religious elite as to the same subject. He was referring to a temporary marriage arrangement called *sigheh*. He believed that *sigheh* was basically a tool for clergy to justify temporary affairs outside of permanent marriage for themselves and their ardent followers. He reminded me that according to Shia's edicts, up to four permanent wives and unlimited temporary *sighehs* were accepted.

Reminding him the *sigheh* in Shia Islam is a form of marriage didn't help. He immediately brought up a good point. *Sigheh*, as a temporary marriage, allows a timetable to be mutually agreed and formally documented in the registrar's office. To drive his point home, he further explained that not only the time limit can be as short as one hour, but also, a compensation for the woman can be agreed upon and fully documented.

Serving the ball, he concluded, "So, basically, it's a formal prostitution blessed and encouraged by the religion. Wake up, man." He returned my serve and continued, "But you are going to America in a few days, so you need to get used to this. Get over your inhibitions.

You're going to the land of the free."

It was confusing. My thoughts circled around the freedom that people who lived in the north of Tehran were enjoying. Why couldn't I stay and join them? The thought didn't last that long, as I quickly remembered that it all was pretend and fake. Real freedom is not just about what the system *allows* you to have. I had to discover what the real freedom was in an open society.

Kahmron's voice broke my thoughts, "Anyway, I'll be right behind you, getting out of here. I'll go to London next month and see if I can get in a university there."

Here he was, a young man who on the surface appeared to have everything; money, glamor, high-level contacts to get him out of any jam. Why did he covet the western civilization? Perhaps he also felt the disingenuousness of what they had in the north. It wasn't the real thing.

Shortly after his earlier comment, he chuckled and continued, "But you know what? It's funny, I lost my virginity in the ghettos where you live."

There it was again, another derogatory comment about where I lived and where my family was placed in the social pecking order. I was sick of it. There was no escape from it in Tehran. I couldn't wait to get out.

I set my mind to exert some physical pain on him, I aimed at his body and hit the ball as hard as possible. After his cry of pain, I helped him remember that my house was in the central part, where the middle class lived, and of course he knew it. He was talking about *Shahr-e-no*, a block of ghetto neighborhood, half an hour south of our place, where many low-cost whore houses operated.

Rubbing his leg where my ball hit, he said, "Yeah, whatever, what a horrible place. Did I tell you what happened?"

Yes, he had. It was three years prior. He came to our house a day later and gave me the details. It was a wonder that he didn't contract a horrible venereal disease. Of course, he used protection, but what followed intrigued me the most.

He claimed that the experience set him free. He became a man, no longer afraid or intimidated by a young man's active imagination.

The two words *free man* bounced in my mind a few times. I liked it. It felt like fresh air, *free man*. But that was three years ago! At that point, he had experienced independence for three years, at least in one aspect of life. At that time, he was just a seventeen-year-old high school brat from ritzy North Tehran. How did he mange to travel an hour and a half south into a crowded, dangerous neighborhood and then into a whore house full of filth, thugs, and shady characters? How did he return home, undetected and unharmed? I asked the question as we hit the tennis ball back and forth.

"Easy. I skipped school and grabbed a cab. I'm telling you, man, that was a liberating experience."

There it was again, *liberating experience,* another set of words that set deep in my mind. All I could say was, "I guess when it comes to liberty, risking one's life becomes irrelevant." I served the ball.

Early that evening, I returned home confused, tired and frustrated. In a society that punished public displays of affection and passion with imprisonment, promiscuity was apparently running rampant in private clubs and affluent areas. I was aware of the Western world's relaxed viewpoint about premarital intimacy. But, it was frustrating to know that in my own city the moral, religious, and civil codes handed out severe punishment to low-income souls who entered in consensual intimacy, while the upper class were given clemency for the exact same behaviors.

The phone rang. Ignoring it didn't help, my mother was rushing for it. Energized by my mother's exertion, I challenged her and successfully picked up the receiver a second before she could. It had become an amusing thing for me to do—to disallow my mother the vantage point of knowing first hand who called our house.

My triumphal smile at my mother turned to a baffled face when I heard the voice on the other side. I turned my back to her for privacy and focus.

"Am I not . . . am I not pretty?" a weeping female voice asked.

My mother stood nearby and acted as if the call was for her and I was wasting her time. The call gave me goose bumps and my mother's presence was a distraction. I covered the handset, and with a slight jerk of my head and a whisper I asked her to leave the area. The call was for me.

She walked away from me, mumbling something. My full attention was pointed at the caller. Softly I asked the caller to identify herself.

"Am . . . I not pretty?" she asked again, between sobs.

"Really, I can't give an honest answer if I don't know who is asking."

"What's the matter with you?" she snapped, "Don't you recognize my voice anymore? This is Bita."

Bita, a younger sister of my brother's wife, was trouble with capital

T. It was not an appropriate time for me to get involved with another one of her dramas. I was only a few days away from leaving the country. She was a year older than me and her well contoured body had been the subject of many of my dreams and fantasies since I first met her at age sixteen. Even her thick glasses and a relatively large mouth did not deter me from fantasizing about her. The only two annoying habits she had, were her cough-like laughs and her overuse of familiar pronouns.

Despite my better judgment, gallantry obliged me to ask why she was crying.

"He says . . . he says . . . that I am ugly!" She erupted into loud crying. "Do . . . do you think I'm . . . ugly?"

I knew she was referring to her bizarre husband. My understanding, up to that point, was that the couple were madly in love. Conversations with Bita were usually centered only on what she wanted. It wasn't clear to me at that moment if her crying was real or if it was to lure me into one of her schemes.

"He is such a con artist," she continued between sobs. "When he married me, he already had a wife with three children! Did you know that? He told me he was divorced, but...but . . . it was a lie! He is still married. He stays with his other family a few nights a week," she howled.

"That bastard!" I reacted to the unwelcome news. But my anger didn't last long. It also triggered the bitter feeling of betrayal I had experienced when she got me involved in one of her well-crafted, tangled webs.

A year prior, as a hopelessly romantic twenty-year-old boy, I wasn't sure if I had any chance with Neilu. She wasn't responding to my affections. As ill luck would have it, Bita called me one Friday afternoon. She caught me off guard, asking if I would go out with her to dinner and a classical music concert.

Forgetting all thoughts of Neilu, I agreed. I was beside myself with anticipation. This was the first time that a popular girl from the privileged upper class of north Tehran was asking me out for a date.

A few hours later, after going through an interrogation like a Q & A session with her father about my intentions with his daughter and the details of the evening, we drove to the concert hall.

Bita wore an elegant, dark green evening gown that covered her body like a well-fitted glove, accentuating her hour-glass figure. A stunning jeweled necklace brought attention to her generous display of cleavage and her heavy makeup. In the car, the aroma of her intoxicating fragrance caressed my face.

My admiration was short lived. As we drove, she explained that the request was nothing but a ruse for her parents, so she could spend a romantic evening with her lover without their suspicions. Her lover was a forty-something- year-old man.

Despite my objections on the grounds of morality, civility, and benevolence, she conned me into proceeding with the evening as she planned.

I drove her to the concert hall. She met her man there. Despite my continuing objections, while I attended the concert, they disappeared under the cover of the night.

Hours later, he dropped her off at the concert hall where I was waiting. During the return trip, she begged me, as her friend, to meet with the man and give her my opinion of him. She was going to marry him!

My motive in accepting the task was unclear to me. Was it my overwhelming curiosity about this man, or did she have some sort of spell on me? Perhaps it was the learning potential and my eagerness to understand how a man of his age and disposition could make a girl like Bita fall madly in love with him. What was his game? Opportunities to solve puzzles like that don't happen often.

A few days later I met with him. We chatted for several hours. He wasn't charming or handsome. He looked old and wrinkled. Something in his beady eyes made me uncomfortable. He was a fast talker and switched subjects often. Something felt creepy about his claim of being madly in love with Bita, but I couldn't pin point it.

My advice to her was to be very careful and think deeply about this matter. I further explained my suspicion about his intentions. But my warnings landed on deaf ears, and despite her family's vigorous opposition, she married that man a few weeks later. It was a quick process in the magistrate's office. No ceremony. Her family was upset and embarrassed about it.

Bita's whimpering in the receiver brought me back to the situation at hand. An alarm went off in my head to stay detached from her. My upcoming journey out of the country was far too important to be impacted by whatever scam she was about to get me involved in. And although I felt a bit sorry for her, she was no picture of virtue and had gone against everyone's advice and wishes to be with this scoundrel.

She whimpered on the phone, "I am going to end my miserable life. I am nothing but an embarrassment to my family. I have no friends left and my husband hates me...."

"Don't even think about it—"

She interrupted me. "I have a knife to my wrist right now. I'm going to end it."

Frantically, I pleaded with her to put the knife away and promised to help her out of the mess. Stopping a suicide was not my forte. In fact, I had never encountered such a thing. Once again, she pulled me into a vortex of potential trouble, this time too close to a pivotal point in my life.

My mother had quietly inched herself near the phone without me noticing it. When she heard my concerned voice, she asked again who it was on the other side. This time her eyes were showing deep concern.

At that point, my focus was on Bita and my mother's snooping was an uninvited distraction. Covering the receiver with my hand again, I begged my mother to go away and leave me alone.

She ignored my warning and continued with her index finger pointing at me. "This is not your private phone. Someone may need to contact us for an important matter. Telephone is only for a short, important conversation—"

With a hand gesture to stop, I interrupted my mother's lecture. Suddenly scuffling and shuffling sounds of struggle came over the phone. A chill went up my spine. "Bita, Bita, what's happening? Talk to me, Bita," I repeatedly asked.

My mother persisted. "What is going on? Is it Bita, your brother's sister-in-law? Why is she calling you?"

I whispered to my mother, "I think she cut her wrist!"

Blood rushed to my head and beads of sweat ran down my forehead as I repeatedly asked Bita to talk to me.

My agitated mother demanded an explanation.

"Bita? Bita, tell me what's going on! C'mon Bita, say something," I asked again.

"I...I . . . uh, I killed it. I killed the damn bastard," Bita answered weeping.

"Killed what?"

"The damn mouse," she replied.

"A mouse?"

She described how her husband leaves his dirty socks, stuffed into each other like little mice, everywhere. "When I ask him to pick them up, he yells and says that it's my job to pick up his socks and clean the house. So, I just stabbed one of them to pieces with my knife," Bita explained.

A sigh of relief came out of my mouth. Wiping the sweat off my forehead, I couldn't stop chuckling, "It felt good, hah?" I asked her. "

So you stabbed a pair of his socks to pieces." "Yeah, I did," she answered.

My mother shook her head, mumbling, "God bless the crazy people," and left.

In a much calmer voice, I talked about the beauty of life and how a few miscalculated steps should not be the end of the world, and comforted her with my promise of help. Yet my help wasn't without a mandate.

She quietly heeded. My intention was to make the most out of the situation. What she had gone through with her husband could be a valuable experience that might help others with a comparable situation. Reminding her of my near departure, I asked her to promise me that she would consider helping others.

After a pause and a few sniffles, she agreed. I sensed a glimmer of hope in her voice. I assured her that help was on the way. The best thing she could do at that moment was to take her mind away from the troubling issues, go outside, and do something fun such as shopping.

"Oh, shopping is a great idea! I love you, like a brother. What a wonderful friend you are!"

Oh boy, here we go again. We hung up.

My mother came back and stood in front of me with her hands on her waist. She was about to say something when I moved away from the phone and with a sheepish smile I said, "It's all yours."

It felt good to calm Bita and get her out of her suicidal mode. She needed a shoulder to cry on, and mine was the only one available. Her older sister, my sister-in-law, was a reasonable and a kind person. She loved Bita despite her mischievousness. I just needed to bring her up to speed about the situation.

I grabbed my jacket and headed out. A few moments later, I found a pay phone and dialed my sister-in-law's office.

Can't wait to leave all these crazy people and start my new life.

20

DEPARTURE

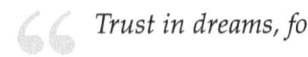 *Trust in dreams, for in them is hidden the gate to eternity.*

— Khalil Gibran, Lebanese-American Poet. (1883-1931)

"*G*ilgamesh." I pronounced the title of the book out loud, as if doing so would help me decide if it belonged in the "go" pile or the "no-go" pile. An important historical figure, it went into the "go" pile, a large brown suitcase that was already full of books. I loved and cherished my books. Each one carried a special part of my collective knowledge. Without them, I felt incomplete.

The clacking of slippers on the stairs echoed in my basement room, alerting me that someone was coming down. A moment later the door opened, and my mother appeared asking if I needed any help packing.

She scanned the room, and without waiting for my answer pointed to the brown one and exclaimed, "*Okh. Okh*, look at all these books in this suitcase! Books are heavy. You won't be able to lift it, Vahid. Why are you taking so many books? What are they?"

After complaining about her asking too many questions, with my hands on my waist, I pointed to the books in the open suitcase and claimed an absolute need for the two volumes of English to Farsi and Farsi to English dictionaries. "I must have them! These other two are about our history, this one is about philosophy, this is about art, this is about music and these are my undergraduate reference books. I still need to add a book of poetry and another of our literature."

Her baffled face was humorous. "Undergraduate reference books? You are going for a graduate degree. Do you really need them?"

She couldn't possibly understand that I was about to embark into a strange new world. One must be ready for any situation. My dramatic justification of taking an entire suitcase of books to the new world was to satisfy her curiosity, so she would leave me alone.

"Don't they have libraries in America?" she asked, unimpressed with my answer.

"Of course, they do! But all their books are in English, a totally different language. That country thinks differently, behaves differently, and basically looks at the world through a different window than the one I am familiar with. I cannot leave my own books behind."

She reminded me of the many stops my flight to America had, shook her head in disbelief, and then like a military commander ordered me to lighten up on the reference books. She bent over the offending suitcase and threw all my carefully selected books onto the floor. "Packing a donkey with books doesn't make it a scholar."

She used a popular Farsi proverb, and she was right, but her action didn't offend me. However, my twenty-one-year-old mind wanted assurances and the security of knowing that my knowledge could travel with me; and my books were my guarantors. I understood her point, though.

How do you pack for a trip of a lifetime?

That night was one of the longest and most exciting nights of my life. Once my suitcases were fully packed with a select number of books and locked, I collapsed onto my bed and wondered if that would be my last night in my basement bedroom—my last night in Tehran--forever. The question plagued my thoughts and I couldn't sleep. My eyes seemed stuck to the dark ceiling, as if wanting to remember even the most mundane aspects of my room.

My thoughts wandered to my friends and then to my immediate family. How would their lives continue without me? My brothers wouldn't care. They both were busy with their day-to-day challenges in a fast changing and unstable world. My older brother's second son was a toddler, and in a year or so his first son would start school. Would he and his wife be able to provide for their children with the economy sinking to a hyperinflation mode and with a strong possibility of the government collapsing? My younger brother had just started college in a university plagued with daily demonstrations, student arrests, and continuous threats of all sorts. He was, like most people in Iran, juggling his daily challenges in an effort to survive.

My father gave an impression of being unfazed. He reminded me of a piece of driftwood on the sea. No storm could sink him. The waves could be high and fierce, the wind could blow relentlessly, but to a piece of driftwood, none of that mattered. It floats in peace and travels with the current.

My mother however, was a different story, I imagined she would cry for a few days, then my first phone calls from the new world would calm her a bit. Her long quest planning to reunite with me would start immediately after my first phone call. She would wonder about me every day.

My thoughts switched to wondering about the exciting things I would discover in the new world, starting with the ocean. I had never seen one. Gently, I closed my eyes and imagined the sensation of standing in front of a great and endless body of water. Then, I got up and frantically started memorizing the images of the things I was leaving behind—my paintings, the poster that I bought in France, and those books that didn't make it into my suitcases.

While shuffling through the books, I found an erotic one that I had bought years ago when I was in high school. I remember, during the tender adolescence years, as a young boy, I had a lot of questions. The force of curiosity was strong. But the only available guidance was mostly from misguided friends. Whispers, chuckles, and random thoughts that seemed not to have conclusions were the most one could get. Culture, religion, or centuries of marginalized openness could be the reason for such a dark "unenlightenment." When I realized there were books that could quench my thirst, my covert operation began. My clandestine effort to locate, obtain, and devour such a book in secrecy began at the age of sixteen. The one I obtained opened a new world to me. How men and women satisfied each other's sexual tendencies, without filters of religion, moral codes, or government censors was what the book offered. Now, it had to be destroyed.

However, the book reminded me of another item of concern. I rushed to my desk drawers in search of a stack of love letters from Neilu. There were bundled and tucked in the back of the middle drawer. With the letters in my hand, I sat on the edge of my bed and read every one of them. Her carefully selected words took me back to the time when love was in the air and every day was a messenger of hope and wonder. My attempt to commit every word to memory was over ambitious. Nevertheless, I found it necessary.

After I finished reading the letters, they were placed on top of a stack of things to be destroyed. Going over the items, I noticed one key piece was missing, an important journal that had been my companion since puberty, my *Journal de Erotiques*.

It was well hidden behind my files in the third drawer of the desk. Chuckling as I flipped the pages, the journal took me back several years ago to the time I was first exposed to print erotica.

I had snooped into my older brother's private stack. For the first time, at age twelve, I discovered the impact that viewing an image of a topless woman can have on man's psyche. Those perfectly rounded C cup, bare white breasts were staring directly at me. And she was smiling! As if she was proud of displaying them for me! Blood surged to my head and I immediately shut the book and ran out of my brother's room.

My confused, twelve-year-old mind was desperate for a refuge. Retreating to a dark and quiet corner of our common room in the old house, with my back pressed against the soft, stored and folded bedding, I closed my eyes. My brain recreated every pixel of the image.

Appreciating her generosity, I smiled back at her. A new paradigm rocked my world: the previously undiscovered and magnificent geography of women.

The experience gave me an idea for my own erotica journal. From that time on, I cut and glued any attractive photos of naked women that came into my possession (which were not many, by the way). A French title, I thought, would be appropriate for such a journal, *Journal de Erotiques*. However, throughout the years, the journal had become a pleasant escape to a forbidden and yet comforting place for me.

We kept a large hibachi in the basement. With great displeasure, I placed the journal, the book, and the letters in it. A moment before lighting them, I had a second thought about the journal and removed it. The rest were burned.

"Good-bye adolescence," I said out loud as flames turned Neilu's words and the book that answered many of my juvenile curiosities to ashes.

Back in bed, I let my mind's eye wander through the mystifying new country I was about to enter. Do they also have any dark, forbidden, and alienated part of their world that is taboo for the public to know or explore? My mind quickly traveled to more fun adventures. Scuba diving, I thought, would be among things that I would love to learn. I closed my eyes and imagined swimming with dolphins. In my mind's eye, I saw myself getting lost while staring at an endless horizon over the ocean; I knew that the magnificent vastness of the Pacific Ocean would inspire me to write many poems . . .

Before too long, my mother's voice woke me with her familiar, folk song imitation of an Isfahani dialect, rising at the end of each sentence. "*Bharkhee, Bharkhee, sobeh sadeghest setareha var-glombidest*, get up, get up, it is a beautiful morning, stars are gone already!"

I sprang up panicking that I had slept for too long, but my mother's smiling face calmed me down. Her look was playful. Since childhood she had awakened me with that song. Would I ever hear it again?

Noticing my panicked behavior, she assured me of ample time, and asked me to go upstairs for breakfast. She seemed happy for me. Her worrisome, motherly nature had not been released on me yet. It must have been hard for a loving and over-protective mother to help her child prepare for the journey of a lifetime.

I moved over to the small window near the low ceiling of my room. The sky was still dark and there was no snow on the ground in our yard.

My mother noticed my examining the outside. She smiled and said, "The sky is clear and there are no storms on the horizon. Perfect weather for a flight." Then she left me to my morning routine.

A perfect day for a flight! Is it really happening? The sentence echoed in my head as butterflies danced in my stomach.

My exercise routine consisted of calisthenics, stretches, and a few Persian pushups, but my arms trembled after only six of those complex Persian pushups. With all the luggage to cart around in foreign airports, I had to be stronger. Ten was a better number.

Psyching myself to press for more, my high school PE teacher's voice bounced in my head, saying we could consider ourselves strong if we completed at least six Persian pushups. I wrapped my grips tighter over the special step board, two inches high and three feet long, built for Persian pushups. Legs wide apart on toes, my head went down first, then shoulders. With shoulders lowered, I turned my body to the right and then twisted to the left. Then the head moved up followed by shoulders and then the arms pushed the body to slide the buttocks to elevate at the highest peak while the hands are gripping the board tightly.

I imagined myself in the center of the circular floor of *zoorkhaneh,* a small indoor arena where Persians conventionally learned the traditional martial arts. The movements of Persian martial art exercises are so well choreographed from centuries of development, that even the pushups look more like dance movements. I twirled and twisted my body with my imagined typical rhythms of a *zoorkhaneh*'s caller. My arms shook and my elbows collapsed at the end of the seventh one. I stopped the exercise and proceeded to the kitchen for my mother's elaborate breakfast spread.

Could this be my last breakfast in Tehran? I certainly hoped for it to be, at least for a few years.

My father was already at the table finishing his breakfast. My brother, visiting for the winter break, was still snoozing in bed. At the table, my mother tracked my every move with her eyes. She had set a soft-boiled egg in its dish, a glass of milk, a dish of butter, jam, a dish of feta cheese, and a bread basket on the table. Our *samovar* at the corner of the table kept a pot of tea warm. She pulled a glass of freshly squeezed orange juice from the refrigerator and put it in front of me. My mother moved every item on the table closer to me as soon as I sat.

My father looked at my mother, pointed to the orange juice and said, "Where did that come from?"

"Never mind, it's his," she replied while standing guard just in case my father tried to steal my glass of orange juice.

"Where is mine?" he asked.

My mother pointed to the refrigerator were oranges were kept and commented on how easily he can juice them himself.

My father looked at me with the face of a victim and shook his head. "See how I get treated? Did you notice how every item on the table moved away from me and was lined up in front of you as soon as you sat down? Just as if you are the sun and all this stuff on the table are planets of the solar system, arranged toward you with the help of your mother's hand."

"You are grown man, you can reach them yourself," my mother replied, but this time she had a hint of teasing in her voice and eyes.

He shook his head again, continued eating, and mumbled, "God only knows what will happen to me when you two boys are gone."

"Well, I for one, am leaving today. In a few days when my brother returns to his school in Shiraz, then you will be the only sun," I joked.

My mother left the room abruptly with her hand covering her mouth. I suppose, it was to cover the sound of her crying. "*Ellah-e-shokr!*" he loudly thanked God after the breakfast, as the tradition dictated, put his dishes in the sink and left the kitchen.

Shortly afterward, my father's thunderous voice boomed from the bedroom ordering my still-snoozing brother to get up.

A few minutes later, I dragged my heavy suitcases upstairs from the basement and lined them up by the front door. With a jubilant voice I announced, "Let's go, everybody!"

"Not so fast," replied my mother as she rushed to the front door with a bundle in her hand. "Not till you go through *ghalyas*."

In a mild protest, I asked if I really had to walk through that loop.

My mother had opened the round loop cloth of a hundred seventy centimeters in diameter and about ten centimeters in width. Verses of Quran and other prayers were written in Arabic all over it. My face must have been clear on revealing my feelings after seeing *ghalyas*.

"Yes, you must," my mother said. "This is our tradition. The traveler must step through *ghalyas's* loop. This will protect you, son."

On the other side of the *ghalyas*, my father held a holy Quran waiting for me to step out of the loop, kiss the Quran, and pass under it toward the door.

My mother warned me to make sure that I have not left anything behind before I go through *ghalyas*. One cannot return once stepped through *ghalyas*. It is considered bad luck and the whole process would have to start over again.

Anxious to start our trip to the airport, I gave the nod. My mother's warning however, reminded me of missing one important part, saying good-bye to my grandmother. How could I forget it? She had lived with us all my life. I rushed to my grandmother's bedroom.

She was in a deep sleep when I entered the room. It was six years ago when we all, including my grandmother, moved from our old house into the current house, which was brand new. Opposite to the traditional style of the hundred-year-old house where we lived before, the new house had a modern layout. My grandmother hated the new house layout. In protest, she stopped walking to her favorite mosque and stores. Therefore, she reduced her daily activities to a minimum. In the old house, just going to the toilet or the kitchen was an exercise, as she had to cross the courtyard and climb down about five steep stairs, and the same with the kitchen. In our new house, the kitchen and the toilet were conveniently located next to her room on the same floor.

"Disgusting! You call this civilized living? The kitchen and the toilet are within a few steps of each other under the same roof!!" She scolded my mother at her first sighting of the new house. Gradually, she lost mobility and the will to live.

This day, her face looked pale but restful. The room smelled sweet but with the slightly pungent odor of urine. My mother kept the room warm and clean.

"*Khoda-hafez Khanjon*, soon you too will start your journey to a new world. Free of pain, you will be greeted by your ancestors and then your new life will begin," I whispered as I kissed her moist forehead good-bye.

I rushed back to my mother's waiting arms, still holding open the *ghalyas* loop.

"Do you *have to* take your guitar, too?" My brother complained just as I was about to begin the traditional *ghalyas* procedure. This was after his grumbling about the heavy weight of my suitcases. My father had ordered him to take my luggage to the car.

"What? How can you say that? My guitar is my best friend. It comforts my soul—"

"Give me a break, you can buy a best friend over there," my brother cut me off.

As usual, arguing with my brother was amusing for me. I answered back, "No, not this one!"

My mother intervened and snapped at both of us to stop bickering. She was right, I didn't know when would I see him again, if ever. Her comment reminded me of something important I wanted to do before I left.

"Sorry, there's one more thing I need to do before *ghalyas*," I apologized sheepishly to my mother with her waiting arms. I approached my brother and whispered, "Follow me."

We hustled to the basement. From my desk drawer, I pulled out my cherished *Journal de Erotiques* and handed it to him.

"Here is my departing gift to you. You may do what you want with it. I just couldn't destroy it."

His sleepy eyes were now wide open along with his mouth. He immediately started to flip the pages. He was speechless.

I asked him to hide it somewhere safe and hustled back up the stairs.

Finally ready, I carefully stepped into the loop of *ghalyas* and kissed the awaiting Quran held by my father. I bent my neck and passed under it toward the door. Everyone except my grandmother followed me. She was in deep, coma-like sleep. We stepped out of the house.

The weather outside was chilly and clear. The crisp air of dawn was refreshing. Birds, welcoming the illumination, were cheerfully chirping and jumping from one branch to another. It was Sunday morning, the second day of the week in Iran. Soon cars and busses would carry millions of reluctant people to work or school. But not me.

My anxiety about possible troubles that could happen on the way to the airport kicked in. Protests, unexpected military activities, road blocks, militia engagements, and the rumor of a strike by airport personnel were among them. I took some deep breaths to calm myself.

My sedan was a newer car compared to our family automobile. It was parked on the street and now a default family car, my father, with the diligence of a pilot's pre-flight check, examined the car to ensure a smooth operation to the airport. Windows wiped clean, engine oil topped off, transmission fluid and other fluids checked and refilled, tire pressures—the works.

Before getting in the car, I turned my head and glanced at the house one last time. My mother carried a bowl full of water with jasmine and rose petals floating in it. She threw the water out on the street in front of our house.

Everyone else was already in the car, I sat in the front. As my father impatiently waited for my mother, he spotted a small smudge on the inside of driver's side window. With a sigh he took a towel from under his seat and with a circular motion wiped it clean. I knew exactly what that smudge was; a trace of me; an imprint of my forehead in despair, saying good-bye to Neilu. I never cleaned it. With every stroke of my father's hand, it faded bit by bit. My thoughts drifted to Neilu's image, her imprint on my heart was there to stay, forever.

My mother placed the pot back in the house, locked the door, and joined us in the car.

"What's the story with the water and flower petals?" I asked.

"Oh, it's just another tradition for a safe trip and a speedy return of the traveler," she replied.

With that, my father started the car. Every turn of the steering wheel took me closer to my lifetime dream and farther away from my roots. Holding my carry-on luggage on my lap, I engraved every street scene and every turn into my memory.

Would I ever return?

21

FLIGHT

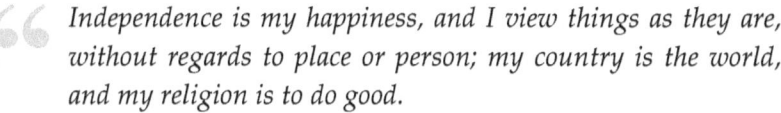 *Independence is my happiness, and I view things as they are, without regards to place or person; my country is the world, and my religion is to do good.*

— Thomas Paine, English-American writer (1737-1809)

The traffic was light on our way to the airport. On that chilly, winter morning, from my front seat window, naked trees and uneven buildings appeared and vanished one by one. Everyone was quiet in the car. I enjoyed watching the typical early morning scenery of Tehran's streets. In the post-dawn calm, before the craziness of day began, shopkeepers calmly tidied the fronts of their stores, delivery trucks unloaded goods, and the city's sweeper crews swept the streets with their long-handled brooms.

Thirty minutes later, the airport complex appeared accompanied by a fluttering in my stomach. This was it! This time, the trip to the airport was for me! Not to see off some relative or welcome them back home. I was just a few hundred meters away from the craft that would take me away to America. To my dream. To my unknown future.

Tehran's airport in 1979 looked similar to a grand train station. There was one great hall for the crowd of passengers and family members to congregate. Loudspeakers echoed announcements in several languages. Davud and his family were not there yet. The flight board showed our flight, Swissair bound for Geneva, with one stop in Damascus, Syria, on schedule.

As we stood in the center of the hall staring at the flight board, my brother spotted Davud's family as they entered. I waved at them so they would see us.

My brother whispered, "What's wrong? How come they all have a funeral face on?"

We all gathered around together. Davud's two sisters and parents did have somber looks on their faces. I knew that Davud's mother was a calculating drama queen who preyed on people's emotions to her advantage whenever possible. I am not sure if it was her constant gossiping or her passive-aggressive behavior that made Davud despise her so much. Sometimes I felt that Davud's move to the U.S. was mostly to put distance between himself and his mother.

Dr. Baahari, Davud's father, broke the somber quiet. "So, you boys are ready to discover the new world, huh?"

"Yes, sir," I replied without hesitation with a big smile. A surge of excitement raced through me.

Dr. Baahari had a kind heart and a true passion for helping people. He was the only one from Davud's entourage that actually showed some excitement. It was clear to me that he was proud of his son for taking this journey.

My father suggested we all take a few group photos and handed the camera to a man standing nearby. We formed a semi-circle. I stood at the end and observed Davud's family's gloomy faces. Even Davud's, which bothered me.

After the photo, I took him aside and asked him about the sad face.

"It's all a game," he whispered. "If I look happy, my mother will nag and will make the next few minutes miserable. It is much easier to have a serious face and get it over with."

I felt the emotional load Davud carried. He received no envy from me.

An announcement echoed over the loud speakers, in three languages, calling the passengers of our plane to proceed to the appropriate gate. My stomach turned as I heard the voice. This was the moment for which I had been waiting for so many years. The start of my new life.

"This is it, folks," I announced excitedly.

Eager to leave, I gave good-bye hugs and kisses to my family. Two kisses, one for each cheek, for each person. Tears could no longer be held back in my mother's eyes. As I gave her two kisses, one for each moist cheek, she wished me a safe and happy journey.

"Remember to write regularly and call once a month," she said, her voice breaking with sorrow. I nodded my head in obedience and moved to my father. It wasn't time to linger and become emotional.

For me, this was an exciting time.

My father's eyes were wet with tears as well, but beyond the tears, I could see a twinkle of excitement. He was not a fan of long trips, but perhaps he knew how important this journey was for me.

As I advanced toward the gate, I looked at Davud's group and gave him the "let's go" head gesture. His family was much nosier than mine. His mother's howling left no doubt on everybody's mind about her talent for drama.

Beyond the gate, a separate large hall, designated only for the travelers and the airport personnel, awaited us. With a last quick glance at my family, I waved and pushed myself through the gate. Bursting with joy, I looked forward to a great adventure and leaving the past where it belonged, behind me.

After a passport check, a luggage inspection, and a final examination of the tickets, we boarded a shuttle for transport to the airplane parked on the tarmac. Davud and I stood in the middle of the bus holding the rails for balance.

As the bus drove away from the main airport building, my eyes feverishly searched for the airplane. A sudden, sharp pain on my ribs turned my attention toward Davud, who had instigated it with his elbow. He smiled, pointed to a Swissair jet parked on the tarmac about two hundred meters away, and said, "There it is, our airplane."

"Our vessel to freedom patiently awaits us," I responded, relieved to see our plane.

Davud advised me to hold the poetry for later. Before getting into a celebratory mood, we had to see if the plane would be permitted to take off with us being inside.

It wasn't more than a moment later, when a sudden jerk threw me into the woman who stood next to me. The bus stopped in the middle of the tarmac. Loud complaints from the other passengers made it difficult to hear the driver's explanation for the sudden stop. I apologized to the woman and lowered my head, scanning the tarmac in search of the reason for the sudden stop.

"There, look out there!" I extended my arm and pointed my finger toward our airplane.

"What the hell is going on?" Davud exclaimed.

The woman next to me asked, "Why all the military vehicles?"

Several military trucks loaded with armed soldiers and accompanied by armored vehicles were speeding toward our airplane sitting on the tarmac.

My stomach couldn't take it anymore. I was about to throw up. Why couldn't this happen one hour later when we are airborne? Why now? Would my hopes be destroyed just at the final seconds? Was the military shutting down the airport?

Everyone watched the unfolding event in silence. That gave the driver a chance to project his voice and encourage everybody to calm down. He explained that this was just a precautionary effort. The military command had ordered all vehicles on the tarmac to stop moving until they positioned themselves. They were there to guard the airplanes and the passengers, nothing else. He promised that we would move shortly.

I sensed a collective sigh of skeptical relief. No sound, not even a single word was spoken after that. We all waited in a total silence. He was right, every airplane received two armored vehicles and several armed soldiers around it. Fifteen minutes later, our bus moved again and stopped near our Swissair plane and we transferred under the watchful eyes of the soldiers.

My guitar and two other carry-on cases slowed my desired speed for climbing the steep stairs leading to the airplane's door. I let Davud go ahead of me. Since we were sitting next to each other, he, with a lighter load, opened the way for me.

Once on top of the steps, before entering the airplane, I turned around for a last glance of the main building. Since I was certain my parents were watching us from behind the large windows of the great hall, I waved.

Inside, the welcoming face of flight attendants and the smell and hum of the cabin gave me goosebumps. After securing my guitar and fitting the two carry-on bags into the overhead bin, I nearly trampled Davud's feet getting to the window seat.

Davud looked at the airplane's emergency exit card. I nudged him with my elbow and asked, "Hey, what are the chances of the air traffic controllers starting their strike before we take off?"

"Let's stay positive," he replied and put his attention back on the pamphlet.

"Five years of dreaming, two years of planning, and a year and a half of actual hard work can be ruined with one stupid, ill-timed strike," I groaned.

Davud was in an uncharacteristically positive mood. "Look at the glass half full," he whispered. "We are just a few minutes away from beginning the greatest adventure of our lives. So, shut up with your pessimistic blab and put some positive thought into it. It will happen!"

The airplane was packed. The pilots finished their preflight tests. Vibrations from the engines and the rush of cool air from the air conditioning vents were all welcome signs of a normal situation.

I asked Davud if he prayed. He shook his head.

"This is a good time for prayers. Would you like me to teach you?"

"No, leave me alone. You talk too much!" Davud complained. We both were anxious for the plane to take off without any further delay.

I looked out my window and could see nothing out of the ordinary on the tarmac. That was good. It was time for me to close my eyes and completely tune myself in with the airplane. My arms were gently resting on the armrests and my hands gripped the ends. My body and my mind were connected to the airplane through the seat. Breathing was the last stage of preparation, gentle and controlled. That way, I could feel the slightest movement in the airplane's hum the moment it happened. It was either going for the takeoff or revving down for possible delay or halting of the flight.

A small jolt, followed by a soft and slow forward motion, put a smile on my face.

"We are moving!" Davud announced quietly with excitement in his voice. I nodded with a smile. The plane taxied down the runway. There were no other planes ahead of us. We assumed, once we took off, we wouldn't be stopped. The only way to bring us back was if the air force fighter jets intercepted and forced the plane back.

Anxiously, we examined all possibilities. Every second felt like a long, drawn-out hour. Mentally we were tired, our souls were exhausted from all the expectations that had been laid upon our young shoulders. We both were weary of lies, deceptions, and instabilities, in addition to all the cultural baggage of an old civilization with thousands of years of superstitions, myths, aggression, and old do's and don'ts.

There were no reasons for the air force jets to intercept our flight. Therefore, the next step was for the plane to take off safely and without interruption.

However, playing the worry game and examining all the possibilities gave us a sense of preparation for the unexpected. We found only one possibility for the intercept, if one or more high-profile members of the government were on the plane and escaping the country. The shah's regime, to calm dissent, had lately turned on his own, arresting the government officials accused by the opposition of corruption, murder, or other crimes. In that case, the air force fighter jets would have a good reason to force the plane to land.

The plane came to a complete stop.

"We will know in a few moments," Davud said, then covered his face with both hands and bent over his knees.

A blanket of silence covered the entire cabin. A moment later the captain announced in English, "Ladies and gentlemen the tower …"

"Oh God," I said out loud.

"Shut up, let me hear him," Davud snapped at me.

The captain's announcement stopped.

Davud, perturbed for not hearing the announcement, turned to a man behind us and asked if the captain announced we were cleared for departure.

"Yes," he answered.

My wild and imaginative mind took a break when I heard the roaring of the jet engines revving up. Sitting up with my back straight, I braced myself for the take off. It started with a big jolt followed by a rapid increase of speed. Then the airplane smoothly lifted from the ground.

A few seconds later, I punched my friend's arm with excitement.

We were airborne! He nodded.

As the airplane gained altitude, houses and roads became smaller. I felt as if my whole face became a giant smile. Thousands of meters above the ground, I was rushing away from the cities, roads, villages and the people that, in my mind, had kept me hostage in a cultural, political, and social chokehold. Happiness permeated my every cell.

I questioned myself, if I should feel sad for the people who were left behind, facing the tumultuous future. But quickly I decided, this was my moment, I was going to enjoy every bit of it.

"Like wind I go," the words muttered under my breath as thin wisps of clouds rushed by my window.

"Coffee or tea?" the Swissair flight attendant's tender voice was a welcoming sign of good things to come.

For hours, the earth below looked the same—brown with occasional patches of green. It was hard to tell exactly where we were. My intent was to memorize the last images of Iran before we moved into Iraq's airspace to the west.

A strange sensation took over me when the pilot announced we had left the Iranian airspace. We were on scheduled to land in Damascus on time. I felt a bizarre combination of goosebumps, jittery stomach, and shortness of breath.

"Good-bye, Iran!" I said aloud, letting go of my anxiety like a locomotive releasing steam.

No reaction from cool and collected Davud. His head was down, surfing a magazine.

I didn't feel sad, and curiously, didn't feel guilty about it. Was it morally wrong not to feel melancholy leaving family and friends for a long period of time? Unsure of it, I asked Davud for his opinion. He shook his head side to side but didn't look up.

He then lifted his head up and looked straight ahead.

His eyes were flooded with tears.

It was a perfect time for some friendly teasing. "Wait a minute," I taunted him, "is that a sad face? What are you choked up about? I thought you couldn't wait to get out of Iran?"

"I miss my Fariba. I won't be able to see her forever now!"

"Oh, God. Not that again. As I recall, she dumped you. Leaving Iran was not an option for her. She wanted to participate in changes and rebuilding Iran. There was nothing you could do to change her mind. Get over it."

"I could've stayed," he whispered as his eyes went back to the magazine.

"Chicken or beef?" asked the flight attendant, standing next to our row with her cart of hot lunches.

The food distracted Davud from moaning over his ex-girlfriend.

Not long after finishing our meals, we entered Syria's air space.

The brown landscape below us didn't change in Syria.

As the airplane descended, my face stayed glued to the window, my eyes devouring every possible detail of the view of the ancient city, Damascus.

Davud didn't share my excitement and complained about the pleasure I took watching so eagerly as we descended over the city. He thought of Damascus as another all-brown, asymmetric, hodge-podge of buildings. A typical Middle Eastern city.

"This place is known to many people as the oldest city in the world," I informed him, eager to show off my knowledge of history. "I mean, the oldest continuously populated city in the world. This city is over eight-thousand-years old. It's an important city for both Muslims and Christians. The shrine of Imam Nasser, the third imam, is here, and according to some, the body of John the Baptist is buried in the Grand Mosque."

"Who cares about all that?"

I stared at Davud, incredulous that he could be so shallow. Perhaps switching to politics would make him more enthused about Damascus. The Syrian dictator, President Hafez al-Assad, had created a large and fearsome military. Politically and militarily, this place had a significant presence. So I mentioned it to him.

Davud argued that Assad with his mighty military lost to the tiny state of Israel. That was true, but still his military power was not to be discounted.

The smooth landing was quickly followed by appreciative applause by the passengers. When we stopped, several military vehicles surrounded the airplane protecting it.

Flight attendants rushed to get the airplane ready for some passengers' departures and arrivals of new ones. An attractive flight attendant with long blond hair helped the passengers near me. Looking for an excuse to justify my affectionate stare, I asked, "Excuse me, are we allowed to get off the plane here?"

"Only, if this is your destination. Otherwise, you are to remain seated as we go through this quick stop," she replied hurriedly, but managed to slip a little smile my way.

"Can I have a beer please?" Davud asked impatiently. His question gave me a few more seconds to admire her blue eyes and well-proportioned lips.

"Once we are in the air, sir. This stop is a short one," she answered, and masterfully moved her well-sculptured body through the narrow corridor among a flock of impatient passengers ready to exit.

"She can't be from the north of Switzerland," I joked with a whisper.

"Yes, you are correct. She actually smiled!" Davud replied and we both laughed. A few people got off and more people got on the plane.

We continued monitoring the military personnel who had surrounded the plane. Davud noticed all-Russian military hardware. We talked about the close relationship between Syria and the Soviet

Union and how astutely Iran had kept a fine balance in being friendly with the two enemies, Israel and Syria.

An officer jumped off one of the armored vehicles and approached the airplane. A few minutes later, one of the pilots went down and talked to him.

"I suppose in this part of the world, we have Palestinian and Kurdish guerrillas in addition to Libyan and Marxist terrorists to worry about. They have hijacked airplanes before," I explained.

After a few short minutes of talk, the pilot rushed back up the stairs into the airplane. All flight attendants went into the pilots' cabin and shut the door.

My anxiety returned, I felt short of breath. I never imagined that we'd be stuck in a foreign land. What if they were grounding our plane?

"Calm down, we don't need to assume the worst every time there is a glitch," Davud whispered.

"Look out the window! We are surrounded by military vehicles. Get up and see if they are blocking us on the other side of the plane too," I ordered.

He hesitated for a moment and then got up. Attempting to peek out of the other side of the plane, he hovered over a girl who was sitting across from us. Right at that moment, flight attendees walked out of the pilots' cabin. One of them noticed Davud.

"Sir, get back to your seat!" she ordered with a firm and projected voice.

Surprised by seeing a group of flight attendees heading toward him, Davud jumped back to his seat and immediately put his belt on.

The flight attendants shut all the open overhead compartments and asked everyone to fasten their seat belts. Soon after, the captain's voice ordered the flight attendees to prepare the plane for an immediate take off.

"Did you see anything on the other side of the plane?" I asked.

"Yes, soldiers are everywhere," he whispered.

A few moments later, I felt a jolt. We were moving, and fifteen minutes later we were airborne again.

With a sigh of relief, I asked, "Man what was that about? What's next?"

Davud ignored my question, reclined his seat and closed his eyes.

About thirty minutes later, the deep blue waters of the Mediterranean Sea appeared below us and delivered a profound calming effect on me. Aside from its comforting color, symbolically I considered it the beginning of my new life away from the dry, brown past.

I elbowed Davud. "Wake up lazy bum, it's official! We are in Europe! I think we are over the Mediterranean Sea."

The Middle East's continuous brown aerial view was gone, and with it went my fear of being entrapped in a dark sandstorm of political unrest and uncertain social climate.

We chatted about our college friends, our girlfriends, parents, and our past. But not much about our future. It was important to validate our departure. At that moment, the clarity of the future did not matter. Where we were on our way and what would happen to us in the strange land did not matter. We knew our final destination was Los Angeles, with a change of plane in Geneva and another one in New York. That is all we needed to know.

"Meat or chicken?" the flight attendant's voice pleasantly interrupted our reminiscence.

Life outside of Iran would expose me to many cultural differences, including dietary variances, I was keenly aware of it. Spontaneously, I asked if the meat was pork.

"Yes," she replied.

Chicken was my choice but Davud ordered the pork. He turned his face to me and said, "We're entering a world where pork is a main staple. Are you going to insist on your old country's habits, like not eating pork and no alcohol?"

"Old country? What do you mean by *old country*? We are not more than few hours away from what you call *old country* and suddenly its morals are passé? Besides, I just don't like pork."

"How do you know? You've never tried it. I think it's delicious," Davud countered.

"Actually, it smells good, but pork is *haram* in Islam. That means it's not healthy for human consumption. I just don't think it's a healthy meat."

Davud shook his head and devoured his pork. Everything about our airplane food was new and unique to us. We were used to large portions of food placed in large plates with metal utensils. Airplane food, in contrast, was neatly wrapped in various colorful packaging, served on clean plastic dishes, and individually wrapped plastic utensils. The way the dessert was wrapped, the butter, the food packaging —all were welcome signs of the new and exciting world, a world far away from our old traditions.

The food took my attention away from the view down below for a while. When I finally peeked out the window, to my delight the terrain had changed from blue water to patches of green, grey, and white.

My jittery stomach was a good indication of my excitement. "We are over Europe for sure now," I reported to Davud.

It wasn't long before the pilot announced the descent, the local time, and the fact that we were landing a few minutes later than the scheduled arrival time in Geneva. Davud and I looked at each other and checked our connecting flight to New York. It was tight.

I changed my watch to match the local time. There it went, the very first change. Moved the time back two and half hours. I mused at the irony of the situation. My journey was to move forward and yet the very first change was to move my watch backward. Davud and I briefly strategized on how we would move about to avoid missing our next flight.

The aerial view of Europe was fascinating. The excitement took away all my worries about the possibility of missing the flight to New York. Houses, with variations of gable and mansard roof tops, much different than the flat ones in Tehran, cars, streets and other parts of Geneva became larger and more realistic as the plane descended closer to the ground.

Davud stopped a passing flight attendant and asked about the gate and location of our flight to New York. She examined the ticket, checked it against her list, shook her head, tightened her lips and gave us the gate information and the new departure time. As she handed back the ticket she said, "You boys need to run fast. You will have only fifteen minutes! Good luck!"

"How can we make it in just fifteen minutes?" I protested.

"Didn't you hear her? We need to run fast! Our luggage will be automatically transferred to the new airplane. We just need to get off this plane and run like hell," Davud explained.

What if the airport was a large one? My two pieces of carry-on luggage plus my guitar would slow me down. Davud had his own two carry-ons.

"What if we don't make it?" I expressed my doubt.

Davud's giant round eyes pumped up even bigger, like those of a pufferfish. His horrified face with his blond afro-style hair was comical. He wasn't an athlete. His smoking and drinking habits made me worry about his ability to run fast enough for us to make it.

The airplane descended, a loud clunk sound came from the landing gears' deployment. A smooth landing brought joyous applause from the passengers.

The airplane doors opened and we were standing in the aisle, ready to deplane. One of the flight attendants asked people in front to allow us to leave first, which I appreciated. We ran as if our lives were depending on it. The beauty, the dazzle, and the charm of a western European airport were mesmerizing to my wondering eyes and curious mind. However, I had to stay focused to make it to the gate on time.

Passing people by less than an inch, Davud and I maneuvered through the crowd. My heart was pumping fast, my face was hot with exertion, my muscles were complaining, but my mind was made up. I was determined to make it.

"We have four minutes left. Do you see the gate?" Davud asked panting behind me.

With my guitar on my back and the carry-on bags in each hand, I couldn't easily check my watch. "It should be here on the left. There!" I answered and turned left.

"Wait up!" Davud shouted at the boarding agent.

The boarding agent waved his hand to us in rapid circular motions, signaling us to hurry up. He was about to close the gate.

The airplane was full, and everyone already seated when we stepped in the airplane, panting.

A flight attendant asked for our boarding passes. Standing inside the plane, we both were bent forward, gasping for air. After a quick glance at our boarding passes, she helped us to find our seats and to stow our carry-ons.

"Boy, that was close!" I exclaimed while wiping the sweat off my forehead. Davud nodded. He was panting so hard that a quick nod was the closest thing to a reply I could get from him.

As the flight attendants prepared the plane for departure, I pulled the aircraft safety card from the pocket of the seat in front of me and studied it carefully. Knowing that most of our flight would be over the Atlantic Ocean, I wanted to know all the exits and also the emergency procedures.

Davud seemed not to care at all. He had leaned back with his neck rested on the seat and his eyes closed.

A few minutes later, the airplane took off and we soared into the sky once again.

On the first drink run of the flight, Davud ordered a Jack Daniels.

"Splurging on a student budget!" I said.

"After what I have just gone through, nothing will soothe me better than a good whisky," Davud replied.

The Jack Daniels was delivered in a miniature replica of the bigger bottle, along with the other things he ordered. Davud's face opened with a big smile and he immediately started mixing his drink like he was an artist engaged in creating a masterpiece.

Hot tea was my drink of choice. The Swissair's flight attendants expertly helped passengers to feel comfortable for their long journey across the Atlantic. A cup of hot tea helped me to settle in my seat and get back to my dream of life in a new world.

At our cruising altitude, the view of Europe was mostly covered in clouds. Majestic white towers floated weightless in the sky, seducing the viewers to dreamland. I was one of them. The vast whiteness below took me away, suspended indefinitely in an imposing realm. I lost track of time. It was the voice of Davud that pulled me back to the present moment.

"Do you think it's strange that I detest my mother?"

I hesitated to answer him directly. We had both taken many psychology courses in college. I asked if he had found any theory that could explain his feelings toward his mother. His gaze passed through me toward the outside the window. To my understanding, his mother had showed passive-aggressive tendencies. I couldn't get along with that type either.

"I'm so happy that I'll be thousands of miles away from her," Davud confessed.

Playfully, I reminded him that she could still call him on the phone.

"If we get a phone, I won't give my parents the number." He had a devilish smile on his face, "And if she starts ranting when I called her, I'd blame a bad connection between continents, and hang up."

In her defense, I prompted him that we were from a patriarchal culture where men rule. With bullies defining the standards of our culture, women are mostly marginalized. At the same time, our corrupt, untrustworthy political system is systematically favoring men. Therefore, passive-aggressive behavior had become a survival tool for some women.

"Another reason that I'm so happy to get away," Davud mumbled.

He then crossed his arms, closed his eyes and dozed off.

At some point, we began flying over the great Atlantic Ocean. Random openings in the clouds gave it away. The enormity of the ocean was impressive. Traveling west delayed the sunset, which finally arrived with a glorious feast of images. The mixture of light, shape, color, and form in the splendid canvas of the universe was breathtaking.

The dinner carts created some excitement in the cabin, but not enough to wake Davud from his slumber. I had to elbow him when the cart came to our seats.

We were grateful that the cost of food was covered within the price of our ticket and we didn't have to pay cash for our meals on the plane. Our money was limited to what we had brought with us until our parents could send more money, assuming the Iranian banks wouldn't collapse because of the turmoil. With no job permit, the closest financial resource was several thousand miles and multiple oceans away.

Davud sensed my qualms about money and in between vigorous bites attempted to calm my worried mind. "Our parents won't forget us, they will send the money regularly," he said.

"What if the unrest in Iran becomes a revolution, the government totally collapses, anarchy takes over, banks close, and no money is permitted to be transferred?"

Davud laughed. "Ah, you are worrying too much." Then he went on a monologue, describing the temporary nature of any potential changes in government and bank shutdowns. With the deep vested interests of the international community, he thought Iran's economy wouldn't collapse.

"Eat your food." He chewed and swallowed another bite. "We can also work and earn our own money. Try to relax."

"We can't work. We don't have a work permit. Our visa is a student visa," I replied.

"Let's take one step at a time. Once we land in New York, we need to figure out how to switch planes and continue our trip to Los Angeles. Then, we need to figure out where to stay, find our school, register, find a bank, open an account and start learning how to live and survive in L.A."

He was right, we had a monumental task ahead of us. Exiting a known universe on the brink of change and entering an unfamiliar world required wit, courage, and calm nerves.

I opened the first food pack on my tray and allowed another new, delightful culinary experience to take me away. The cup of hot tea that followed our pleasant in-flight dinner was a soothing segue to the next part of the trip. The jitters in my stomach had not settled yet, partly due to the excitement of the new adventure, and partly from anxiety of the unknown.

Moments later, the captain's voice announced the customary information about the altitude, speed, location, estimated time of arrival, custom procedures, and that he was going to turn off the cabin lights for passengers who wanted to rest.

As the plane flew in the dark of the night, our twenty-two-plus hour journey entered its second trimester. I couldn't stop thinking about the friends I left behind. Firoozeh's kind and patient demeanor, Neilu's unsettling spirit, Farhad's mysterious new life, and others. Thoughts of my friends' uncertain future in Iran occupied most of my time. But I wasn't sad. Quite the opposite. I couldn't wait to face the future. My understanding of this new world was mostly based on movies, TV shows, what I read, my uncle Raahmat, and a few Americans whom I had met in Iran.

It was exhilarating to think of it as a rebirth into a society where I could be who I wanted to be, and not who others wanted me to be—a kind new world with a spirit of individual respect; a world with no limits on personal growth. A society whose moral foundation was based on equality and dignity for all mankind.

"This is the captain speaking. We have started our descent into New York..."

Startled by the announcement, I checked my surroundings. Everything looked unfamiliar. Then I realized the comfort of the plane had lulled me into a deep sleep. As the captain's voice echoed through multiple speakers, the cabin lights went on. The jet engines changed pitch. My forehead was glued to the window, my eyes searching for light beyond the darkness.

"Do you see anything out there?" Davud asked.

"No, it's pitch dark."

The flight attendants distributed warm, wet towels. The sounds of hundreds of clicks and clacks from passengers getting ready for landing echoed throughout the entire cabin.

Davud brought his head close to the window, looked out and said, "What are you looking for?"

I wasn't sure, just maybe some sprinkles of lights, some good old fashioned hope, or perhaps I was searching for a confirmation that this new world I was entering would indeed be the promised land.

After what seemed to be hours, but was really only ten or fifteen minutes, the plane took a sharp turn. When it straightened, there she appeared, majestic as she was promised, welcoming the travelers as she was intended.

Turning my head, I elbowed Davud and said, "There she is, the Lady Liberty."

Davud hovered over me to peek at the view. "Did you ever think we could really make it to America?"

The sky below us was clear. It was hard not to be mesmerized by the fantastic night view of New York City, but my eyes were fixed on the Statue of Liberty. I wasn't letting it disappear into the gleaming lights of New York. My mind traveled fast to the past, already feeling as if it were stored in a closet far away. A sudden surge of energy took over my body and caused me to tremble. I took a deep breath and kept my eyes on the statue. The jittering in my stomach and a faster, more energetic heartbeat were welcoming signs of a new me. Shackle free and thirsty for hope, I had finally arrived.

"I knew we could," I replied.

Only later was I told that our plane was the last commercial flight out of Tehran's International Airport. After our departure, the airport was shut down in preparation of the last Iranian king's departure. On January 16, 1979, the shah's private jets carried the royal family and their entourage out of Iran forever. The airport was closed until Ayatollah Khomeini's historical return to Iran on the first day of February 1979. Iran was changed forever, and so was I.

AUTHOR'S NOTE

No major life decision is without sacrifices and no sacrifice is ever easy.

Any key social upheaval, whether fueled by political or religious ambitions, that inflicts violence and civil unrest on ordinary citizens bears human suffering and sacrifice.

In my belief, superstitions, traditions, cultural fallacies along with their older siblings, religion and nationalism, and their more modern cousins, fashion and social trends, have always served as tools for oppressors and bullies to manipulate young and old minds alike.

My struggle for independence was two-fold. One was about bursting the shackles of manipulation that are deeply embedded under the cover of familiar and often beloved terms such as traditions, religion, and cultural innuendos. The second was ridding myself of the chains that the repressive political machinery of the time imposed on individuals. Sacrifices had to be made to liberate my very basic human rights from the tyranny of both evils.

In the attempt to explain the predicaments of my journey to liberty, this project casts some light on the myriad of questions from Westerners about what went wrong in Iran during the 1978 revolution.

Events are best depicted when relayed by a person subjected to the upheaval. Where personal accounts may lack accuracy, they certainly add color and unique views of the world surrounding the subject.

It is obvious that no complete tale about the Iranian revolution and/or any personal struggle during the mayhem, can avoid subjects such as Iranian culture, history, politics, religion and even Persian cuisine. It is my hope that the reader will come to understand that many aspects of the culture are delightful.

In closing, I find Steve Jobs' and Rumi's insights among the most illuminating. Both have eloquently described the struggle we each face in regard to inner and outer battles over our personal freedom.

"Your time is limited, so don't waste it living someone else's life. Don't be trapped by dogma - which is living with the results of other people's thinking. Don't let the noise of others' opinions drown out your own inner voice. Most important, have the courage to follow your heart and intuition."

— STEVE JOBS

"Your task is not to seek for love, but merely to seek and find all the barriers within yourself that you have built against it."

— RUMI

ACKNOWLEDGMENTS

An old road is full of memories, good and bad, but where it ended made the journey complete.

This memoir is my story of many trails in places that not many of you have traveled. The twelve years it took for its completion with all the research, edits, and revisions would not have been possible without the help of others. My gratitude and appreciation go to the many people who were instrumental in encouraging me to push through the ups and downs of this complex project.

Jeanette Morris, my editor from California walked with me shoulder to shoulder, or better said, chapter to chapter, on this trail for most of these years. Her wisdom, patience and guidance made the journey possible.

Carole Eckhardt for being my steady guide from the beginning until a year before the completion of this project, when cancer took her away from us. Her handwritten note, encouraging me to finish the project, just before being taken away to the hospital will be cherished forever.

Susan Leon, my editor from New York for her astute critique and edits. My team of readers who helped me navigate this road with their enthusiasm and cheers, and my children who took many hours from their busy life to advise and provide me with resources for the countless issues involved in this project.

However, none of this would be possible without my wife,

Kathryn's, encouragement, guidance and patience during the entire length of this project; I'm eternally grateful for her support.

For images related to this era and additional background information visit: www.LiketheWindIGo.com

ALSO BY VAHID IMANI
IN THE SHADOW OF THE KINGMAKERS

This post-WWI historical fiction reflects on an igniting conflict between the West and East. Inspired by actual events in 1924 Persia, this action-packed historical thriller (espionage, spy fiction) brings voice to the human sufferings of the political lust of the West for domination.

The novel transports the reader to an era that had a significant role in shaping the political world we live in now.

For more information visit:
www.shadowkingmakers.com
Available in eBook and print

ALSO BY VAHID IMANI

Naji and the mystery of the dig

An award-winning children book for middle graders.

This award-winning cultural book is inspired by a true story. One summer morning, 8 year old Persian girl, Naji woke up to an unusual sound. Three strangers were digging in her courtyard. Naji's sixth sense warned her: something suspicious was lurking down there. As events unfold and suspense rises, readers will enjoy the many colors of Persian culture, cuisine, folklore, history, geography, religion, language, and intrigue through Naji's eyes and heart. No one was prepared for the ending.
Not even Naji.

For middle graders to adults.
Includes glossary, study projects and discussion questions sections.
Lexile® Measures 690L.
Available in eBook and print
For more information visit:
www.NajiStories.com
Facebook: www.facebook.com/NajiStories
Twitter: https://twitter.com/najistories
Pinterest: www.pinterest.com/najistories

ABOUT THE AUTHOR

Vahid Imani was born in Tehran, Iran, and made the United States his home in 1979. He earned his master's degree in 1980 from Gonzaga University's School of Business in Spokane, Washington. At the turn of the century, he transitioned to the world of fine arts after a career in high-tech as a business executive. His opinions and insights about the arts, history, and international politics have been shared in articles, public lectures, and mass media. In 2014, he debuted as an author with his award-winning middle-grade novel *Naji and the Mystery of the Dig*. In 2019 he published his historical fiction *In the Shadow of the Kingmakers*. Imani is the father of three children, grandfather of three, and lives with his wife in California.

PHOTO BY: LAURIE ZANDER PHOTOGRAPHY

www.ingramcontent.com/pod-product-compliance
Lightning Source LLC
Chambersburg PA
CBHW020416010526
44118CB00010B/281